5th Edition

ACCOUNTING

NON-ACCOUNTANTS

A Manual for
Managers and Students

GRAHAM MOTT

KOGAN
PAGE

First published in 1984 by Pan Books
Second edition 1990
Third edition published in 1990 by Kogan Page
Fourth edition 1993, reprinted with revisions 1994, 1995
Fifth edition 1999

Kogan Page Limited
120 Pentonville Road
London N1 9JN

British Library Cataloguing in Publication Data

A CIP record for this book is available from the British Library.

ISBN 0 7494 2859 7

Typeset by Saxon Graphics Ltd, Derby
Printed and bound by Clays Ltd, St Ives plc

Contents

Contents

Preface

Accounting and finance have a language of their own with a variety of statements and techniques that can mystify non-accounting colleagues. This new edition, like its predecessors, is written primarily for those non-financial students and managers who need to know about finance and accounting in any organization. The aim is to cut through as much of the jargon as possible and explain the various statements and techniques in a straightforward manner that requires no prior training.

This fifth edition is being updated after a period of public debate as to the manner in which a firm's financial affairs are reported. A number of company failures and alleged wrongdoings among large companies, such as BCCI, Polly Peck and the Maxwell empire, have posed various questions about the reliability of published accounts. In the early 1990s, many well known companies were putting the best face on their financial performance by the use of what is called creative accounting.

From the mid-1990s the Accounting Standards Board introduced Financial Reporting Standards (FRSs) which have made great inroads into this practice. It will take some time before all contentious areas are covered, but a good start has already been made with 14 new standards relating to the profit and loss account, the balance sheet, the cash flow statement, accounting for subsidiary undertakings, acquisitions and mergers, associated companies, goodwill and other clarifications.

There are three parts to this book. The first part deals with the types of statement found in the annual report and their interpretation. These include profit and loss account, balance sheet, cash flow, inflation adjustments and performance measures. Some chapters have been rewritten to provide a sharper focus on each financial statement and to reflect recent changes in accounting practice. Not only is the purpose of these statements explained, but also the principles underlying their preparation and their limitations. A new chapter has been included here on performance measures to embrace the topics of benchmarking and non-financial indicators.

The second section of the book deals with the nitty-gritty of management accounting and introduces terminology and techniques likely to confront an operational manager. To play a team role in the planning and control of those resources for which they are held responsible, managers need to know about the costs of products and the running costs of their departments. We therefore need to look at how firms cost products and services before progressing to the planning and control techniques of standard costing and budgetary control. Many decisions are based on an *ad hoc* analysis of costs to determine the best course of action and marginal costing is an appropriate technique here.

The final part of the book deals with the techniques of financial management, which concentrate on the efficient use of capital. This covers the cost of capital for the particular capital structure adopted by a business; the management of working capital; and the procedures for capital investment appraisal. Also included in this third part of the book are chapters on business taxation and overseas transactions.

The efficiency with which a company carries out all these operations is reflected in its profit and loss account and ultimately in the value of that company's shares. Financial management also has wider ramifications in a company's ability to attract new capital and offer career development opportunities to its personnel.

Most of the book is relevant to any form of business organization, large or small, in both public and private sectors. Employees of public bodies will, however, find the chapters on financial ratios, share values and taxation, largely irrelevant, although their organization may come into contact with the private sector or with its accounting techniques.

I am very pleased that this book has been used for 15 years as an introductory text on finance and accountancy for non-financial students and managers. It is recommended reading on a variety of business and management courses, and technical degree courses, at a number of colleges and universities.

I hope you enjoy this new fifth edition.

Graham Mott
October 1998

Part 1
The annual accounts

1
Financial reporting

INTRODUCTION

This book is all about accounting and the uses to which it is put. When discussing any topic it is advisable that both writer and reader are on the same wavelength, so I repeat here the Chartered Institute of Management Accountants' (CIMA's) definition of accounting as:

- the classification and recording of monetary transactions;
- the presentation and interpretation of the results of those transactions in order to assess performance over a period and the financial position at a given date;
- the monetary projection of future activities arising from alternative planned courses of action.

To illustrate, let us consider a company's annual accounts. Manual or computerized bookkeeping systems are used to record all monetary transactions throughout the year. These transactions are grouped and classified before presentation in the two key financial statements of profit and loss account and balance sheet. The profit and loss account measures financial performance over the year whilst the balance sheet states the financial position as at the year-end. Looking ahead now, top management will prepare for their own internal use a budgeted profit and loss account and balance sheet, based on a set of projected financial transactions for the coming year.

USERS OF ACCOUNTING INFORMATION

The aim of all accounting information is to provide the particular user with relevant and timely data to make decisions. Who are these users of accounting information and what decisions do they need to take? Possible users include:

- shareholders;
- owner-managers;
- management;
- suppliers;
- customers;
- employees;
- government;
- competitors;
- lenders.

1. *Shareholders* of limited companies will be influenced in their decision to remain investors or to increase/decrease their holding by receiving information about the financial performance and financial position of their company. This usually occurs twice a year in the form of a profit and loss account and a balance sheet relating to the first half-year and, later on, the full year.
2. *Owner-managers* of non-incorporated businesses will require the above information but they will also be privy to more detailed and more frequent information about the business's financial affairs.
3. *Management* in companies range from director level down to supervisor level. Each person requires accounting information to help them in their role. Supervisors may be concerned with operating costs for a very small part of the undertaking. Directors need to control the overall performance of the company and make strategic financing and investment decisions. Middle management need feedback on whether they are meeting their financial targets.
4. *Suppliers* need to assess the creditworthiness of potential and existing customers when setting the amount and period of credit allowed. This will partly, if not mainly, be based on the financial history of each customer so the supplier's accountants will assess the latest profit and loss account and balance sheet. Other data on payment history may be obtained from credit agencies, for example, Dun & Bradstreet, to assist in this decision.
5. *Customers* also need to be reassured, in this case to minimize the risk of their supplies drying up and disrupting their own output. Firms entering into a joint venture will also need mutual reassurance. Similar checks to those outlined above for suppliers will need to be carried out. This approach is outlined in Chapter 18.
6. *Employees* and their representatives have a vested interest in the financial health and future prospects of their employer. They rely on an assessment of the published accounts by experts for this.
7. *Government* levies tax on the profits earned by businesses and value added tax on the sales value of most industries. Tax authorities rely on the information provided by companies for these purposes.
8. *Competitors* can make some comparisons, for example, sales per employee, from published accounting data in a process known as benchmarking. This may provide clues to areas where performance may be improved particularly if explanations of differences in operating systems can be obtained.

9. *Lenders* need to be assured that their capital is safe and that the borrowing company can service the loan or overdraft adequately, so again the financial statements of profit and loss account and balance sheet will be examined from this viewpoint.

It can be concluded from the above that most users of accounting information are drawing on that provided in the published accounts. Only management have access to more detailed, non-published financial information within a company.

BRANCHES OF ACCOUNTING

Different users of accounting information will require different information and use it for different purposes. Accounting can be broken down into three main branches:

- financial accounting;
- management accounting;
- financial management.

1. *Financial* accounting is the preparation of financial statements summarizing past events, usually in the form of profit and loss accounts and balance sheets. These historic statements are mainly of interest to outside parties such as investors, loan providers and suppliers.
2. *Management accounting* is the provision of much more detailed information about current and future planned events to allow management to carry out their roles of planning, control and decision-making. Examples of management accounting information are product costs and cost data relevant to a particular decision, say, a choice between make or buy. Also included in management accounting is the preparation and monitoring of budgeted costs relating to a product, activity or service. All the above management accounting information is rarely, if ever, disclosed to outside parties.
3. *Financial management* covers the raising of finance and its deployment in the various resources needed by a business, in the most efficient way. The cost of capital is influenced by both the capital structure adopted as well as the riskiness of the investments undertaken. Part 3 is devoted to this theme.

Within these three broad areas of accounting there may be further sub-sets of accounting relating either to one specific activity, or across the whole spectrum. Examples of these are:

- treasury;
- taxation;
- audit.

1. *Treasury* is a finance function usually only found in a very large company or group of companies. It embraces the management of bank balances so as to raise the maximum interest on positive balances, or minimize the payment

of interest on negative balances. This might entail lending money overnight on the money markets. Also included here is the management of exchange risk where financial transactions are denominated in foreign currencies.

2. *Taxation* in a small company will be included in the duties of the financial accountant who may need to call on outside professional advice from time to time. Corporation tax on company profits is not straightforward and the system of capital allowances can be complex for some large companies, groups of companies, or multinational companies. Mention should also be made of the ramifications of value added tax (VAT) and the taxation of employee and director benefits in kind. A specialist accountant, or team of accountants, is often appointed in large companies to minimize the pain and maximize the gain from the various taxes and allowances affecting such organizations.

3. *Audit* is another accounting function mainly found in larger organizations. Internal auditors monitor that accounting procedures, documents and computerized transactions are carried out correctly. This work is additional or complementary to that undertaken by external auditors who take a broader approach in providing an independent report to shareholders in the annual report.

PROFESSIONAL ACCOUNTANCY BODIES

A number of failed attempts have been made in recent years to unify the accountancy profession in the UK by merger of various member bodies. The aims of any such amalgamation may be seen as the need for the profession to speak with one voice, at a time of criticism of their work resulting from some spectacular company failures in the early 1990s. Also important is the possibility of reduced administration costs if there were not so many separate bodies and the opportunity to rationalize student training and continuing professional development.

All qualified accountants in the UK belong to one (or more) of the following professional bodies:

- The Institute of Chartered Accountants comprises three separate bodies representing England & Wales (ICAEW), Scotland (ICAS), and Ireland (ICAI).
- The Association of Chartered Certified Accountants (ACCA).
- The Chartered Institute of Public Finance and Accountancy (CIPFA).
- The Chartered Institute of Management Accountants (CIMA).

Only members of the first two groups, referred to as chartered and certified accountants respectively, are allowed to act as professional auditors when reporting back to shareholders in the annual accounts. CIPFA members are usually found in local government, central government departments and quasi-government bodies. Management accountants belonging to CIMA are found in trade, industry and commerce where the emphasis is on the provision of relevant and timely information to management at various levels.

Other than the legal barrier restricting professional audit work to chartered and certified accountants, the only other limitations to a professional accountant entering into a particular type of accounting relate to training, experience and aptitude. For example, chartered accountants can be found in trade and industry as financial accountants or management accountants whilst CIMA members may hold the post of financial accountant or financial director.

UK GENERALLY ACCEPTED ACCOUNTING PRACTICE (UK GAAP)

When preparing financial statements for its own internal use, a company is not obliged to follow any prescribed formats or methods of calculating individual figures. This is not the case with the preparation of the financial statements contained in the annual accounts and circulated to shareholders and other interested external parties. In the UK these published accounts have to conform with certain regulations, and specifically with:

- *company law* as laid down by Parliament in various Companies Acts, notably 1985 and 1989;
- *accounting standards* which comprise a set of professional rules governing the detailed calculations and presentation of information in published financial statements;
- *stock exchange* regulations augmenting the above in the case of a listed company.

UK GAAP incorporates the detailed requirements of all of the above, but it also embraces other accounting conventions that are generally accepted by the profession. The term 'UK GAAP' has no statutory or official backing which is not the case with the GAAP of some other countries. One aspect that is universal is that GAAP is constantly changing, primarily as new accounting standards are introduced and as the pressures for international harmony increase.

ACCOUNTING STANDARDS

Accountancy standards are a most important source of guidance in the detailed presentation of accounting information to external parties. All professional accountants are obliged to follow the rules laid down in Financial Reporting Standards (FRSs) when preparing or auditing company accounts for publication.

These standards have changed significantly since 1990 when a new organization structure was introduced. The aim is for companies to provide more meaningful information that is less capable of manipulation by creative accounting. This reorganization was given added impetus by some well-known failures such as BCCI, Polly Peck, Maxwell and others, though some of these were the victims of outright fraud as opposed to creative accounting which in itself is (just) legal.

The structure for standard-setting in the UK and compliance monitoring of those standards is:

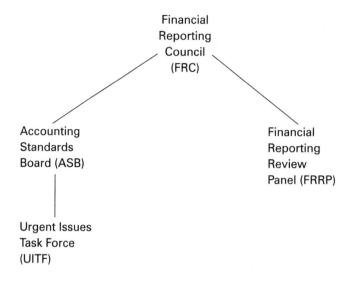

The Financial Reporting Council is the governing body, overseeing and financing the work of its two main subsidiaries – the Accounting Standards Board and the Financial Reporting Review Panel. It liaises with the government and acts as the public voice of the profession with regard to standard setting. Its 25 or so members are drawn from the professional accountancy bodies, the wider financial community, industry and commerce.

The Accounting Standards Board is charged with preparing and issuing accounting standards which are referred to as Financial Reporting Standards or FRSs. Since its inception in 1990, 14 new FRSs have been issued to date, some replacing the old Statements of Standard Accounting Practice (SSAPs) which started back in the 1970s. A list of the new FRSs is at the rear of the book in Appendix 1.

Included in this list is the *Financial Reporting Standard for Smaller Entities* (FRSSE) which is a composite standard for any non-public companies falling within its compass, based on size. Entities that apply FRSSE are exempt from applying all other accounting standards. An important point to recognize here is that the full accounting standards (FRSs) apply only to a few thousand public companies, whereas the FRSSE is applicable to many times more smaller companies.

An offshoot of the ASB is the Urgent Issues Task Force. As its name implies, the UITF deals with any issues arising that require quick attention, relating to a matter not covered by an existing standard.

The Financial Reporting Review Panel was set up in 1991 to ensure that companies comply with all relevant standards. Larger companies have to make such a declaration in their published accounts and draw attention to any material deviations and the reasoning behind them; this directs the Panel's attention to possible cases for investigation. The Panel also receives complaints from interested, and sometimes anonymous, parties!

Ultimately the FRRP has the power to apply to the courts for changes to be made to a company's published accounts. So far, the existence of this sanction has been sufficient without it having to be carried through, so that any required changes have been made voluntarily!

International accounting standards

The International Accounting Standards Committee (IASC) was 25 years old in 1998. Its aim is to produce its own accounting standards and to promote their worldwide acceptance and observance. Members are the professional bodies of accountants throughout the world. They are required to use their best endeavours back home to get domestic standard-setters, auditors, government and stock exchanges to comply with the international standards.

In the UK there is a large degree of conformity of our domestic standards with the international standards and the Accounting Standards Board considers each new international standard carefully before deciding whether or not to include it in the domestic standard. Topics that have been the cause of disagreement in the recent past are the treatment of goodwill, deferred tax and pension costs.

With the growth of multinational companies and international listings on multiple stock exchanges, there is a growing need for acceptance of one international set of standards. At one time there was a move towards the development of an EC set of standards, but this has since diminished. The emphasis now in Europe is on reducing differences in accounting disclosure and measurement. The EC is now thought to be supportive of the new international standards. Some countries are considering legislation to allow particular companies to comply with the international standards in place of domestic standards.

If the IASC can reach agreement with IOSCO (an organization representing the world's stock exchanges), UK companies will be able to adhere to international accounting standards on all stock exchanges bar London, where local standards still have to be followed. This will put pressure on our own ASB to reconcile all remaining differences between UK and international standards.

THE ANNUAL REPORT AND ACCOUNTS

The contents of the annual report and accounts for a listed company, being one that is quoted on a stock exchange, is more comprehensive than the requirements of unlisted companies which reduce in line with their size. Disclosure requirements of listed companies derive from three sources:

- statutory law embodied in Companies Acts;
- accounting standards as laid down in FRSs and SSAPs;
- listing regulations specified by the Stock Exchange.

9

The following main items are disclosed in the annual report and accounts:

1. *Chairman's statement* – a broad review of progress, changes in strategy and management and a guide to future prospects. This may be supplemented by a Chief Executive's review of each individual business's performance.
2. *Operating and financial review* – a detailed commentary on the financial results and influential factors.
3. *List of directors* – details of service, responsibilities and other directorships.
4. *Directors' report* – a formal report on specific required items, eg dividend declaration, principal activities, share capital and substantial shareholdings, political and charitable contributions, directors' shareholdings, employment policy, creditor payment policy, close company status and appointment of auditors.
5. *Report of the remuneration committee* – policy statement on how the total remuneration package of executive and non-executive directors is set.
6. *Corporate governance* – a statement of compliance, or otherwise, with the Code of Best Practice on board structure and directors' remuneration. The original report by Cadbury was later supplemented with reports by Greenbury and then Hampel and was finally published by the London Stock Exchange in June 1998 after seven years of discussion.
7. *Auditors' report* – a statement of auditors' responsibility and their report on whether or not the financial statements give a true and fair view of the state of affairs.
8. *Financial statements* – comprising consolidated profit and loss account, balance sheet, cash flow statement, statement of total recognized gains and losses and parent company balance sheet only.
9. *Notes to the financial statements* – additional breakdown and analysis of figures appearing in the main financial statements.
10. *Historic record of financial performance* – a 10-year summary of the main financial figures and ratios reflecting profitability, dividends and shareholders' funds.
11. *Notice of meeting* – notice of the time and venue of the annual general meeting and the business to be conducted.

ACCOUNTING CONVENTIONS

An accounting convention is a basic principle or concept underlying the preparation of financial accounts. These statements of profit and loss, balance sheet and cash flow are usually prepared monthly for management purposes, but particular emphasis is placed on the annual and half-yearly accounts which are the only ones that inform shareholders and other interested external parties.

Although the basic recording of financial transactions using double-entry bookkeeping is a mechanical exercise, there is, however, also a subjective side to accountancy. The production of the financial accounts is not totally automatic and various rules, principles or conventions are followed in addition to statutory and financial reporting standard requirements. By way of illustration, let us consider some examples where conventions are required, before we can proceed to answer them.

Examples
1. A company buys a new machine for £10,000 and expects it to last for five years. Does it charge this cost to the profit and loss account in the year it buys it, or in the year when it will be scrapped?
2. A retail store buys a quantity of washing machines one month for £4,000 and sells three-quarters of them for £3,600 in the same month. The remainder are sold in the following month for £1,200. Should the total cost of £4,000 go into the first month's profit and loss account or should it be £3,000?
3. Now suppose that the washing machines in the previous example were bought on credit and the agreed credit terms with the supplier do not require payment until the end of the following month. Should the cost to go into the first month's profit and loss account be nil, or £4,000, or £3,000?

Answers to these questions will be given after discussing the main accounting conventions used by accountants. These are now listed and then each one considered separately:

- separate entity;
- going concern;
- money measurement;
- double-entry bookkeeping;
- realization;
- matching;
- accrual;
- capital and revenue expenditure;
- depreciation;
- stability of the value of money;
- historic cost;
- materiality;
- consistency;
- objectivity;
- prudence.

1. *Separate entity.* Every business is regarded as an entity on its own. We need to keep its financial transactions separate from those of other businesses, and from the personal transactions of its owners, to enable accountants to measure the financial performance of each business.
2. *Going concern.* When preparing financial statements, the assumption is made of continuity; that the business is a 'going concern'. If a firm ceases to trade, its possessions are sold off to the highest bidder, but it would be very unlikely they would fetch their cost price. Buildings may fetch more, but stocks, work-in-progress and specialist equipment may fetch much less on a forced liquidation. Unless any information is known to the contrary, the

assumption is made that a business will continue trading. This is particularly important regarding the valuation of assets which might have very different values placed on them in the event of a liquidation.

3. *Money measurement.* Accountants can only record transactions that have a money measurement. Money is the means of adding transactions together, which is only possible when we can express transactions in money terms. For this reason, internally generated goodwill never appears in a list of assets as its value is unknown until someone wants to take over the business and buy the goodwill. Only if we buy up another company and pay £x for its goodwill will it appear as a financial transaction.

4. *Double-entry bookkeeping.* Most people have heard of this even if they are hard put to define it precisely! It refers to the dual aspects of recording financial transactions. By this is meant that every transaction is recorded twice, in two different ledger accounts, recognizing the giving and receiving aspects separately. This topic is examined in the following chapter.

5. *Realization.* With the exception of some retail trade, most business-to-business sales are done on credit rather than for immediate cash settlement. It is therefore important to define when exactly a sale takes place. Is it when goods or services change hands or when the cash is finally received by the supplier? The realization concept adopts the former timing, so we place a sale in the month the goods and services are delivered to the customer, regardless of when the cash is received.

6. *Matching.* This principle requires accountants to match the cost of sales against the value of those same sales in the same time period when determining the profit or loss. In the first example at the beginning of this section, the cost of sales is £3,000 and is matched against the sales value of £3,600 to show a gross profit of £600. The unsold goods costing £1,000 are carried forward as stock and shown in the next month's profit and loss account when they were sold for £1,200, thus realizing a profit of £200. The answer to the third example is the same £3,000 based on the accrual convention below.

7. *Accrual.* Expenses which relate to any accounting period must be included in that period's profit and loss account irrespective of when they are paid for. If an invoice has been received for goods or services supplied to the business, the bookkeeping system will automatically include that expense in the profit and loss account. However, if the goods or services have been received but no invoice received by the period end, then an 'accrual' is raised to get the cost into the bookkeeping system. Conversely, if an expense has been paid for but not yet received, then an adjustment is made for the prepayment. The two principles of realization and accrual are crucial to measuring business performance accurately over short periods of time.

8. *Capital and revenue expenditure.* The expenditure that is consumed and has no value remaining is charged to the profit and loss account as revenue expenditure and matched against revenue or income. Some expenditure,

however, lasts for many accounting periods. Buildings and equipment are examples of items which it would be unfair to charge in full to any one accounting period. This is deemed to be capital expenditure and is placed in the balance sheet.

9. *Depreciation.* The value of most capital expenditure reduces as the assets wear out over time. Depreciation is the process of reducing the value in the balance sheet by transferring part of it to the profit and loss account each period. Hence capital expenditure becomes revenue expenditure bit by bit over the asset's expected lifetime. This process is explained more fully in Chapter 3. Referring back to the first example earlier, it should now be appreciated that neither of the solutions offered as alternatives is correct. The £10,000 cost of the equipment should be depreciated by, say, £2,000 in each of the next five years.

10. *Historic cost accounting.* In general terms, accountants ignore inflation and assume the stability of money in financial statements. We tend to prefer the certainty of what things cost, to some other subjective estimate. We may amend this approach for certain items, such as land and buildings, and revalue them from time to time. *Current cost accounting* is when due allowance for inflation is made on all financial transactions in the profit and loss account and balance sheet. Historic cost accounting, however, is the norm, not least because it is adopted by the Inland Revenue.

11. *Materiality.* This convention might be used to overrule a strict interpretation of another convention. For example, the installation of coat hooks in a room is an improvement of an asset and should be treated as capital expenditure and depreciated each accounting period. Such administrative effort for a trivial sum of money is pointless, so businesses usually set a minimum sum below which capital expenditure is treated as revenue expenditure for expediency. Another example of materiality might be not bothering to count and value small amounts of stationery left at the end of each period to include them in stocks. In this case stationery is charged as revenue expenditure on purchase regardless of when it will be used.

12. *Consistency.* Where there is a subjective judgement made in accountancy, this will be adhered to from one year to another. An example of this might relate to the method used to calculate depreciation. Alternative methods are available, as discussed in a later chapter, but the chosen method should be consistently applied year after year.

13. *Objectivity.* Accountants try to produce financial accounting statements as objectively as possible, but as a number of items require an element of judgement this may not always be achieved.

14. *Prudence.* A salesperson will count a sale when an order is received whereas the realization concept used by accountants requires the product to first be delivered to the customer. This is one example of prudence where a profit is not anticipated before it is realized. This might seem at odds with the treatment of a loss to be incurred in the future when an accountant provides for the estimated loss immediately. Accountants view prudence as anticipating a loss but never anticipating a profit.

All these accounting conventions find their way into the financial statements of profit and loss account and balance sheet. We first need to find out how all the information going into those statements is recorded, and then see how we sort out which information goes into which statement. These topics are discussed in the following chapter.

Further reading

Glautier, MWE & Underdown, B (1997) *Accounting Theory and Practice,* FT/Pitman.
Melville, A (1997) *Financial Accounting*, FT/Pitman.

Self-check questions

1. Name the two key financial statements that measure a business's financial performance and financial position.
2. List as many users of accounting information as you can and the purposes to which they put that information.
3. What are the main two or three branches of accountancy?
4. What does the acronym GAAP stand for?
5. Which accounting standards apply to smaller entities?
6. Are international accounting standards mandatory on companies in all countries?
7. What are the contents of a listed company's annual report and accounts?
8. List as many accounting conventions as you can, stating their purpose.

2
Financial recording

INTRODUCTION

To enable a business to produce financial statements of any kind it is essential that every financial transaction is meticulously recorded. This aspect of accounting is very mechanistic and requires a thoroughly systematic approach, regardless of whether the bookkeeping is done manually in ledgers or by using computers. There are two systems of bookkeeping to consider: single entry bookkeeping and double entry bookkeeping.

SINGLE ENTRY BOOKKEEPING

If you have ever been the treasurer of a small club or society, you most probably kept your financial records in a small cash book, entering cash receipts on the left-hand page and cash payments on the right. In both cases the date and a brief description would be given against each item. A *receipts and payments account* is a summary of such a cash book.

This statement is prepared by small, non-profit-seeking organizations with few, if any, assets and liabilities. The cash balance at the beginning of the accounting year heads the receipts and the cash balance at the year-end is the balancing figure between total receipts and total payments. A typical example of a receipts and payments account for a drama club is shown in Figure 2.1.

Many small businesses use a system of recording similar to that described above for the small club or society. In their case a larger cash book, say with 16 columns each side, is required to analyse the purpose of each receipt and payment. Figure 2.2 gives a simplified example of this approach.

The great advantage of this system of recording is its simplicity. You do not have to be a trained bookkeeper to keep records this way! If the small business comes within the VAT system, some further analysis of sales and purchases will

Cash receipts	£	Cash payments	£
Cash balance at start	257	Hire of hall	50
Members' subscriptions	50	Hire of costumes	180
Sale of tickets	385	Refreshments	45
		Printing and stationery	65
		Advertising	120
		Sub-total	460
		Cash balance at end	232
Total	£692	Total	£692

Figure 2.1 *St Mary's Drama Club receipts and payments account*

be required. A decision will have to be made whether to treat the VAT tax point as at the time of sale or purchase, or at the time of cash settlement at some later date. The UK Customs and Excise allow small businesses to choose either point, but larger organizations must adopt the former.

There are some disadvantages of this simple way of recording transactions. Most firms buy and sell on credit. When a statement of cash receipts and payments is prepared, it will not disclose the amount of money still owing to suppliers nor the amount owed by customers. This will be the case at both the beginning and the end of the year. Nor is any distinction made between expenditure on running costs that have been used up in the period, as opposed to expenditure on such assets as equipment, which still have value remaining for future use.

We need to take account of all these aspects when preparing statements describing a firm's financial performance and position. It is for this reason that most business organizations use a system of double entry bookkeeping. This system automatically discloses amounts owing and other assets and liabilities so all information is readily available to prepare the financial statements.

	Receipts					Payments				
Date	Description	Cash sales	Credit sales	Other receipts	Date	Description	Purchases	Wages	Office expenses	Other payments
May 10	F. Smith		200		May 11	B. Gas			320	
11	J. Brown		175		11	ABC Co.	510			
11	Cash sale	25			13	XYZ Co.	293			
14	Loan			1,000	14	Payroll		990		

Figure 2.2 *Small company cash book*

DOUBLE ENTRY BOOKKEEPING

Most companies employing more than a handful of staff use the system of recording called double entry bookkeeping. This system records both cash and credit transactions as they occur at their different times. The name *double entry* derives from the fact that each individual transaction is entered twice, recognizing two aspects. These two aspects are referred to by accountants as *debits* and *credits*.

Double entry bookkeeping has a long history. Back in 1494 an Italian monk called Pacioli documented a system of double entry bookkeeping in a work entitled 'Summa de Arithmetica, Geometria, Proportioni et Proportionalit a' involving the use of journals and ledgers.

In the old days when firms recorded transactions in books or ledgers, the left side was the debit side and the right the credit side. The left side got all expense items and assets of value to the business. The right side got the sources of income and any liabilities to repay money in the future. Cash received went on the left and cash paid out on the right. To summarize so far:

Debit side	Credit side
Expenses	Income
Assets (including customer debts)	Liabilities (including owing to suppliers)
Decrease in a liability	Decrease in an asset
Cash received	Cash paid out

Accounts are opened in a ledger for each item of expense, asset, income, and liability. Think of an account as a letter T, with the name of the account on the cross bar and any entries of figures on the left or right side of the vertical bar. Each financial transaction is entered in two separate accounts in a double entry system. One entry will be on the debit (left) side in one account while the other entry will always be on the credit (right) side of the second account involved. Let us look at a few simple examples.

Example
Paid £200 wages on 2 Aug with money from the bank account.

The two T accounts involved here are the wages account, abbreviated to *wages a/c* and the *bank a/c.* Wages are an expense so the entry goes on the debit side of the wages a/c. Money paid out for any reason is always a credit entry in the bank a/c as it is shown here. You will notice that the name of the other account involved is always given as a cross reference and as an explanation of what happened, and the date is included to record when it happened. The two entries will now appear as:

Wages a/c		Bank a/c	
Aug 2 Bank a/c200			Aug 2 Wages a/c 200

Example

The purchase of £900 goods on credit from A. Supplier on Aug. 5.

The two accounts involved here are the purchases a/c (an expense item) and that of A. Supplier a/c (a liability). Note that in practice every credit customer and every supplier will have their own separate account in the sales ledger and purchase ledger respectively, so that we can keep track of all amounts owed to and by the business.

Purchases a/c		A. Supplier a/c	
Aug 5			Aug 5
A. Supplier 900			Purchases 900

Example

The part payment of £600 to A. Supplier on Aug. 29.

The two accounts now involved are A. Supplier a/c which gets a debit entry to reduce the liability, and the bank a/c which gets a credit entry for cash paid out.

A. Supplier a/c		Bank a/c	
Aug 29			Aug 29
Bank 600			A. Supplier 600

Trial balance

At the end of an accounting period, say at the end of a month, we need to total up each account to find out how it stands. If entries are only on one side of the account, as will be the case with wages, we add up the weekly entries and arrive at the total or *balance* as it is called. When an account has entries on both sides, as will A. Supplier's a/c and the bank a/c in the above examples, we need to deduct the items on the smaller side from the larger side to find the balance.

In the case of the A. Supplier a/c, this balance will be £300 on the credit side as there is still a remaining liability of £300 to pay some time in the near future. This is illustrated now:

A. Supplier a/c					
Aug. 29	Bank	600	Aug. 5	Purchases	900
			Aug 31	Balance	300

All accounts are balanced off at the end of the month, or other accounting period. All accounts with a balance on them (some may not have) are then listed in what is called a *trial balance*. In the few accounts that we entered transactions above, the trial balance would come out like this:

Trial balance as at 31 August

Debit balances		Credit balances	
Purchases a/c	900	Bank a/c	800
Wages a/c	200	A. Supplier a/c	300
	£1,100		£1,100

The trial balance must always balance because we have entered each transaction in two separate accounts, on opposite sides, and in balancing each account have cancelled out a like amount on both sides. This is some proof of numerical accuracy, but it does not prove we have entered amounts in the right accounts! It is also possible to enter an identical wrong amount in both accounts!

The T accounts are not seen as such when computers are used to record double entry, but the basic principles of debit and credit are still observed. Accounting packages are available to do all the double entry bookkeeping, extract the trial balance and go on to produce the profit and loss account and balance sheet statements. As students or managers, our interest in bookkeeping is not for its own sake but as an explanation of why a balance sheet balances and where all the information comes from to produce the monthly and annual accounts.

This can be shown diagrammatically as in Figure 2.3.

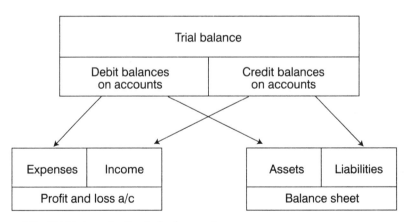

Figure 2.3 *Trial balance leading to final accounts*

Let us now take the example of the trial balance shown in Figure 2.4 relating to a market trader and produce a profit and loss account and balance sheet from it. Profit is the difference between income and expenses, but to keep the double entry principle going we will show the second entry of profit as an increase in the business owner's capital. This is true if the owner retains all the profit in the business.

Trial balance

Debit balances		Credit balances	
Cash a/c	400	Capital a/c	500
Purchases a/c	4,000	A. Supplier a/c (creditor)	200
Wages a/c	1,300	Sales a/c	8,200
Rent a/c	1,000		
Equipment a/c	1,500		
Customer a/c (debtor)	700		
	£8,900		£8,900

Profit and loss account

Expenses		Income	
Purchases	4,000	Sales	8,200
Wages	1,300		
Rent	1,000		
Total expenses	6,300		
Profit (8,200–6,300)	1,900		
	£8,200		£8,200

Balance Sheet

Assets		Capital liabilities	
Equipment	1,500	Original capital	500
Debtors (A. Customer)	700	Retained profit	1,900
Cash	400	Total capital	2,400
		Creditor (A. Supplier)	200
	£2,600		£2,600

Figure 2.4 *Final accounts from trial balance*

No matter how large the organization, these principles still apply, although more detailed descriptions of expenses, assets and liabilities will result in more complex statements than those in Figure 2.4. The type of business organization also affects the title and layout of the statements. We look at the details of the profit and loss account and balance sheet in the following chapters.

CHART OF ACCOUNTS

In computerized accounting systems a particular ledger account is identified by a unique number with the whole list of numbers being referred to as the *chart of accounts*, somewhat akin to a telephone directory. The UK is different to most other European countries in that we have no national chart of accounts and therefore no requirement for all organizations to use a standardized numbering system for financial accounts. Each company can invent its own unique chart of accounts although member companies of a group of companies may find it useful to use a common system to aid consolidation.

An example can be found in France with their Plan Comptable General (PCG) which is a standardized numbering system or chart of accounts plus account formats which are required to be used by all companies. Other numbering systems can be used in France, but they must be capable of conversion back to the national system code by code.

Other European countries have similar broad structures, but these may differ in the detailed analysis. For example, Belgium, France and Spain use the same seven broad classes:

Class 1	Equity, provisions and long-term loans.
Class 2	Fixed assets.
Class 3	Stocks, work-in-progress and long-term contracts.
Class 4	Debtors and creditors.
Class 5	Investments and cash.
Class 6	Purchases and expenses.
Class 7	Revenues.

Each of these classes is broken down into more detail by a further digit for each sub-class. For example, Class 3 in Belgium accords 30 to raw materials stocks, 32 to work-in-progress, etc, but these code numbers do not necessarily have the same meaning in the other two countries.

These European charts tend to have statutory backing and are geared up to producing financial accounting statements in the stipulated form. These differ from the UK also in that we analyse costs objectively by function (eg distribution costs, administrative costs, etc) whilst they analyse costs subjectively by source (eg wages, salaries, materials, depreciation, etc).

ORGANIZING THE BOOKS OF ACCOUNT

Ledgers

Each account code represents an individual T account. In a manual accounting system used by the smallest of businesses all T accounts may fit into one book or ledger. In most businesses, however, the volume of transactions, and the need for more than one person to have access to make entries, means that similar transactions are entered into one particular ledger. This is also true of computerized accounting systems. Typically there are three main ledgers:

- sales ledger;
- purchases ledger;
- nominal ledger.

The sales and purchases ledgers contain the T accounts for each individual credit customer and supplier whilst the nominal ledger contains the T accounts for total sales, total purchases and every other expense, income, asset and liability.

Journals

Double entries are not made directly into the ledgers, but are first entered in a book of prime entry from which *postings* to the two relevant ledger accounts are made later. These books of prime entry are:

- sales day book or sales journal;
- purchases day book or purchases journal;
- journal;
- cash book(s).

The sales and purchase day books act as a kind of diary where all sales and purchases are entered in chronological order. At a later date each transaction is entered in the named account of the customer or supplier in the sales or purchases ledger respectively whilst the total of a batch of similar transactions is entered in the sales account or purchases account in the nominal ledger, so completing the double entry. Since the advent of value added tax (VAT) some years ago, a further entry in the sales and purchase journals is needed to record these tax amounts which are posted to the relevant side of the VAT account in the nominal ledger in batch totals. In this way large volumes of individual sales and purchases are kept out of the nominal ledger by only posting batch totals for a day or a week at a time.

In a similar way, large amounts of cash transactions are first entered in a cash receipts book or a cash payments book, both of which act as books of prime entry and as ledgers. These cash transactions are later posted to the named account of the customer or supplier in the sales ledger or purchases ledger respectively. This again completes the double entry.

The journal proper is a book of prime entry used to make the initial record of non-routine transactions which are later posted to two ledger accounts to preserve the double entry principle. Typical entries in a journal might relate to:

- the correction of errors;
- adjustments for prepayments and accruals;
- the creation of provisions for bad debts or any other purpose;
- adjustments for stocks on hand at the end of an accounting period.

We have now seen how financial transactions are routinely recorded in journals and ledgers, and how a chart of accounts identifies each ledger account in a double entry bookkeeping system, all enabling the final accounts to be produced. The following chapters now examine each of these financial accounting statements in turn.

Further reading

Cox, D *et al* (1998) *Business Record Keeping,* Osborne.
Melville, A (1997) *Financial Accounting,* FT/Pitman, London.
Wood, F and Robinson, S (1997) *Book-keeping and Accounts,* FT/Pitman, London.

Self-check questions

1. Which system of bookkeeping is most suited to a self-employed plumber?
2. Define a receipts and payments account.
3. Prepare a receipts and payments account from the following information for Gosforth Gardeners Association, showing the cash balance at the end of the year:

Cash at start of year	£1,270
Bulk purchase of seeds and fertilizers	£2,510
Members" annual subscriptions	£560
Sales of seeds and fertilizers to members	£2,250
Purchase of equipment for hire	£1,500
Hire fees received	£450

4. Identify whether the following are debit or credit account balances:

   - expenses;
   - liabilities;
   - assets.

5. Name the two T accounts you would use to record the payment of a sum of money owed to a supplier (for goods bought on credit).
6. Prepare T accounts and a trial balance for John Deel, a market trader, who has provided you with the following information relating to his first year in business:

   Opened a business bank account with £1,500 of his own capital.
   Paid £1,200 for a stall and scales.
   During the year he purchased goods worth £17,000 from A. Wholesaler on credit.
   Received £28,000 from cash sales to customers during the year.
   He hired a van for business use at a cost of £300 per month inclusive of all running costs.
   During the year he made drawings of £6,000 cash to live on.
   Paid A. Wholesaler a total of £16,000 during the year.
   He had no stock left at the year-end. Assume there was no depreciation.

Trial balance

Fixtures and fittings a/c	6,300	Capital a/c	6,000
Purchases a/c	47,200	Creditors a/c	3,500
Wages a/c	22,700	Sales a/c	86,500
Rent, rates, electricity a/c	7,300		
Sundry expenses a/c	2,700		
Bank balance	9,800		
	£96,000		£96,000

7. Prepare a profit and loss account and balance sheet from the above trial balance relating to a baker's shop. Ignore depreciation. Assume there was nil stock at the year-end and that any profit is retained in the business.
8. What is meant by a chart of accounts?
9. Explain the difference between a journal and a ledger.

3

The profit and loss account

INTRODUCTION

The annual accounts consist essentially of an income statement and a balance sheet, which are also usually produced each month for internal use by management. In addition, there is a third, less well-known cash flow statement, but this seems to generate less interest than the other two statements. The most well-known income statement is a profit and loss account, but a *revenue account* or an *income and expenditure account* are alternatives used by non profit-seeking organizations. All three statements compare income with expenses consumed in the same period and broadly follow the same accounting principles.

One difference between the three income statements relates to their sources of income. For example, a local authority will have rates, council tax and government grants as its main sources of income in its revenue account. Any charges for services provided will be a minor source of income for a local authority, but in a profit-seeking company will be the main, or only, source of income.

The other main difference between types of income statements is the treatment of the resulting profit or loss. Non-profit-seeking organizations will use the terms surplus or deficit. Profit-seeking enterprises will have to account for tax on the profit, and reward the owners of the business with dividends, if a limited company, or a share of profits if unincorporated. Any profit remaining after these appropriations is left in the company as extra capital. Having highlighted the differences, we are going to concentrate our attention on the profit and loss account relating to companies. The income statements of the other business organizations are addressed in Chapter 6.

DEFINITION OF PROFIT OR LOSS

We now need to examine exactly what is meant by a profit or a loss. The layperson's definition of a profit or loss being the difference between what something cost and its sales value is true overall. However, this definition has to be considerably tightened up when accountants come to measure profit or loss during specific time periods of one month; so much so that the layperson may not recognize the original definition!

A profit and loss account is a summary of a firm's trading income from its customers, offset by the cost of the goods or services sold, plus other running expenses for the same period of time. Therefore:

Income is defined as sales to customers and also includes rent or investment income received. The realization principle states that we count income when delivery of the goods or services takes place, and not at the time cash is actually received in settlement of credit sales.

Example
If credit sales were £120,000 during a year, while cash received from those same sales amounted to only £110,000 by the year-end, it is the former figure of £120,000 which counts as income. Double entry bookkeeping will have recorded all the sales as £120,000 and the cash received as £110,000, while the outstanding balances on various customer accounts will total the other £10,000 and be shown as debtors in the balance sheet.

Expenses are the cost of wages, materials and overheads used up during the period on the goods and services sold to customers. Accountants refer to these costs as *revenue expenditure*, as opposed to the purchase cost of assets, such as buildings, vehicles and equipment, which last a number of years and which are termed *capital expenditure*.

There are two tests as to whether or not an expense goes into the profit and loss account (the alternative location being the balance sheet). First, it must relate to the time period covered by the statement irrespective of whether the cash payment has been completed (any bills waiting to be paid are shown as creditors in the liabilities section of the balance sheet). This is the accrual principle at work.

Second, the expense must relate to goods and services included as sales income in the same statement. This is the matching principle at work. Expenses incurred for a later period, or on goods or services not yet sold to customers, go into the balance sheet as assets – the first as a prepayment and the second as stocks.

It is a common misconception to think of the profit and loss account as a summary of all cash flowing into and out of the business, and that the excess of cash receipts over payments represents the profit. Such thinking ignores all the cash transactions that affect the balance sheet, for example, when a company receives a bank loan, or when it buys new equipment.

A loan is a cash receipt, but it cannot be counted as income in the profit and loss account as it must be repaid at some future time. It is therefore shown as a liability in the balance sheet. When the loan is eventually repaid, such repayment is not an expense in the profit and loss account, but a reduction of the asset cash in the balance sheet. Before looking at a comprehensive example of a profit and loss account we need to discuss the treatment of stocks and the concept of depreciation.

TREATMENT OF STOCKS

In most businesses, goods purchased or manufactured are rarely all sold in the same accounting period and therefore give rise to stocks at the month or year-end. A basic principle of the profit and loss account is that sales must be matched with the cost of goods sold, not with the cost of goods purchased.

In ongoing companies we therefore have two stock figures to contend with – the opening stock at the beginning of the period and the closing stock at the end of that same period. Opening stock is an expense brought forward from a previous period to the present one, while closing stock is an expense to take from this period and carry forward in the balance sheet list of assets to the next period.

Example
A retail firm sold goods for £50,000 one month when purchases cost £30,000. Stock at the beginning of the month was £12,000 and this had increased to £15,000 by the month end.

	£	£
Sales		50,000
Opening stock	12,000	
Purchases	30,000	
	42,000	
Less Closing stock	15,000	
Cost of goods sold		27,000
Gross profit		23,000

Figure 3.1 *Trading account showing treatment of stocks*

This figure shows the part of a profit and loss account called the *trading account*. Instead of using the two-sided format based on double entry, we have now switched to the more usual vertical format. This approach is used in almost all published financial statements. Although companies do not publish a trading account as such, they are free to use whatever formats they like for internal consumption.

DEPRECIATION

A business spends cash in one of two ways – either on expenses or on assets. The expenses of labour, materials and overheads go into the profit and loss account, but not so the cost of fixed assets, such as vehicles or equipment. All may be thought of as necessary expenditure, but the crucial difference is that of time.

Labour, material, and overhead expenses are used up almost immediately unless expended on items remaining in stock. Fixed assets usually last for a number of years and it would be unfair to charge their whole acquisition cost against one month's, or even one year's, income. This problem is overcome by the simple expedient of charging a proportion of the cost, called *depreciation*, in each period's profit and loss account over the whole life of the asset.

The amount of depreciation to charge each month, or each year, is based on the expected life of an asset. To take a simple example of a machine costing £10,000 and expected to last five years before being scrapped, this would result in a depreciation charge of £2,000 each year for five years.

The actual life may not turn out to be five years. If shorter, then additional depreciation will be needed in the last year of its life. If longer, then the business gets a free ride after the fifth year. This evens itself out to some extent, taking a swings-and-roundabouts view of things. It is better to be, say, 90 per cent correct with the yearly depreciation charge than not attempt to calculate depreciation at all, so charging the profit and loss account with the full cost of the asset in the year it is scrapped.

There are two main methods used to calculate depreciation in the UK:

- the straight-line method; and the
- reducing balance method.

The method described earlier reduced the value of the machine by the same £2,000 each year. This is called the straight-line method because the depreciated value of the asset falls in a linear fashion. The reducing balance method charges a smaller amount of depreciation year after year. This is because a fixed percentage is applied to the falling value each year. On this basis we never get an asset value down to zero until it is scrapped. These two methods of depreciation can be contrasted in a simple diagram showing how the remaining value of the asset varies year by year, as in Figure 3.2.

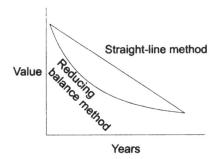

Figure 3.2 *Asset values under different depreciation methods*

If the remaining value varies on the two methods, so must the yearly depreciation charge. Let us apply the two methods to an example, now bringing in a residual value of the asset at the end of its life.

Example
A machine costs £11,000 and has an estimated value of £1,000 at the end of its five-year life.

The straight-line method takes the residual value from the original cost and divides by five, giving a depreciation charge of £2,000 per annum as follows:

$$\frac{\text{Cost of machine} - \text{resale value}}{\text{Expected life}} = \frac{£11,000 - £1,000}{5}$$

$$= £2,000 \text{ pa}$$

A variation of this straight-line method is to calculate the life in hours rather than years, so expressing the depreciation charge as £x per hour. This *machine-hour rate method* is often used in internal costings.

To calculate the reducing balance method of depreciation we need to find what percentage rate which, when applied to the reducing value of the machine each year, will reduce its value to £1,000 by the end of the fifth year. This is found from the formula:

$$r = 100 - \left(\frac{\sqrt[n]{\text{Residual value}}}{\text{Original cost}} \times 100 \right)$$

where n equals the estimated life in years and r equals the depreciation rate. Using the previous example we can solve the equation:

$$r = 100 - \left(\frac{\sqrt[5]{£1,000}}{£11,000} \times 100 \right)$$

$$\therefore r = 38\%$$

The calculations are now set out side-by-side in Figure 3.3 for the two methods, both resulting in approximately the same residual value of £1,000 after five years.

	Reducing balance method £	Straight-line method £
Original cost	11,000	11,000
First-year depreciation (38%)	4,180	2,000
Balance sheet value – end year 1	6,820	9,000
Second-year depreciation (38%)	2,592	2,000
Balance sheet value – end year 2	4,228	7,000
Third-year depreciation (38%)	1,607	2,000
Balance sheet value – end year 3	2,621	5,000
Fourth-year depreciation (38%)	996	2,000
Balance sheet value – end year 4	1,625	3,000
Fifth-year depreciation (38%)	618	2,000
Balance sheet value – end year 5	1,007	1,000

Figure 3.3 *Calculating depreciation*

Under the reducing balance method, the depreciation charge is greater for the first two years than under the straight-line method. After that the roles are reversed with straight-line depreciation being more in the last three years than under the reducing balance method. Both methods are acceptable, but the reducing balance method is not normally used to depreciate buildings or leases. Either method can be used on plant, equipment and vehicles but it is on motor cars that the reducing balance method is most commonly seen.

The Inland Revenue ignore a company's own depreciation charge when calculating how much tax is chargeable on the profit made, and substitute their own tax or capital allowances in its place. Basically, for most industries and locations there are only three rates of tax allowance:

- 4 per cent pa based on the original cost of industrial buildings and calculated on a straight-line basis;
- 25 per cent pa on the reducing balance of plant, equipment, fixtures, furnishings and vehicles with a life not exceeding 25 years.
- 6 per cent pa on the reducing balance of plant and equipment with a life exceeding 25 years.

Special rates of capital allowances apply at times when economic incentives are needed to boost investment, and differential rates may be applied to specific industries. These tax allowances, and other aspects of taxation, are further discussed in Chapter 21.

We can now look at a fuller version of an internal profit and loss account, suitable for a trading organization where stocks are relevant. This is shown in Figure 3.4. A service organization could use a similar format, but omit the stocks items and the reference to gross profit.

Strictly speaking, what we are calling the profit and loss account comprises four stages, of which companies select those relevant to their business. The four stages are as follows:

- Stage 1 *Manufacturing*. When appropriate to a business, this shows the cost of goods manufactured.
- Stage 2 *Trading*. This shows the gross profit earned by matching the income against the cost of sales.
- Stage 3 *Profit and loss*. The overhead expenses of running the business are deducted from the gross profit to arrive at the net profit.
- Stage 4 *Appropriation*. This shows how the profit is appropriated in tax provisions; payment of dividends to shareholders; and the amount of profit retained in the business.

Manufacturing companies need a more detailed statement to take account of the three possible kinds of stock – raw materials, work-in-progress and finished goods as illustrated in Figure 3.5.

Further examples of internal profit and loss accounts for specific industries are shown in Chapter 15 which discusses their use in a budgeting context.

	£	£
Sales		50,000
Opening stock	12,000	
Purchases	30,000	
	42,000	
Less Closing stock	15,000	
Cost of goods sold		27,000
Gross profit		23,000
Less Wages and salaries	7,500	
Directors fees	2,500	
NI and pension contributions	2,300	
Rent, business tax	3,500	
Depreciation	1,400	
Electricity, gas, etc	700	
Stationery, postage, telephone	650	
Vehicle running expenses	2,500	
Auditors fees and other professional fees	200	
Bank interest and charges	360	21,610
Net profit		£1,390

Figure 3.4   *Example of a monthly profit and loss account*

PUBLISHED PROFIT AND LOSS ACCOUNTS

Published profit and loss accounts never disclose the degree of detail about expenses shown in Figures 3.4 and 3.5, although some individual expense items are shown tucked away in the notes to the accounts to comply with the legal requirements on disclosure.

Very often, expenses are grouped together under a limited number of functional headings, for example cost of sales; distribution costs; administrative expenses. The most popular Format 1 of the four types prescribed by the Companies Acts is shown abbreviated as Figure 3.6. Format 2 requires more detail on the face of the profit and loss account, but these extra details are contained in supplementary notes to Format 1, so in reality there is little difference between them. Formats 1 and 2 use a vertical form of presentation whilst the rarely seen Formats 3 and 4 use a horizontal presentation that reflects double entry bookkeeping.

	£000	£000
Sales		
Less Cost of sales:		1,000
Raw materials used	200	
Direct wages	<u>400</u>	
	600	
Add Opening work-in-progress	<u>100</u>	
	700	
Less Closing work-in-progress	<u>200</u>	
Prime cost	500	
Add Other factory expenses	<u>100</u>	
Gross cost of production	600	
Add Opening stock of finished goods	<u> 50</u>	
	650	
Less Closing stock of finished goods	<u> 55</u>	<u>595</u>
Gross profit		*405*
Less Administration expenses:		
Salaries	30	
Printing stationery, postages, telephone	10	
Rates, heat, light and power	10	
Bank charges and sundries	<u>10</u>	60
Selling and distribution expenses:		
Salaries and commision	40	
Advertising	10	
Carriage and packing	20	
Motor expenses	<u>20</u>	<u> 90</u>	<u>150</u>
Balance before charging		255
Depreciation	20	
Auditors' remuneration	10	
Debenture interest	10	
Directors' remuneration	<u>80</u>	<u>120</u>
Net profit before tax		135
Corporation tax		<u>60</u>
Net profit after tax		75
Dividends		<u>20</u>

Figure 3.5 *Example of a manufacturing, trading and profit and loss account*

	This year £m	Last year £m
Turnover	37,900	35,600
Cost of sales	(30,000)	(33,800)
Gross profit	7,900	1,800
Distribution costs	(400)	(350)
Administrative expenses	(3,500)	(4,100)
Operating profit/(loss)	4,000	(2,650)
Interest receivable	250	60
Interest payable	(100)	(400)
Profit/(loss) on ordinary activities before taxation	4,150	(2,990)
Tax on profit on ordinary activities	(650)	—
Profit/(loss) on ordinary activities after taxation	3,500	(2,990)
Dividends paid and proposed	1,350	—
Retained profit/(loss) for the financial year	2,150	(2,990)
Earnings/(loss) per share	7.0p	(5.7)p

Figure 3.6 *Published profit and loss account in Format 1 style*

The Financial Reporting Standard (FRS No 3) issued in 1992 and entitled *Reporting Financial Performance* aims to make the profit and loss account statement more reliable an indicator of financial performance and less vulnerable to creative accounting. It specifically requires companies:

- to separate turnover and operating profit between continuing operations, acquisitions, and discontinued operations;
- to disclose profits and losses resulting from restructuring/reorganization or from the disposal of fixed assets or parts of the business;
- to disclose extraordinary items (which should now be a rare event) as opposed to exceptional items (which could be quite commonplace);
- and to calculate earnings per share after taking them into account.

In addition, the standard requires a note to the profit and loss account statement disclosing what the profit would have been if revaluations of property were excluded, and the amount of any consequent adjustment to depreciation charges. This is to enable comparison to be made with other organizations that have used historic cost accounting throughout their lives. You may wish to refer to Chapter 7 dealing with historic/current cost accounting to follow up this point.

Finally, FRS 3 requires a statement showing the *total recognized gains and losses* in the period, comprising the profit for the period plus any other movements in balance sheet reserves. The purpose of this requirement is to give a picture of the overall performance, which previously was obscured (as in the case of Polly Peck plc) by items being reported in the separate accounting statements; in that case, the two items being interest receivable and exchange rate losses.

Further reading

Accounting Standards Board (1992) *Financial Reporting Standard No 3*, London.
Glautier, MWE and Underdown, B (1997) *Accounting Theory and Practice*, FT/Pitman, London.
Laidler, J and Donaghy, P (1998) *Understanding UK Annual Reports and Accounts*, ITP, London.
Melville, A (1997) *Financial Accounting*, FT/Pitman, London.

Self-check questions

1. Name three possible kinds of income statement.
2. A profit and loss account is a statement of all monies received during a period less all monies paid out. True or false? Give reasons.
3. Define depreciation.
4. What is the balance sheet value of an asset after three years if its original cost of £16,000 is depreciated at 20 per cent pa on the reducing balance method?
5. On inheriting £9,000, you decided to open a shop and paid three months' rent, in advance, on 1 October. The annual rental is £6,000.

   In the first week you fitted out the shop at a cost of £4,800 and you expect the fittings to last about four years.

   You started trading in the second week by buying £3,000 of goods for resale; £1,000 of which you managed to get on credit for settlement by the end of November; the other £2,000 you paid for in cash immediately.

   During October you paid out £600 in assistant's wages/ NI and £200 on sundry expenses. The previous tenant had paid about £450 this quarter for electricity, but you have not had the meter read yet. By the end of October your sales (all for cash) amounted to £3,600 and you still had half your purchases left in stock for sale the next month. How much profit or loss did you make in October?

4

The balance sheet

INTRODUCTION

When we talk about a set of accounts we are essentially talking about the profit and loss account statement (discussed in the previous chapter) and the balance sheet statement, to which we now turn. This is not to deny the existence of a third statement dealing with cash flow, which also plays an important role in informing managers and other parties as discussed in Chapter 5.

A balance sheet is a snapshot picture at a moment in time. On the one hand it shows the value of assets (possessions) owned by the business and, on the other, it shows who provided the funds with which to finance those assets and to whom the business is ultimately liable. Here we have an example of the dual aspects of recording which explains why a balance sheet must always balance.

DUAL ASPECTS OF RECORDING

Another way of expressing the dual aspect of a balance sheet is by the equation:

Assets	=	Liabilities

This balance sheet equation can best be understood by showing a few simple examples of how a balance sheet will look after transactions that affect either assets or liabilities, or both at the same time.

Example 1

Joe Bloggs starts up a business and pays £l,000 into a newly opened business bank account. The balance sheet now reflects the asset of £1,000 cash and the liability of the business to the owner who provided the £1,000 capital. This is to reflect the accounting convention of *separate entity* when the accounts of each

The annual accounts

business enterprise are kept apart and distinct from the proprietor's personal transactions.

Balance sheet for Joe Bloggs

Assets		Liabilities	
Cash	£1,000	Owner's capital	£1,000

Example 2

If some of the cash is now spent on stock costing £400, there is no change to the balance sheet totals on either side, but a switch from cash to stocks on the assets side as follows:

Balance sheet for Joe Bloggs

Assets		Liabilities	
Stock	400	Owner's capital	1,000
Cash (1,000–400)	600		
	£1,000		£1,000

Example 3

Further stock costing £200 is now bought on credit. The asset of stock is now increased in value by £200, which is balanced by the new liability of creditors on the other side for the same amount, as follows:

Balance sheet for Joe Bloggs

Assets		Liabilities	
Stock (400 + 200)	600	Owner's capital	1,000
Cash	600	Creditors	200
	£1,200		£1,200

Example 4

Some stock originally costing £l00 is now sold for cash of £150, making a profit of £50. This shows as a switch from one asset to another asset, but also partly shows as an increased liability. Stock reduces by £100, but cash increases by £150. The seeming imbalance of £50 is corrected by showing the owner's capital increasing by £50 to £1,050 on the liabilities side. This is because retained profits in any business belong to the owner(s) who would ultimately get that amount if all the assets were turned back into cash and the liabilities were then paid off. The balance sheet now looks like this:

Balance sheet for Joe Bloggs

Assets		Liabilities	
Stock (600 – 100)	500	Owner's capital (1,000 + 50)	1,050
Cash (600 + 150)	750	Creditors	200
	£1,250		£1,250

Having justified (it is hoped!) why a balance sheet must always balance, let us return to examining this statement in some detail. Assets are of two main types and are classified under the headings of either *fixed assets* or *current assets*. Fixed assets are the hardware or physical things used by the business itself and which are not for sale to customers. Examples of fixed assets include buildings, plant, machinery, vehicles, furniture and fittings.

Other assets in the process of eventually being turned into cash from customers are called current assets, and include stocks, work-in-progress, debts owed by customers and cash itself. Therefore we can say:

Total assets	=	Fixed assets	+	Current assets

Assets can only be bought with funds provided by the owners or borrowed from someone else, for example, bankers or creditors. Owners provide funds by directly investing in the business (say, when they buy shares issued by the company) or indirectly, as we have seen earlier, by allowing the company to retain some of the profits. Therefore for a limited company:

Total liabilities	=	Share capital and reserves	+	Borrowings and other creditors

This same identity is also true for non-incorporated businesses when the owner's capital comprises the initial investment plus any retained profits, while further finance is provided by borrowings and, indirectly, by credit from suppliers.

Borrowed capital can take the form of a long-term loan at a fixed rate of interest or a short-term loan, such as a bank overdraft, usually at a variable rate of interest. All short-term liabilities owed by a business and due for payment within 12 months are referred to as *creditors falling due within one year,* and long-term indebtedness is called *creditors falling due after one year.* Having identified all the items in a balance sheet, we can show the total picture as in Figure 4.1, keeping to the balance sheet equation of assets equal liabilities for the moment. You may be correct in thinking that assets and liabilities are on the wrong sides, but the convention grew up for some unknown reason that the sides were reversed in the balance sheet. This is now all irrelevant as explained below.

Balance sheet

	£000		£000
Capital and reserves	200	Fixed assets	100
Creditors falling due after 1 year	50	Current assets	250
Creditors falling due within 1 year	100		
	350		350

Figure 4.1 *Balance sheet structure (horizontal format)*

This horizontal presentation is rarely used, certainly in the case of published accounts that have to comply with the relevant standards. A vertical presentation is now the norm and the same balance sheet items shown in Figure 4.1 are now represented vertically in Figure 4.2:

Balance sheet		
	£000	£000
Fixed assets		100
Current assets	250	
Less		
Creditors falling due within one year	100	
Net current assets (ie working capital)		150
Total assets *less* current liabilities		250
Less		
Creditors falling due after one year		50
Net assets (wealth owned by shareholders)		200
Capital and reserves		200

Figure 4.2 *Balance sheet structure (vertical format)*

ASSETS

A business's possessions or assets are normally divided into two broad categories based on a time distinction: fixed or long-term assets, and current or short-term assets.

These various categories of asset are normally valued at the original cost of the items which is referred to as the *historic cost convention*. Sometimes a valuable building may be revalued to its current value, but this is the exception rather than the rule. *Current cost accounting*, where assets are revalued regularly, and the profit adjusted for the effects of inflation, is the subject of Chapter 7.

It may come as a surprise but some assets are not disclosed in a balance sheet. Internally generated goodwill, including the value of many brands that have been developed over many years, never appear in a balance sheet. The skills of the workforce, probably any firm's most valuable asset, do not appear at all in a balance sheet. This is because the firm does not own its employees, who can leave and go to work for someone else. There would also be a valuation problem here as it can not be assumed that training costs incurred by a current employer equate to skill value. An exception here might be the transfer fees paid to recruit professional football players which some clubs are treating as a capital asset. Other clubs pass transfer fees paid and received through their profit and loss account as expenditure and income respectively.

These two factors – historic asset values and missing assets – are the main reasons why a balance sheet as published, has limited economic meaning. It certainly does not purport to show the value of a business or what a company's shares are worth. It merely records what assets the organization has spent its money on and who provided that money. With this big proviso in mind, let us now examine the balance sheet in detail.

Fixed assets

These are assets held in the business for use rather than for resale and can be regarded as long-term assets to be used for a number of years. Fixed assets are grouped under three possible headings:

- tangible assets;
- intangible assets;
- investments.

1. *Tangible assets* are likely to appear in every balance sheet. They embrace land and buildings, plant and machinery, motor vehicles and furniture and fittings. They are normally shown in the balance sheet at their original cost reduced by the amount of depreciation written off to the profit and loss account so far.

The main object of depreciation is to spread the original cost of the asset over its expected life so that the profit and loss account for any period bears a fair share of the original cost of fixed assets. Consequently, the value of fixed assets in the balance sheet may not reflect their saleable value at that time because of inflation, or because of changing technology, or other reasons.

This practice of depreciating owned fixed assets is extended to some leased assets. First, a distinction has to be made between *operating leases* and *finance leases*. The former would describe the short-term hire of an asset, for example, the renting of a vehicle or piece of equipment for a few weeks or months. These operating lease payments are charged to the profit and loss account when incurred, and no entry is needed in the balance sheet.

Finance leases, however, are seen as conferring all the benefits of outright ownership except that the asset is financed in a way somewhat akin to hire purchase. In this case, the assets being leased are originally shown in the balance sheet at their full cost together with the capital amount outstanding on the finance agreement. The asset value is then depreciated each year and the outstanding liability is reduced by the element of capital repaid.

It is a mammoth task in large organizations to keep records of all fixed assets showing their cost and depreciation amounts over time. In a business of some size, maintenance of the asset register is computerized, and accounting packages for this specific purpose are available.

2. *Intangible assets* embrace goodwill, brands, patents, trade marks, licences, etc. Such items will only appear on a balance sheet if they are separately identifiable and money is spent on their acquisition. Goodwill and brands have been very contentious items where UK accounting standards have not been in accord with international standards.

When FRS 10 becomes effective at the end of 1998, it will bring UK accounting practice on goodwill and intangible assets much closer to international practice.

It requires purchased goodwill and intangible assets to be capitalized as assets on the balance sheet. Any internally generated goodwill will not be capitalized (as before) and any other internally generated intangible assets should be capitalized only if they have a readily identifiable market value.

Intangible assets with limited lives will be amortized to the profit and loss account over their expected lives, but not if they are deemed to have infinite lives. In this case they need to be written down in the balance sheet only if their value has suffered impairment.

In general it is presumed that the useful economic lives of purchased goodwill and other intangible assets do not exceed 20 years from the date of acquisition. This can be rebutted if the asset is capable of measurement so that an impairment review can be carried out annually. For assets with an expected life of less than 20 years and therefore subject to amortization, impairment reviews are only needed after one year or if there are grounds for believing that the asset's value has fallen below the balance sheet value. The accounting rules on impairment are contained in FRS 11.

3. *Investments* only appear under the umbrella of fixed assets if they are long-term in nature and represent stakes in subsidiaries, joint ventures, or related companies. Sometimes this part ownership of another business relates to a supplier, competitor, or customer and the stake is held for strategic reasons and, possibly, eventual takeover.

Current assets

These are short-term assets which are already cash or which are intended to be turned back into cash in the course of normal trading activity. There are three main types of current assets, namely:

- stocks;
- debtors;
- investments, cash and bank balances.

Here we briefly examine each in turn, although the detailed management of these items is the subject of Chapter 18.

1. *Stocks* can be of up to three main types, depending on the nature of the business. The three categories are:

- raw materials;
- work-in-progress;
- finished goods.

A manufacturing firm will have all three kinds whereas a retail outlet will only have finished goods for resale. Service industries may also carry stocks. For example, an architect has considerable work-in-progress, consisting of labour and overhead charges on the drawings and supervision of building not yet charged out to clients.

Stocks are valued on the basis of their cost, or realizable value, if lower.

Realizable value means their value to the trade not their sale value to a customer. This rule can be important for firms holding stocks of commodities, for example, tin, lead, cocoa whose prices can be volatile at times. Valuing these stocks at the year-end may result in a loss if market value happens to be lower than cost at that particular moment. Engineering firms and confectionery manufacturers can see their profits affected either way by sharp changes in commodity prices.

The valuation of work-in-progress and finished goods may also not be quite so straightforward as valuing at cost would suggest. In this context it is debatable what constitutes cost. Obviously, the direct costs of labour and materials which went into making the product are part of the cost. So too is a share of some overhead costs of running the firm. It can be argued that all production and administrative overheads should be charged to all products, whether part or wholly finished. Selling and distribution overheads, however, should only apply to the goods sold and not by definition to the goods in stock. Fortunately, some rules have been formulated by the accountancy bodies and these are found in SSAP 9.

The value of stocks held in store is also influenced by the stores pricing policy. A few alternative systems of pricing stores issues are available, all of which affect the value of items not yet issued. This is discussed in Chapter 11 which explains costing matters.

2. *Debtors* arise only when firms sell on credit but, as credit sales are normal for all industries except some retailing, it means debtors are found in most balance sheets. Also included under this heading are payments made in advance of the goods or services being received when, say, rates were already paid for a further period after the balance sheet date. These are termed *prepayments*.

The basis for valuing trade debtors is to take the value of the customer invoices outstanding at the date of the balance sheet from the sales ledger. A small adjustment to this value is then made to reflect past experience that all invoices never get settled in full. Usually this is because some dispute about the goods or services delivered can arise at a later date, or some customers go bankrupt, or into liquidation, and cannot pay their debts.

For these reasons, firms make a small provision, based on past experience, of the amount which they should classify as doubtful debts. This provision for bad debts is charged as an expense in the profit and loss account and the global value of the debtors reduced accordingly in the balance sheet. Depending on the actual bad debts occurring within the year, the provision is topped up to a suitable level again at the next year-end.

3. *Investments* are not uncommon in the list of current assets and are of a different nature to those investments already discussed in fixed assets. Current asset investments relate to short-term investments of monies that are not immediately required and have been placed temporarily in the money markets, or elsewhere, to get a good return. If the investments are quoted securities, such as

shares or gilts, then their current market value must be disclosed on the balance sheet or by way of a supplementary note.

4. *Cash and bank balances* include cash floats, petty cash balances and any takings not yet banked. Businesses always have at least one bank current account (which will be a liability if overdrawn!) and may also have a deposit account. All these cash and bank balances pose no valuation problems.

Balance sheet sequence

The foregoing groups of assets are normally listed in order of permanence. Fixed assets are therefore listed before current assets and within each group the same practice is recognized. This results in the sequence land and buildings, plant and equipment, motor vehicles, fixtures and fittings for fixed assets. The sequence for current assets becomes stocks of raw materials, work-in-progress, finished goods, debtors, investments, ending with the least permanent assets of cash and bank balances.

LIABILITIES (OR SOURCES OF FUNDS)

We now turn our attention to a business's sources of funds – where the money comes from with which the assets are bought. The three main sources are:

- shareholders (or owners);
- borrowings;
- creditors excl. borrowings.

Each of these sources can be further divided as we shall see. In addition, a source of finance is usually found in trade credit. This occurs when a firm buys goods or services from other firms, but is allowed a number of weeks to pay. These trade creditors reduce the amount of working capital needed to be provided from shareholders and borrowings. It is for this reason that creditors falling due within a year are deducted from the total current assets to show the net amount of working capital in the balance sheet. We now look at each source of finance in turn.

Equity ie shareholders funds

Essentially this consists of the issued share capital and reserves of various kinds. It represents the amount of money that shareholders have invested directly into the company by buying shares, together with retained profits that belong to shareholders but which the company uses as additional capital. We look at each of these sources of finance separately.

1. *Ordinary shares* form the bulk of the shares issued by most companies and are the shares which carry the ordinary risks associated with being in business – indeed, they are often referred to as risk capital or *equity*. All the profits of the business, including past retained profits, belong to the ordinary

shareholders once any preference share dividends have been deducted. Ordinary shares have no fixed rate of dividend, but companies hope to increase its size in line with the growth of company profits over the years.

A company does not have to issue all its share capital at once. The total amount it is authorized to issue must be shown somewhere in the accounts, but only the issued share capital is counted in the balance sheet. Although shares can be partly paid, this is a rare occurrence. Partly paid shares on privatization of a publicly owned organization are not the same, as any outstanding monies are owed to the government and not to the company concerned.

2. *Preference shares* get their name for two reasons. First, they receive their fixed rate of dividend before ordinary shareholders. Second, in the event of a winding up of the company, any funds remaining go to repay preference share capital before any ordinary share capital. In a forced liquidation this may be of little comfort as shareholders of any type come last in the queue after all other claims from creditors have been met.

3. *Reserves* is probably the most misleading term in all accounting! In general terms it means profits of various kinds that have been retained in the company as extra capital. Also important is what the term reserves does not mean. It does *not* mean actual money held back in reserve in bank accounts or elsewhere. Reserves come from retained profits over many years but are probably reinvested in buildings, equipment, stocks, or company debts, just like any other source of capital.

The main categories of reserves are as follows:

- *Profit and loss account*, ie cumulative retained profits from ordinary trading activities.
- *Revaluation reserve* being the paper profit that can arise if certain assets are revalued to current price levels without the assets concerned being sold.
- *Share premium account*, ie the excess over the original par value of a share when new shares are offered for sale at an enhanced price. Only the original par value is ever shown as issued share capital.

Creditors

This term means any money owed to other parties at this time, that is payable at some future date. It embraces all borrowings and all money owed to suppliers plus other items mentioned below. The main distinction of creditors in a published balance sheet is based on time, with one year hence being the critical moment. Therefore, the two main headings of creditors in the balance sheet are:

- creditors falling due after one year;
- creditors falling due within one year.

1. *Creditors falling due after one year* fall into three main categories:

- borrowed capital;
- provisions or charges;
- other creditors.

Borrowing is attractive to a company if it thinks it can earn a greater return on the money used in its business than it costs to service the interest payments. When the government throws in tax relief on the interest payments, it becomes irresistible, although excessive borrowing gets risky if pushed too far. This relates to the topic of *gearing* which is discussed later in Chapters 9 and 16.

Firms sometimes also make provisions against future events, say, a restructuring or reorganization and redundancy programme. A provision is made by charging an estimated future cost as an expense in the profit and loss account now. The money has not yet been spent as this action anticipates a future event. Meanwhile, both the cash and the potential liability are shown in their respective places in the balance sheet reflecting the dual aspects of recording.

2. *Creditors falling due within one year.* As well as bank overdrafts or other short-term borrowings, these creditors are liabilities incurred in the normal course of trading. Examples are:

- bank overdrafts;
- amounts owing to suppliers (trade creditors);
- Employer's National Insurance contributions (NIC);
- payroll deductions of employees' National Insurance and Income Tax;
- corporation tax and VAT not yet due for payment;
- dividends declared but awaiting the payment date.

As already indicated, it is the normal practice now for these *current liabilities*, as they are also known, to be regarded as a negative current asset in the working capital cycle. This shows them as a deduction from current assets which they help to finance rather than as a separate source of funds in their own right. This working capital cycle is explored more in Chapter 18.

Other borrowings and sources of funds

There are various hybrid types of finance that are neither pure share nor pure borrowing. A *convertible loan* or a *convertible preference share* are cases in point. In both cases the original security is convertible into ordinary shares at some future date(s) on predetermined terms. The accounting standard FRS 4 entitled *Capital Instruments*, details how capital instruments and their associated costs are to be disclosed in the financial statements.

There can also be various types of borrowing, some being secured on assets of the business, some not. Loans, debentures, mortgages are all kinds of borrowing with different rights and obligations for the parties concerned. *Mezzanine finance* provided by venture capitalists is a loan subordinated to major finance and is common in management buy-outs or buy-ins.

It is possible to raise finance by the special use of existing assets. Occasionally one hears of a company selling off its valuable premises to a financial institution, but continuing to occupy them on a long-term lease. This is known as *sale and leaseback*. Capital previously tied up in the premises is now released for investment in other fixed assets or in more working capital. Future profits earned in this way will be partly offset by the rent charges hitting the profit and loss account.

Another asset which can be turned into cash is trade debtors. This is done by selling the invoices to a specialist finance house who collect the money from the customer later. *Factoring*, as it is called, is discussed in Chapter 18 and is a very fast-growing source of funds.

Mention has already been made of leasing or hire purchase. By this means, a business can acquire the use of fixed assets immediately but pay for them by instalments (plus interest) over a number of years. The differences are mainly legalistic ones regarding the terms of eventual ownership of the assets. When financed this way, both the assets and the capital debt are included in the balance sheet in much the same way as if they had been purchased from borrowed capital.

When deciding which sources of funds to use, companies have to consider such factors as availability, cost, risk, repayment burden if appropriate, and so on. This is touched on in Chapter 16.

We can now look at a complete balance sheet in Figure 4.3, incorporating all the items we have discussed.

Balance sheet

	£m	£m
Fixed assets		
Tangible assets:		
Buildings	40	
Plant and machinery	26	
Motor vehicles	8	
Fixtures and fittings	6	80
Intangible assets:		
Patents, licences		6
Investments		14
		100
Current assets		
Stocks and work-in-progress	120	
Debtors (customers' debts)	110	
Short-term investments	5	
Cash and bank balances	15	
	250	
Less		
Creditors falling due within one year		
Bank overdraft	35	
Other creditors	65	
	100	

continued overleaf

Balance sheet *continued*

Net current assets (ie working capital)		<u>150</u>
Total assets less current liabilities		250
Less		
Creditors falling due after one year		
Borrowings	40	
Provisions and charges	<u>10</u>	<u>50</u>
Net assets (wealth owed to shareholders)		<u>200</u>
Capital and reserves		
Issued share capital	120	
Retained profits (accumulated P & L a/cs)	<u>80</u>	<u>200</u>

Figure 4.3 *Balance sheet structure (vertical format)*

AUDIT

Limited companies must submit their annual accounts to audit by an independent, qualified accountant. The trend is towards minimizing the cost and procedures for small unquoted companies, but their larger brethren face big fees for audit services.

The audit report in a company's annual accounts is usually a very brief but important statement. In it, an independent report is made to the shareholders about whether the accounts give a *true and fair view* of the company's state of affairs. This means that adequate records have been kept and that the accounting statements comply with the Companies Act 1985 and professional standards laid down in SSAPs and FRSs.

A qualified report draws some irregularity to the attention of the shareholders for them to pursue at the annual general meeting or elsewhere. If it relates to a technicality that is not significant to the company's financial health, it will not attract much attention. A qualification on a serious matter, such as keeping inadequate records, overvaluation of stock, or using creative accounting to misinform shareholders, would lead to repercussions on the share price initially, followed by pressure on the directors to take immediate action or resign. Depending on the nature of the matter raised, it might also attract the attention of the Financial Reporting Review Panel or the Department of Trade and Industry.

Concern has been voiced about the reality of an auditor's independence. The directors of a company are usually empowered to fix the auditor's remuneration; they can recommend a change in auditor to the members; they also negotiate with the auditors about the presentation of the accounts. These factors may seem to leave auditors susceptible to pressure from directors.

External auditors have the legal responsibility for audit but many large organizations, not just companies, also employ internal audit staff on complementary work. The external auditor is reporting on the accuracy of the financial statements and any supporting systems and should bear the work of internal auditors in mind in performing this role. Internal auditors will have a much wider brief, taking them into issues of stewardship, costing, and computerized systems, to name but a few.

Further reading

Glautier, MWE, and Underdown, B (1997) *Accounting Theory and Practice,* FT/Pitman, London.
Laidler, J and Donaghy, P (1998) *Understanding UK Annual Reports and Accounts,* ITP, London.
Melville, A (1997) *Financial Accounting,* FT/Pitman, London.

Self-check questions

1. Why must a balance sheet always balance?
2. What are the two main groups of assets called?
3. What are the main two sources of long-term capital for a company?
4. Why is the goodwill of a company, built up over many years, not shown as an asset in its balance sheet?
5. Distinguish between operating leases and finance leases.
6. Name the three main types of stocks.
7. Why will there be a difference between the total value of customers' invoices outstanding and the amount shown as debtors in a company's balance sheet?
8. Differentiate between ordinary shares and preference shares.

5

Cash flow statement

INTRODUCTION

Readers of annual reports need some training to understand profit and loss accounts and balance sheets. They may be heartened by this further statement whose title does accurately describe its contents. The cash flow statement is quite literally a statement of the amounts of cash flowing in and out of the company during the period, analysed by the reason and purpose of the flow.

This statement is the third of the trio of statements found in company published accounts (the others being the profit and loss account and balance sheet). Its preparation is mandatory under FRS 1 for all but small companies, but even they are encouraged to prepare one under their own reporting standard (FRSSE). In addition to these external reporting requirements, a cash flow statement is likely to be prepared monthly, along with the other two statements, for the board and top management.

A cash flow statement summarizes exactly where cash came from and how it was spent during the year. Superficially, it would therefore, seem to draw on a mixture of transactions included in the profit and loss account and balance sheet for the same period end, but this is not the whole story.

Because there is a time lag on many cash transactions, for example, tax and dividend payments, the statement is a mixture of some previous year and some current year transactions; the remaining current year transactions go into the following year's cash flow statement during which the cash actually changes hands. Similarly, the realization and accrual conventions relating to sales and purchases respectively result in cash transactions having a different timing to when they were entered in the profit and loss account.

Example
A company had sales of £5 million this year and £4 million last year and these figures appeared in the profit and loss accounts of those years. Debtors at the end of

this year were £1 million and at the end of the previous year were £0.8 million. The cash inflow arising from sales this year is £4.8 million (£0.8 million +£5 million – £1 million) whereas the sales figure in the profit and loss account is £5 million.

For these reasons it is not possible to look at just this year's profit and loss account and balance sheet to find all the cash flows without reference to the previous year's accounts. The balance sheet will show the cash balance at the period end but will not easily disclose the multitude of ways in which it was achieved.

Compiling a cash flow statement is quite a technical job and some training plus inside information is needed to complete the task. Nevertheless, the bulk of the items can be identified from an examination of the other two accounting statements for both the current and previous years. However, managers are interested in how to read the statement, not how to compile one, so we shall concentrate on its interpretation.

CASH FLOW HEADINGS

The summarized cash flow statement in Figure 5.1 gives an illustration of what it looks like in outline, using the FRS 1 format and headings, as revised in 1996. All the detailed items which would normally be included under each heading are omitted at this stage. Cash outflows are shown bracketed; cash inflows are without brackets.

	£000
Operating activities	1,400
Returns on investment and servicing of finance	(150)
Taxation	(400)
Capital expenditure and financial investment	(550)
Acquisitions and disposals	(220)
Equity dividends paid	(200)
Management of liquid resources	(100)
Financing	300
Increase in cash during the period	80

Figure 5.1 *Summarized cash flow statement*

Descriptions of headings

We now examine exactly what is contained under each of the headings in turn, running through all of the items.

1. *Operating activities* shows cash generated or paid out from transactions relating to its trading activities with its customers, and includes operating profit, depreciation and changes in stocks, debtors and creditors during the period.

A prime source of cash for any company should be the sale of goods and services for more than their cost, thus leading to a cash inflow from profit. When depreciation is charged as an expense in the profit and loss account, it lowers profit but does not lead to any cash outflow, unlike all other expenses. For this reason depreciation must be added back to profit to find the cash inflow from trading operations.

Other operating activities that lead to inflows or outflows of cash are changes in the levels of stocks, debtors, and creditors by the period end. For example, a decrease in stocks allows a company to generate cash from sales without a corresponding cash outflow on purchases. This stock decrease is therefore a cash inflow. To take another example, any decrease in creditors can only be achieved by paying off creditors, which results in an outflow of cash.

If not shown on the face of the cash flow statement, a note reconciling the operating profit with net cash inflow from operating activities (£1.4 million in Figure 5.1) is required as shown in Figure 5.2:

	£000
Operating profit	1,340
Depreciation charge	280
Increase in stocks	(170)
Increase in creditors	70
Increase in debtors	(120)
Net cash inflow from operating activities	1,400

Figure 5.2   *Indirect method of reconciliation*

The net cash flow from operating activities of £1,400,000 above is arrived at by what is termed the *indirect method*. The alternative, but less popular *direct method* is shown below in Figure 5.3. FRS 1 allows thse two alternative ways to disclose the net cash flow from operating activities. The indirect method (Figure 5.2) seems to be the more popular, which may be because when the direct method is used a reconciling note to the indirect method is still required.

The indirect method derives the cash flow from operating activities by taking the operating profit plus depreciation and the changes in working capital items. These figures are all easily traceable from the last profit and loss account and the last two balance sheets. The direct method expresses the cash flow from operating activities in gross cash flow terms, not differentiating between current year's profit and working capital changes.

	£000
Cash received from customers	9,900
Cash payments to suppliers	(5,200)
Cash paid to and on behalf of employees	(2,700)
Other cash payments	(600)
Net cash inflow from operating activities	1,400

Figure 5.3   *Direct method of calculation*

2. *Returns on investment and servicing of finance* refers to the payment of interest on any loans, overdrafts, or finance leases and all interest received. The section also includes all dividends received, but only dividends paid to non-equity shareholders and minority interests. Dividends paid to the parent's equity shareholders are shown as a separate item below.

3. *Taxation* referred to here is UK corporation tax on company profits or similar taxes overseas on profits earned abroad. Such home and overseas tax cash flows will normally be payments, but tax recovered in certain circumstances could result in a cash inflow.

4. *Capital expenditure and financial investment* refers to the purchase and sale of fixed assets during the period except those included in the next section – acquisitions and disposals. It also includes loans made or repaid that are not part of an acquisition or disposal nor short-term in nature when they are classed as liquid resources.

5. *Acquisitions and disposals* relates to payments to acquire and receipts from the sales of an associate, joint venture or subsidiary business.

6. *Equity dividends* paid are dividends paid to the reporting entity's (or parent in the case of a group) equity shareholders.

7. *Management of liquid resources* relates to payments and withdrawals of short-term deposits or other investments held as liquid resources that are readily convertible into cash and held as current asset investments.

8. *Financing* includes receipts and repayments of any form of external finance, for example, shares, loans, debentures and finance leases.

9. *Increase/decrease in cash during the period* is the final result of all the above cash inflows and outflows when totalled. The resulting total will be reflected in the cash and bank balances as at the period end. The net cash flow for the period will explain the difference between net debt at the start of the period and net debt at the end of the period and a note reconciling the net cash flow to the movement in net debt is required.

PUBLISHED STATEMENT

Having discussed the detailed contents of each heading in the cash flow statement, it is now time to look at a complete example and how the figures contained in it might be interpreted. This is shown at Figure 5.4

Cash flow statement		
		£000
Net cash inflow from operating activities (see Fig 5.2):		1,400
Returns on investments and servicing of finance:		
Interest received	25	
Interest paid	(95)	
Preference dividends paid	(80)	
Net cash outflow from returns on investment and		
servicing of finance		(150)

continued overleaf

Cash flow statement *continued*

Taxation:		
Corporation tax paid		(400)
Capital expenditure and financial investment:		
Payments to acquire tangible fixed assets	(670)	
Sale of fixed asset investment	120	
Net cash outflow on capital expenditure and financial investment		(550)
Acquisitions and disposals:		
Sale of interest in joint venture	60	
Purchase of subsidiary undertaking	(280)	
Net cash outflow from acquisitions and disposals		(220)
Equity dividends:		
Equity dividends paid		(200)
		(120)
Management of liquid resources:		
Sale of treasury bills	40	
Purchase of treasury bills	(140)	
Net cash outflow from the management of liquid resources		(100)
Financing:		
Issue of ordinary shares	450	
Repayment of loan	(150)	
Net cash inflow from financing		300
Increase in cash during the period		80

Figure 5.4 *Cash flow statement in FRS 1 format*

INTERPRETATION OF THE STATEMENT

The example shown in Figure 5.4 discloses near the end that the company had a net cash outflow of £120,000 *before* the management of liquid resources and financing. An issue of £450,000 new share capital was undertaken, partly to finance this deficit, partly to repay an old loan of £150,000, and most of the remainder temporarily going to purchase treasury bills. The remaining £80,000 went to swell the cash and bank balances. Looking higher up the statement, we now want to find reasons why this net cash outflow of £120,000 occurred.

The first calls on operating profit are interest charges, taxation, and dividends – in that order. Payments for all three combined amount to £750,000 – just over one-half of the £1.34 million operating profit earned. The remaining profit plus depreciation provisions are available for new investment in working capital (stocks, debtors, etc), new fixed assets and acquisitions.

It would appear to be the high level of investment in tangible fixed assets, amounting to £670,000, that has resulted in the company not being totally self-financing in the period and having to resort to new financing. This capital expenditure is well in excess of the £280,000 depreciation charge for the period. Some of the difference may be explained by the inflation effect on the cost of replacement assets, but the remainder is likely to be explained by the purchase of additional assets.

Dividend distributions of £200,000 do not look excessive in relation to the £850,000 profit after interest and taxation. If the new acquisition and investment in working capital and additional fixed assets reflects growth in the scale of operations, the new financing may be quite justified, provided an adequate return is earned on those assets.

This third financial statement augments the view users get from looking only at the profit and loss account and balance sheet of a company. It adds another perspective of cash flowing into and out of the company during a period of time, together with explanations and reasons for them. The first two statements have various limitations and subjective judgements attached to them which makes their interpretation less precise than users may wish. The cash flow statement has few, if any, such limitations and tells us literally what its title says it does.

Further reading

Accounting Standards Board (1996) *Financial Reporting Standard No. 1*, London.
Glautier, MWE and Underdown, B (1997) *Accounting Theory and Practice*, FT/Pitman, London.
Laidler, J and Donaghy, P (1998) *Understanding UK Annual Reports and Accounts*, ITP, London.
Melville, A (1997) *Financial Accounting*, FT/Pitman, London.

Self-check questions

1. Why do companies prepare a cash flow statement in addition to a profit and loss account and balance sheet?
2. What is the difference between the operating profit and the net cash inflow from operating activities?
3. Which figures would you compare in a cash flow statement to discover whether a company was merely replacing old fixed assets or making additions to them?
4. If a cash flow statement shows a final cash inflow for the period, is it therefore trading profitably?

6
Accounting for different business organizations

INTRODUCTION

For most practical purposes, the layouts of the profit and loss account for the self employed, partnerships, limited companies (and even public authorities) are identical. The exception comes at the very end of the statement, which shows the disposition of the profit (or surplus) in taxation, rewards to the owners and profit retained in the business.

The layouts of the balance sheet are also nearly identical except for the section showing the owner's funds invested in the business. There is more conformity with the assets owned by any type of business, which are capable of analysis into the now familiar fixed or current asset categories.

Example
We will compare identical basic information for the year ended 31 December throughout this chapter and see how it is treated in the different types of business organization. The standard data is:

	£
Capital originally introduced	30,000
Profit retained at 1 January	18,000
Net profit before tax for the year ended 31 December	24,000
Tax due on profits	9,000
Personal drawings or dividends	10,000
Profit retained in the business	5,000

SELF-EMPLOYED

The sole trader or self-employed situation is the simplest. All the profit belongs to the one person and it is usual to show the profit before any personal drawings are charged. This accords with the profit which the Inland Revenue use to levy income tax as, otherwise, drawings would not be taxed.

In the balance sheet the original capital and retained profit are merged into a combined *capital account* which is reduced by any personal drawings of the proprietor. As income tax is levied on the owner rather than on the business it is not usually shown in the accounts, but treated as drawings when actually paid. These transactions are illustrated in Figure 6.1.

	£
End of the profit and loss account:	
Net profit for the year	24,000
Balance sheet:	
Capital account:	
Balance at 1 January (£30,000 + £18,000)	48,000
Add Net profit for the year	24,000
	72,000
Less Personal drawings	10,000
Balance at 31 December	62,000

Figure 6.1 *Extracts from accounts for the self-employed*

The apparent increase of £14,000 in the owner's capital account will be reduced by further drawings at a later date when the £9,000 tax is paid, leaving capital of £53,000 – an increase of £5,000.

PARTNERSHIPS

The partnership agreement or, in its absence, the Partnership Act 1890, may allow for interest on the original capital, for the payment of salaries to partners, and state the proportions in which remaining profits are to be shared. Interest and salaries paid to partners are still regarded as shares of the profit for tax purposes.

It is necessary to show these items in an appropriation section at the end of the profit and loss account together with the agreed division of remaining profit. Tax is dealt with in the same way as in sole trader's accounts. If interest is paid only on the original capital and not on profits retained in the business then it is necessary to have separate capital and current accounts for each partner in the balance sheet.

Example

In the illustration in Figure 6.2 it is assumed that the two partners, A and B, each receive salaries of £6,000 and £4,000 respectively; that 10 per cent interest is allowed on their capital accounts; and that any balance of profit is shared equally between them.

		£	£
End of profit and loss account:			
Net profit for the year			24,000
Interest on capital accounts	A	1,000	
	B	2,000	
Salaries	A	6,000	
	B	4,000	
Balance divisible equally	A	5,500	
	B	5,500	24,000
Balance sheet:	A	B	
Capital accounts:	10,000	20,000	30,000
Current accounts:			
Balance as at 1 January	5,700	12,300	
Add Interest on capital	1,000	2,000	
Salary	6,000	4,000	
Share of profit	5,500	5,500	
	18,200	23,800	
Less Personal drawings	4,600	5,400	
Balance on current accounts as at 31 December	13,600	18,400	32,000
Total of partners' capital and current accounts	23,600	38,400	62,000

Figure 6.2   *Extracts from accounts of a partnership*

The same principle applies here as in the note on self-employed, that the apparent increase in the partners' current accounts will be reduced by further drawings of £9,000 when they make their personal tax payments. The increase in current account balances will then be £5,000 more than the figure at the start of the year.

LIMITED COMPANIES

A company is a separate entity from its individual owners or shareholders so that corporation tax payable by the company is shown as an appropriation of profit together with the dividends paid and proposed for the year. Any balance of profit remaining, after tax and dividend have been provided, is not added to the original share capital, but is shown as a *revenue reserve.*

Companies are legally obliged to show the issued share capital and reserves separately in their balance sheets, although together they form the total shareholders' funds invested in the business. Tax owing and dividends declared, but unpaid at the year-end, appear as current liabilities if the tax is due for payment within the next 12 months. See Figure 6.3 for an example.

End of profit and loss account:	£	£
Net profit for the year		24,000
Corporation tax payable on year's profit		9,000
Profit after tax		15,000
Dividends on ordinary shares		10,000
Retained profit added to revenue reserves		5,000
Balance sheet:		
Authorized and issued ordinary share capital		30,000
Revenue reserves (retained profits)		23,000
Current liabilities:		
Corporation tax payable	9,000	
Proposed dividend	10,000	19,000
Total		72,000

Figure 6.3 *Extracts from accounts for a limited company*

The revenue reserve of £23,000 comprises £18,000 + £5,000. If an interim dividend has been paid during the year, only the proposed final dividend appears as a current liability.

LOCAL AUTHORITIES

The income statement of a local authority or other public body is prepared on the same principles and conventions as a company profit and loss account. Their format, however, must take account of the different way each is financed and the treatment of surpluses or deficits.

A local authority will publish a *revenue account* as its income statement. The format of this statement is intended to inform readers of the cost of providing various services and how expenditure on them was financed. The precise format is laid down by statute and guidelines from the relevant professional bodies.

Local authorities use a system of fund accounting for reporting on their activities. Typical funds will include the general rate fund, the housing account, the loans fund, the insurance fund and the capital fund. When all funds are aggregated, a consolidated revenue account and consolidated balance sheet emerges for the authority.

Of the various funds, the general rate fund embraces many of the functions traditionally associated with local authorities, so an illustration of this is shown in Figure 6.4.

Revenue account for the year:		
	£000	*£000*
Income (not specific to any expenditure):		
Rates		50,300
Block grant		49,000
		99,300
Expenditure (net of specific fees, charges, and grants):		
Cultural and leisure activities	7,400	
Education	58,300	
Environmental health	5,600	
Finance	4,100	
Housing	200	
Social services	14,400	
Planning	8,900	
		98,900
Surplus transferred to balance sheet (revenue balances)		400
Balance sheet at year-end:		
Fixed assets		110,000
Current assets	53,400	
Creditors due within one year	(23,700)	29,700
		139,700
Financed by:		
Long-term borrowing		127,000
Provisions for liabilities and charges		900
Revenue balances (including 400 for this year)		11,800
		139,700

Figure 6.4 *Local authority – general rate fund accounts*

CONSOLIDATED OR GROUP ACCOUNTS

Shareholders of limited companies are not necessarily individuals. As a company is a separate legal entity, it follows that it can be a shareholder in another company. When the shareholding exceeds 50 per cent of the voting capital, then that other company is called a subsidiary of the parent or holding company. This is very commonplace in the UK, where many public and private companies wholly, or partly, own other (subsidiary) companies.

Each individual company must produce and distribute to its shareholder(s) a set of annual accounts. However, the various companies in a group are parts of one single undertaking and the consolidated accounts are the means of informing the parent company's shareholders of the financial position and performance of the combined companies which it controls. The legal requirements are to present:

- a consolidated profit and loss account;
- a parent company balance sheet;
- a consolidated balance sheet.

The precise requirements are very complex and are contained in FRS No 2, *Accounting for Subsidiary Undertakings*, but the basic elements of consolidation are now described below.

Consolidated profit and loss account

This statement combines all the separate profit and loss accounts of the parent and subsidiary companies. Where the subsidiary companies are wholly owned, then sales, trading profit, interest, tax, etc, are aggregated item by item. Sales to other group companies which have not been resold to third parties must be eliminated, as must any profits on such sales or interest on inter-group loans. The logic here is that a company cannot sell to, or profit from, itself.

In the case where all subsidiary companies are not wholly owned then all of the profit does not belong to the parent company. The proportion of the profit after tax belonging to the outside shareholders is deducted to arrive at the profit attributable to the parent company's shareholders. These outside or minority shareholders in subsidiary companies are called *minority interests*. An abbreviated example of a consolidated profit and loss account showing a share of profits going to such minority interests is illustrated in Figure 6.5

	£
Sales	10,000,000
Cost of sales	(5,600,000)
Gross profit	4,400,000
Distribution costs	(2,670,000)
Administrative expenses	(1,133,000)
Income from interests in associated undertakings	130,000
Operating profit	467,000
Income from investments	50,000
Net interest payable	(103,000)
Profit on ordinary activities before tax	414,000
Tax on profit on ordinary activities	(140,000)
Profit on ordinary activities after tax	274,000
Minority interests	(15,000)
Profit attributable to ordinary shareholders	259,000
Ordinary dividends	(57,000)
Retained profit of parent company	202,000
Earnings per share	31.6p

Figure 6.5 *Example of a consolidated profit and loss account*

Sometimes companies own shareholdings in other companies or joint ventures, over which they can exert significant influence but which they do not control. Typically, this is when they own between 20 per cent and 50 per cent of the voting capital, so that they are not classified as subsidiary companies but are called *associated undertakings*.

When producing a consolidated profit and loss account, the holding company must disclose its proportionate share in associated company profits and losses, irrespective of whether or not it receives such profits as dividends. This is illustrated in Figure 6.5 as *income from interests in associated undertakings* of £130,000. However, it does not disclose its share of the turnover and expenses of such associates in the consolidated profit and loss account.

When a company owns less than 20 per cent of another company, this is treated as a *fixed asset investment* and only the income received from such investments (as opposed to a proportionate share of profits) is shown in the consolidated profit and loss account. This amounts to £50,000 in the example shown in Figure 6.5.

Parent company balance sheet

This has all the appearance of a normal balance sheet except that included in the assets will be the cost of shares owned in subsidiary (and associated) companies plus any amounts owed by them. Conversely, if the parent company has borrowed money from a subsidiary company this indebtedness will also be disclosed.

Consolidated balance sheet

A consolidated balance sheet is prepared by adding together the individual balance sheets of the parent company and its subsidiaries. This is achieved as follows:

1. All fixed and current assets and external liabilities are amalgamated item by item.
2. Inter-company indebtedness is eliminated.
3. The cost of the investment in subsidiary companies cancels out the proportion of the shareholders' funds acquired in those companies.
4. If there is an excess purchase cost over the value of shareholders' funds acquired, this is called *goodwill*. Conversely, a *capital reserve* occurs when the purchase cost is less than the value of shareholders' funds acquired.
5. The amount of shareholders' funds in subsidiary companies owned by outside shareholders is shown separately as minority interests.

Example

The simplest situation is where a parent company (P Ltd) sets up a wholly owned subsidiary (S 100% Ltd) from the beginning. In this case there are no minority interests and no goodwill to concern us. The relevant balance sheets are set out in Figure 6.6, together with the resultant consolidated balance sheet. These are shown in horizontal format for ease of illustration.

P Ltd balance sheet

	£000		£000
Issued share capital	22,000	Fixed assets	11,000
Reserves	1,300	Investment in S 100% Ltd	10,000*
	23,000	Loan to S 100% Ltd	2,000†
Current liabilities	1,200	Current assets	1,500
	£24,500		£24,500

S 100% Ltd balance sheet

	£000		£000
Issued share capital	10,000*	Fixed assets	17,300
Reserves	15,400	Current assets	21,100
	25,400		
Loan from P Ltd	2,000†		
Current liabilities	11,000		
	£38,400		£38,400

P Ltd consolidated balance sheet

	£000	£000		£000	£000
Issued share capital		22,000	Fixed assets	11,000	
Reserves	1,300			17,300	28,300
	15,400	16,700			
Current liabilities	1,200		Current assets	1,500	
	11,000	12,200		21,100	22,600
		£50,900			£50,900

Note The items cross-referenced with symbols † and * cancel each other out in the consolidated balance sheet.

Figure 6.6 *Consolidated balance sheet – wholly owned subsidiary*

When a subsidiary company is only partly owned, then all the assets (less debts) are not owned by the parent company even though they are all shown in the consolidated balance sheet. Therefore the value of these assets, which equals the value of shareholders' funds owned by outsiders in the subsidiary company, is shown as a liability on consolidation.

Example
We will now assume that parent company (P Ltd) owns only 80 per cent of a subsidiary company (S 80% Ltd) which was set up in conjunction with another company who provided the other 20 per cent of the share capital. The relevant balance sheets are now set out in Figure 6.7.

P Ltd balance sheet

	£000		£000
Issued share capital	30,000	Fixed assets	22,000
Reserves	15,000	Investment in S 80% Ltd	20,000*
	45,000	Loan to S 80% Ltd	5,000†
Current liabilities	5,000	Current assets	3,000
	£50,000		£50,000

S 80% Ltd balance sheet

	£000		£000
Issued share capital	25,000*	Fixed assets	35,000
Reserves	10,000		
	35,000		
Loan from P Ltd	5,000†		
Current liabilities	20,000	Current assets	25,000
	£60,000		£60,000

P Ltd consolidated balance sheet

	£000	£000		£000	£000
Issued share capital		30,000	Fixed assets	22,000	
	15,000			35,000	57,000
Reserves (80%)	8,000	23,000			
		53,000			
Minority interests					
(20% × 35,000)		7,000			
Current liabilities	5,000		Current assets	3,000	
	20,000	25,000		25,000	28,000
		£85,000			£85,000

Note The inter-company loan cross-referenced † cancels itself out. The investment in the subsidiary of £20,000 cancels out 80% of the issued share capital of the subsidiary; the other 20% being part of minority interests.

Figure 6.7 *Consolidated balance sheet – partly owned subsidiary*

If the subsidiary had been bought at a later stage then the cost of the investment must be matched against the value of shareholders' funds acquired, including the pre-acquisition profits held in reserves. This comparison determines whether goodwill or a capital reserve arises on consolidation at the year-end. Only post-acquisition profits in the subsidiary are included in the consolidated reserves. The distinction of profits of the subsidiaries into 'pre-' and 'post-acquisition' is also important for dividend purposes. The parent company must not pay dividends to its shareholders from pre-acquisition profits of subsidiaries. These matters are more complex than the purpose of this book allows us to pursue, so interested readers should follow them up elsewhere.

In this chapter we have examined the final accounts for differing types of organization and shown how the statements are usually presented in a modern format. We have also looked at the principle of consolidation because most published accounts of quoted companies represent the activities of a group rather than a single company.

Further reading

Accounting Standards Board (1992) *Financial Reporting Standard, No. 2*, London.
Glautier, MWE and Underdown, B (1997) *Accounting Theory and Practice*, FT/Pitman, London.
Jones, R and Pendlebury, M (1996) *Public Sector Accounting*, FT/Pitman, London.
Melville, A (1997) *Financial Accounting*, FT/ Pitman, London.

Self-check questions

1. Why does a self-employed person not normally show drawings in his or her profit and loss account list of expenses?
2. Subject to any partnership agreement, in what ways may partners share out the profit between themselves?
3. Is the retained profit for the year of a limited company, the profit before or after charging tax and dividends?
4. Why are consolidated accounts prepared for a group of companies?
5. What are minority interests in a group balance sheet?

7
Accounting for inflation

INTRODUCTION

Unfortunately inflation is like the poor – always with us. Economic historians can point to times past when the value of money actually increased but these have been short-lived. In the present inflationary era, albeit at a relatively low rate, we need to be able to distinguish between the apparent profit of a business and its real profit after allowing for inflation. Top management of companies certainly need to know what the real profit is in order to form rational dividend and investment policies. This chapter explains the problems caused by inflation before explaining how accountants can deal with them in accounting statements.

THE PROBLEM OF INFLATION

Inflation has been present in the UK, as in the world economy, throughout the whole post-war period. When the rate of inflation is at a mild rate of, say, less than 4 per cent per annum, accountants along with others largely ignore its existence when preparing the annual accounting statements of profit and loss account and balance sheet. This is not necessarily the case when accountants consider the effects of inflation on pricing, dividends, new investment and other management decisions.

Over a number of years, however, even a modest rate of inflation like 4 per cent per annum has a dramatic effect on the value of the assets of a firm. Even more important is the effect on the replacement cost of such assets when they eventually wear out and have to be renewed, and whether or not the business has allowed for this in its calculation of profit.

Example
A company buys fixed assets costing £2 million and expected to last five years. It

charges depreciation on their historic cost at £400,000 pa in each of the five years. Profits are fully distributed to shareholders each year so that no additional capital is retained. Assuming inflation at 5 per cent pa the replacement cost of the fixed assets is £2,552,000 at the end of five years, but only £2 million depreciation has been accumulated. Therefore, over £0.5 million new capital may have to be raised just to continue in business.

A number of basic problems are presented by inflation when preparing the annual accounting statements of profit and loss account and balance sheet. Profits are overstated when the costs of depreciation and stock consumed during the year are based on their original acquisition cost and not on their current replacement cost. The values of fixed assets and stock shown in the balance sheet are understated when based on their original cost. In turn this undervalues the capital employed in the company. The combination of these factors means that the *return on capital* is considerably overstated, as the following example illustrates:

Example

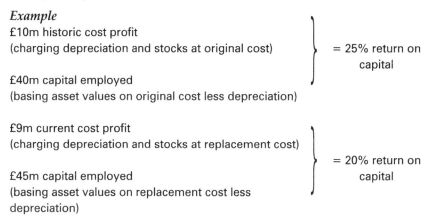

£10m historic cost profit
(charging depreciation and stocks at original cost)   } = 25% return on
                                                              capital
£40m capital employed
(basing asset values on original cost less depreciation)

£9m current cost profit
(charging depreciation and stocks at replacement cost)   } = 20% return on
                                                              capital
£45m capital employed
(basing asset values on replacement cost less
depreciation)

Another problem caused by inflation is that assets held in the form of money lose some of their value over time. Debtors and cash itself are cases in point. Conversely, firms gain by borrowing money and owing creditors for supplies because no allowance for inflation is made at the time repayment takes place. These gains and losses are excluded from a conventional profit and loss account.

If real profits are not measured, there is the danger that firms will be too generous with wage increases, dividend payments and other benefits to the detriment of new investment. Some companies may pay dividends they have not really earned because they have not allowed for the extra costs of inflation in their profit and loss accounts. If inflation is ignored in the day-to-day running of the business, there is also the danger that selling prices may not reflect the up-to-date costs of stock and asset replacements. Hence insufficient cash will be generated to maintain the same trading level without recourse to more and more borrowing.

DIFFERENT ACCOUNTING SYSTEMS

In the 1970s when the rate of inflation in the UK rose into double figures, and by the mid-1970s threatened to turn us into a banana republic, the professional accountancy bodies were involved in a long debate about how best to show the effects of inflation in accounting statements. One contentious point was whether to use general or specific price indices when revaluing stock or fixed assets. Another issue was whether to show the whole effects of inflation as falling on the firms' owners or whether to apportion it to different providers of capital. Some members of the profession preferred to ignore inflation and advocated continuing to provide statements based on the original value of transactions, ie historic cost accounting, on the basis that no subjective judgements were required.

Broadly speaking, there are three options available:

- historic cost accounting;
- current purchasing power accounting;
- current cost accounting.

Historic cost accounting (HCA)

This is the system still adopted by virtually all UK companies for external reporting purposes. No adjustments are made in the profit and loss account or balance sheet to recognize the effects of inflation. This does not exclude the occasional revaluation of a specific fixed asset, for example, property, when the fixed assets are described as modified historic cost. One purpose of this revaluation may be to enhance the security available for taking on increased borrowing.

Only one company traditionally did not present its accounts in historic cost form. British Gas uses replacement cost for its asset values and charges depreciation on these values in its profit and loss account. The combined effect is to lower the return on capital compared to what it would be when calculated on an historic cost basis. However, the published accounts disclose profit in historic cost terms in supplementary notes to the accounts.

Current purchasing power accounting (CPPA)

This system was recommended by the Sandilands Committee in the 1970s whereby all transactions in the financial statements would be adjusted to the present time by reference to changes in the Retail Price Index (RPI) – a general measure of inflation calculated monthly by the National Statistical Office. This did not find favour with accountants particularly, as it was felt that a general price index would not accurately measure the effects of inflation on individual businesses. This was because the resources used by them varied so much from one industry to another, as well as from the basket of goods and services used in the RPI. The CPPA system never really came into effect.

Current cost accounting (CCA)

In March 1980 the accountancy profession published its Statement of Standard Accountancy Practice No 16, entitled *Current Cost Accounting*. This SSAP required listed companies and larger private companies to clarify the effects of inflation on both the profit earned in the year and on the value of assets held at the year-end. This was achieved by the company producing supplementary statements to the historic cost profit and loss account and balance sheet. Although this SSAP was withdrawn in 1988 for reasons explained later, it is useful to examine the processes involved in CCA to gain a better insight into the effects of inflation. The system is still used by companies in industries such as electricity distribution and supply which are subject to regulation, and where the regulator requires both HCA and CCA information.

CURRENT COST ACCOUNTING STATEMENTS

Current cost profit and loss account

A supplementary profit and loss account statement contains four adjustments to the historic cost profit to arrive at the current cost profit attributable to the owners as Figure 7.1 illustrates. It is important to realize that the thrust of the statement is to show the effects of inflation on the profit earned for the shareholders, rather than the effects of inflation on the business as a whole.

	£000	£000
Profit as per 'historic cost' profit and loss account		1,000
Less: Depreciation adjustment, being the extra cost of depreciation calculated on the replacement cost of assets instead of their original cost.	200	
Less: Cost of sales adjustment, being the extra cash needed to replace stocks at prices ruling at the time of sale.	300	
Less: Monetary working capital adjustment, being the additional cash needed to give credit to customers for the inflated value of goods and services provided, less any extra credit received from suppliers.	100	600
Equals:		
Current cost operating profit		400
Add: Gearing adjustment, being the proportion of the above three adjustments not required to be borne by the shareholders if part of the company's capital is borrowed (assumed 40% here).		240
Equals:		
Current cost profit earned for shareholders		640

Figure 7.1 *Example of current cost profit and loss account*

The historic cost profit of £1,000,000 is shown as being overstated when compared to the current cost operating profit of £400,000, which allows for the inflated costs of replacing fixed assets and stocks and giving more credit to customers. Some of these additional costs are offset by not having to recompense the providers of borrowed capital for the effects of inflation, so that the current cost profit earned for the owners comes out at £640,000.

The way the first three adjustments are calculated largely makes use of index numbers supplied by the National Statistical Office to track the price movements of various assets and materials used in a variety of industries. In the event of a suitable index not being published a firm can construct its own in-house index.

Example

To illustrate the basic approach, the depreciation adjustment is calculated from the following information. A firm bought some fixed assets during 1996 at a cost of £2 million and expected them to have a five-year life. Depreciation on a straight-line basis amounts to £400,000 per annum. The average price index for this type of asset was 120 in 1996 and 160 in 1999. The depreciation adjustment for 1999 gives the additional depreciation required to supplement the original £400,000 depreciation charged in the historic cost profit and loss account. In this example the extra depreciation amounts to £100,000 for 1999 and this figure appears in the supplementary current cost profit and loss account.

The calculations are as follows:

Total depreciation based on current cost of £400,000 × $\frac{160}{120}$	= £500,000
Depreciation already provided in historic cost profit and loss account	= £400,000
Depreciation adjustment for 1999	= £100,000

Current cost balance sheet

The supplementary balance sheet values all assets at their current replacement cost at the balance sheet date. When inflation increases the value of an asset in money terms, it might appear that the balance sheet will no longer balance. This is remedied by creating a special reserve called a *current cost reserve*, or *revaluation reserve*, which is part of the shareholders' funds and effectively updates the value of the shareholders' investment in the business. If, for example, the value of fixed assets rose by £1 million by the year-end then this reserve will also be increased by £1 million. This keeps intact the balance sheet equation that assets must always equal liabilities.

Example

Let us take the example of a firm owning £1 million assets financed totally by share capital. The financial position can be set out as:

Balance sheet (HCA)

Total assets	£1,000,000	Share capital	£1,000,000

Assume now that because of inflation the assets increase in value by £50,000. The current cost balance sheet now is:

Balance sheet (CCA)			
Total assets	£1,050,000	Share capital	1,000,000
		Revaluation reserve	50,000
			£1,050,000

The differences between a current cost balance sheet and an historic cost one are limited to the valuation of assets and the revaluation reserve. All assets are revalued to their replacement cost at the balance sheet date while debtors and cash remain unaffected. All liabilities are unaffected by inflation except for the revaluation reserve which accumulates the asset revaluations and the four profit adjustments shown in the current cost profit and loss account.

REACTIONS

SSAP 16 was introduced for a trial period of three years to be reviewed in 1983. Its use was extended until 1985 when it ceased to be mandatory due to lack of support from within and without the profession. Accountants found it an expensive and time-consuming task to produce the required data in another form. They also found a mixed response from intended users of the additional information either on the grounds of its complexity or disagreement with the rationale, and it is now applied by few firms. British Gas plc is one of those few companies publishing current cost accounts as its main financial statements, although a number of other privatized utilities produce them for their regulators.

There was hope that the Inland Revenue would accept the current cost procedures outlined in SSAP 16 as a basis for taxing real profits. They appeared to reject this, possibly on the grounds of the subjectivity allowed to individual companies when choosing relevant price indices and asset lives.

It is doubtful if company managers, investors, employees and possibly even accountants, understood all the ramifications of the current cost adjustments. The effects of inflation on pricing policy, working capital requirements, corporation tax assessments, dividend policy, the cost of capital and wage claims are complex, and not easily understood. The tendency was for companies, unions and the financial press to concentrate on the well-known, but misleading, HCA figures and ignore the more accurate supplementary CCA information.

In 1980 a leading firm of stockbrokers estimated that 40 per cent of UK companies were paying dividends not covered by *current cost earnings*, ie excessive dividends were eroding the real capital base of these companies. With inflation down to below 5 per cent in the 1990s, this is no longer the case, especially as many companies pay less than half their profit out as dividends.

This chapter has concentrated on the effects of inflation on information contained in the annual accounting statements of the profit and loss account and balance sheet. It demonstrates how, if inflation is ignored, profits are overstated and assets are understated in terms of the current value of money.

Accountancy procedures used in the early 1980s to correct this, by producing supplementary CCA statements, have been explained. These allow a more correct assessment of the return on capital, of the profits available for distribution as dividends and of the book value of company shares. It is assumed that companies' top management and city analysts use this way of thinking when making judgements about financial performance.

Inflation has other effects on company finances. Questions as to what values to use when pricing, budgeting, setting standards and appraising investments are left until the relevant chapters containing these techniques. Even if inflation adjustments are not shown in their published annual accounts, organizations will consider the effects of inflation when making these policy decisions.

Further reading

Accounting Standards Committee (1980) *Current Cost Accounting: SSAP No 16*, London.

Glautier, MWE and Underdown, B (1997) *Accounting Theory and Practice,* FT/Pitman, London.

Lewis, R and Pendrill, D (1996) *Advanced Financial Accounting*, FT/Pitman, London.

Self-check questions

1. What is the difference between an historic cost profit and a current cost profit?
2. What happens if a firm distributes all of its historic cost profit as dividends at a time of high inflation?
3. Name the four adjustments to historic cost profit that appear in a current cost profit and loss account.
4. If an asset is revalued, how does a balance sheet still balance?

8
Value added

INTRODUCTION

The value of the wealth created in any country during a period of time is called its *gross domestic product* (GDP) and increases in this wealth are referred to as economic growth. In the UK and other developed countries, GDP is measured each quarter, building up to an annual total.

This wealth is the value of the goods and services produced by measurable economic activity – in other words, the money value of the output of firms of all sizes in all industries. There are some problems posed for the official statisticians when they tackle this exercise. One is the existence of the black economy whereby there is no recorded economic activity for what in the UK is deemed to be billions of pounds of economic activity.

The other main problem lies in avoiding double counting the same output when it passes from one firm to another and one industry to another. The answer lies in calculating the size of output on a value-added basis.

Example
Consider the coal industry. Coal is used to generate electricity, which is used to produce steel, which in turn is used to manufacture cars. If we take the total final value of coal, electricity, steel and cars produced in the UK in a year, we would be counting the value of coal four times over and not just once. But if we deduct the value of all the bought-in goods and services from the sales of each industry, we are left with the value added by that industry alone. This avoids all double counting.

DEFINITION OF VALUE ADDED

Just as we can measure the wealth created by a country or an industry, so we can for a single company. The wealth created by any business is the value of its sales less the cost of all the bought-in goods and services (which is wealth created by other firms).

Value added = Sales *less* all bought-in goods and services

All firms are creators of wealth. They buy in raw materials and services, which they then convert or process into a product or service, which in turn they sell to their own customers. The difference between the final sales value and the original bought-in materials and services is the value added by that firm. It is this wealth a company has available for distribution to the four interested parties:

- employees;
- government;
- providers of capital;
- the company itself.

We can think of a firm as a kind of partnership between these four parties. Employees bring their various skills while the government provides the environment in which firms and employees more easily prosper from the various services provided. Shareholders and loan providers allow their capital to be used to finance the production process while the firm brings together all the assets needed to carry out its economic function. It is these four partners who always share in the wealth created by themselves, although the shares are by no means equal.

VALUE ADDED STATEMENT

A typical value added statement for a firm appears in Figure 8.1, but it should be remembered that the four-way split differs from firm to firm and industry to industry.

		£000
Sales		230
Less: Bought-in goods and services		130
Value added		100
This was distributed as follows:		
To employees – as wages, salaries, pension, and NI contributions	70	
To government – as taxes on profits	8	
To providers of capital – as interest and dividends	10	
To reinvestment – as depreciation and retained profits	12	100

Figure 8.1   *Typical value added statement*

COMPARISON WITH A PROFIT AND LOSS ACCOUNT

The principles on which a value added statement is prepared are the same as for a profit and loss account. The conventions of realization and accrual are followed, as is the concept of matching the *cost of sales* with *sales* in the same accounting period. Therefore, any increase in stocks of work-in-progress and finished goods is not counted as part of the wealth created in this period because the sale has not yet taken place. Conversely, a decrease in such stocks counts as wealth created in this period.

Statisticians, however, do take these stock changes into account when calculating the total value of national output. Companies likewise would also have to take these stock changes into account when basing incentive payments on value added. If not, this might appear to be a perverse way of looking at things from an employee's viewpoint if an individual month's added value bonus does not exactly reflect employee productivity in that same period of time.

Value added statements and profit and loss accounts are both prepared from the same financial data. Their difference lies in the presentation and orientation of the contents. A profit and loss account gives a narrow, shareholder-centred view of company performance, unashamedly so, because this is the design concept.

Part (a) *Profit and loss account:*

	£000	£000
Sales		1,000
*Less:*Materials used*	300	
Services purchased*	130	
Wages and salaries	350	
Depreciation	90	
Interest on loan	50	920
Profit before taxation		80
Corporation tax on profit		30
Profit after taxation		50
Dividends		30
Retained profit		20

Part (b) *Value added statement:*

	£000
Sales	1,000
Less: Bought-in materials and services (*300 + *130)	430
Value added	570

This was distributed as follows:

	%	£000
To employees – wages, salaries, pensions and NICs	61.4	350
To government – corporation tax on profit	5.3	30
To providers of capital – interest and dividends	14.0	80
To reinvestment – depreciation and retained profit	19.3	110
	100.0	570

Figure 8.2 *Comparison of (a) profit and loss account with (b) value added statement*

However, the very word *profit* does have an emotive and political undertone when viewed by parties other than shareholders. A value added statement, however, concentrates on wealth creation rather than profit and shows its distribution to all four parties, not just one, who have contributed. In addition to the absolute values, the percentage share of value added going to each of the four parties is shown.

We can see both the similarities and the differences if we examine the two statements, both of which are prepared from the same basic data as in Figures 8.2 (a) and (b).

Very few companies are producing value added statements as an integral part of their annual report, although the Corporate Report issued way back in 1975 recommended that practice.

There are no fixed percentage shares of value added applicable to all companies. In a capital-intensive industry, the share of wealth going to labour should be smaller to allow for the servicing of large amounts of capital and a high level of reinvestment to replace worn-out plant. Conversely, in a labour- or material-intensive industry, the proportion of value added going to labour will be higher because the amount of capital to be serviced and the replacement investment are not so large.

It can be argued that in some firms the proportion of wealth going to one party has been too large resulting in too small a distribution elsewhere. The classic trade-off is between labour and capital reinvestment. Some financial experts have commented that, in many of our declining industries, the level of reinvestment has been much too low to keep the UK competitive internationally. Others have pointed to poor productivity, which results in low value added, low reinvestment and an apparently high distribution of wealth to labour.

This debate lies at the heart of how we are to continue to improve our economic performance as a nation, particularly on the manufacturing front. Some improvement in productivity and in reinvestment levels was starting to be evident in the 1980s, sometimes aided by Japanese capital and changed methods of manufacturing. This has carried on through the 1990s and must continue, with international competition now coming from all corners of the globe.

USES OF VALUE ADDED

There are two main uses to which value added statements can be put. Shareholders reading the statement can note the trend of distributions to themselves, to the labour force and to reinvestment for growth. Any tendency to an increased labour share at the expense of reinvestment may lead them to reconsider their continued shareholding.

Trade-union officials and employees will find the value added statement more helpful than the profit and loss account. The size of value added puts an absolute maximum on employee remuneration even if one could ignore the legal claims for interest and tax. Employees are shown to be the recipients of the lion's share of wealth in many companies and the debate on conflicting claims is more easily conducted using the value added statement. Perhaps more emphasis needs to be placed on increasing the size of the cake (value added) than on squabbling about the size of the four slices which in reality boils down to three, or even only two.

The other main use of the value added concept is in measuring performance. Chapter 9 introduces the idea of using ratios to measure aspects of cost control and asset utilization aimed at improving the return on capital. In a similar way we can examine the trend of *value added per worker*, or £ *wages per £ value added* to monitor labour productivity. Likewise, we can appraise capital productivity via the ratio £ *value added per £ capital employed*. Comparisons of these ratios between similar firms can only stimulate a more informed debate on efficiency and productivity.

Consideration should also be given as to whether the value added statement is produced on an historic or current cost basis. The latter would seem more appropriate because only after allowing for the cost of sales, depreciation and monetary working capital adjustments can we talk about the real wealth created at today's prices.

Employee reports

This topic is introduced here because of its affinity to the value added statement, which is often used to communicate basic financial information to employees in place of the profit and loss account. Most employees (and many shareholders for that matter) find the annual accounts totally confusing and, increasingly, firms prepare a short, salient financial report just for their employees' consumption.

The cornerstone of this report is usually a value added approach, describing the wealth created in the year and how it has been distributed. Sometimes an abbreviated profit and loss account is given, but it is perhaps confusing to present both. Balance sheets are rarely given except in a highly summarized manner. The whole purpose of employee reporting is to communicate a few key facts on company performance which can be readily understood, rather than a morass of accounting detail which can thoroughly confuse the untrained reader.

Further reading

Wood, F and Sangster, A (1996) *Business Accounting Vol 2*, FT/Pitman, London.

Self-check questions

1. Define value added.
2. A value added statement is based on the same concepts, and uses the same information, as which statement?

3. How might a firm use the value added to measure changes in productivity and efficiency?
4. Name the four parties to whom value added is distributed.
5. Even when firms do not include a value added statement in their annual reports, they may distribute one to which party?

9
Financial ratios

INTRODUCTION

Earlier chapters have examined the two most important financial statements of profit and loss account and balance sheet. To recapitulate – the trading performance of a company for a period of time is measured in the profit and loss account by deducting running costs from sales income. A balance sheet sets out the financial position of the company at a particular point in time, namely, the end of the accounting period. It lists the assets owned by the company at that date matched by an equal list of the sources of finance.

A person experienced in reading company accounts can get some insight into a company's affairs by examining these financial statements. Changes in some of the key items can be identified by comparing the current year's figure with the previous year's figure, but conclusions drawn from this approach can be misleading. Consider the following situation.

Example
Consider a company whose profit increased by 5 per cent over the previous year. This might appear to be a good performance until one considered that a 4 per cent rate of inflation existed during the year, and that an extra 10 per cent of capital employed was needed to earn that extra profit.

Analytical approach

Experienced and inexperienced readers of accounts will benefit from a more methodical analysis of the figures. The main analytical approach is to examine the relationship of pairs of figures extracted from the accounts. A pair may be taken from the same statement, or one figure from each of the profit and loss account and balance sheet statements. When brought together, the two figures are called ratios, although this term is not always used in the normal sense of the word. Some of the ratios are meaningful in themselves, but their value mainly lies in their comparison with the equivalent ratio last year, a target ratio, or a competitor's ratio.

All too frequently one sees television or newspaper reporting that some leading company made £x million profit last year. As a sum of money the figures sound very large and more naive audiences might be tempted to think of excessive prices being charged. Such reporting is almost meaningless without reference to last year's figure, the size of the company's sales, or the amount of capital employed. In other words, the absolute value of profit is not as meaningful as, say, the return on capital employed or the profit margin on sales, both of which are expressed as percentages.

Forms of ratios

Ratios can be expressed in one of three forms although it is mainly convention which determines which form one particular ratio will take. The three forms are:

- a percentage – say when profit is expressed as a percentage of sales turnover;
- a multiple – for example, sales being three times the size of the capital employed;
- a true ratio – as when the ratio of current assets to current liabilities was 2:1.

KEY RATIOS

Most of the main ratios are concerned with aspects of profitability and, like any personal financial investment we might make, the key concern is with the return on capital invested. We calculate this by expressing profit as a percentage of capital. This in turn is influenced by two further ratios comprising the profit margin (profit as a percentage of sales) and the rate of turnover of capital (sales divided by capital).

Example
Using sample figures when profit is £l million, sales are £10 million, and capital is £5 million, then:

Return on capital	=	Profit margin	x	Turnover of capital
$\dfrac{\text{Profit £1m x 100\%}}{\text{Capital £5m}}$	=	$\dfrac{\text{Profit £1m x 100\%}}{\text{Sales £10m}}$	x	$\dfrac{\text{Sales £10m}}{\text{Capital £5m}}$
20%	=	10%	x	2 times

The typical return on capital will vary from one industry to another (and firm to firm), but wider variations may be found in their profit margin and rates of turnover of capital. Figure 9.1 shows various assumed ways in which, say, a 20 per cent return on capital could be achieved in different industries.

Industry	Return on capital	=	Profit margin	x	Turnover of capital rate
Contracting	20%	=	2%		10 times
Food retailing	20%	=	4%		5 times
Heavy engineering	20%	=	10%		2 times

Figure 9.1 *Sample performance ratios*

Profit margins in contracting may be only 2–3 per cent, but this is offset by a very high rate of asset turnover. In more capital-intensive industries, with a long production cycle, the low rate of asset turnover is compensated for by a high profit margin.

These three key ratios are only the starting point from which a number of subsidiary ratios can be calculated relating either running costs or assets to sales. Figure 9.2 shows this approach in diagrammatic form.

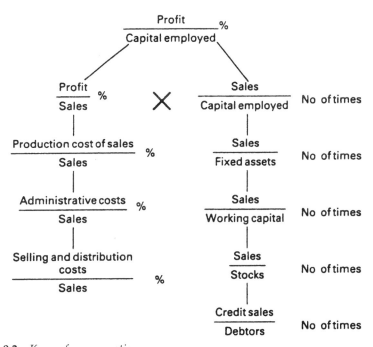

Figure 9.2 *Key performance ratios*

Financial ratios can be broken down into groups that are used to analyse specific aspects of a company's financial performance and standing. Typical ratio groups examine the areas of:

- profitability;
- efficient use of assets;

- liquidity (short-term);
- liquidity (long-term);
- financial investment.

A more precise definition and meaning of the most important ratios are now given.

PROFITABILITY RATIOS

Return on equity

This ratio is usually expressed as a percentage in the way we might think of the return on any personal financial investment. Both profit and capital may be defined in different ways, the choice of which depends on the use to which the ratio is put. From the owners' viewpoint, their concern is with the profit earned for them relative to the amount of funds they have invested in the business. The relevant profit here is *after* interest, tax (and any preference dividends) have been deducted. This is expressed as a percentage of the equity which comprises ordinary share capital and reserves. Therefore:

$$\text{Return on equity} = \frac{\text{Profit after taxation} \times 100}{\text{Ordinary share capital} + \text{reserves}} \ \%$$

The above ratio will be influenced not only by the trading performance but also by the mix of owners' and borrowed capital used by that particular company. A company which fails to achieve a return on equity commensurate with shareholder expectations has a doubtful future in its present form.

Return on capital employed

This takes a wider view of company performance than return on equity by expressing profit *before* interest, tax, and dividend deductions as a percentage of the total capital employed, irrespective of whether this capital is borrowed or provided by the owners. This states:

$$\text{Return on capital employed} = \frac{\text{Profit before interest, tax and dividends} \times 100}{\text{Total capital employed}} \ \%$$

Capital employed is defined as share capital plus reserves plus long-term borrowings. This should also be equal to total assets less current liabilities, which amount is disclosed as such in the balance sheet. Where, say, a bank overdraft is included in current liabilities every year and in effect becomes a source of capital, this may be regarded as part of capital employed. If the bank overdraft varies considerably from year to year, a more reliable ratio to use may be return on total assets. This will facilitate the year-by-year comparison of this ratio and show a more reliable trend.

There is no one precise definition used by companies for capital employed. The start- and end-year figures should be averaged if the information is available. Also, some companies adjust their capital employed figure to allow for cash balances and tax and dividend liabilities.

Further points to bear in mind are that a revaluation of fixed assets in one year will affect the value of equity and capital employed and hence distort year-on-year comparisons. Goodwill written off to reserves in previous years depresses the true value of both equity and capital employed and result in higher percentage returns on capital than are really the case. This can make inter-company and international comparisons less meaningful unless adjustments are made to correct any different treatment of such items.

Gross profit margin

This ratio measures the margin earned on its sales and in effect acts as a monitor of buying (or manufacturing) and selling prices. It can also be influenced by a change in product mix when different product lines have different gross margins. Any change in the mix of volumes will affect the overall gross margin.

$$\text{Gross margin} = \frac{\text{Gross profit} \times 100}{\text{Sales}} \, \%$$

Net profit margin

In effect this ratio measures the net profit after the cost of sales and all overheads have been deducted from sales and expresses the resultant figure as a percentage of sales.

$$\text{Net profit margin} = \frac{\text{Net profit before tax, interest, and dividends} \times 100}{\text{Sales}} \, \%$$

It is usual to take the profit before tax, interest and dividends because all are subject to influences which have nothing to do with the basic trading performance. We are really saying that profit margins are determined by the cost of sales, overhead costs and selling prices rather than the capital mix or effective tax rate at any point of time. An extension of this ratio is to express every profit and loss item as a percentage of sales. Figure 9.3 is an example of this approach:

	%
Direct labour/sales	23
Direct material/sales	25
Production overheads/sales	14
Administration overheads/sales	15
Selling and distribution overheads/sales	13
Profit/sales	10
Total sales	100

Figure 9.3 *Percentage analysis of profit and loss account*

As previously stated, the absolute value of these ratios has little meaning. Ratios are like fingerprints in detective work. They point in a direction that appears to merit further investigation when shown to compare adversely with previous experience, targets or competitors' ratios. Some of these themes are discussed in later chapters.

EFFICIENCY RATIOS

This group of ratios is concerned with asset management and its efficiency. The assets concerned may be a group total, say, fixed assets, or it may be an individual item, say, stocks or debtors. First we start with an overall measure, bearing in mind the dual aspect of bookkeeping that assets are of equal value to their sources of finance.

Turnover of capital

This ratio is usually expressed as a rate of turnover. Total sales is divided by the amount of capital employed to find the number of times each £1 of capital employed has generated £1 of sales.

Example
A company has capital employed of £2 million and annual sales of £4 million. Capital employed has been turned over twice during the year. Another way of expressing this would be to say each £1 of capital has generated £2 of sales.

$$\text{Turnover of capital} \quad = \quad \frac{\text{Sales £4m}}{\text{Capital employed £2m}} \quad = \quad 2 \text{ times}$$

Capital employed is the total amount of issued share capital, reserves and long-term borrowing, which is equal in value to total assets less current liabilities. We could equally say in the above example that assets are being turned over twice.

Turnover of fixed assets

Subsidiary ratios may relate groups of assets, or an individual asset, to sales. In capital intensive industries it is important to measure how many pounds of sales are generated by each £1 of fixed assets. It is possible in some industries to find the answer expressed in pence rather than pounds, particularly when long-life assets are involved.

Example
Scottish Hydro-Electric plc in their 1997 group accounts had annual sales of £951 million and tangible fixed assets of £1,548 million at the accounting year-end, giving a turnover rate of 0.61 times. Put another way, it achieved £0.61 sales for every £1 invested in tangible fixed assets.

Turnover of working capital

A similar calculation could be performed on working capital to identify the velocity of circulation of each £1 of working capital when it is used over and over again during the year. Sales turnover for the year is divided by the amount of working capital at the year-end to calculate this turnover rate. Alternatively, an average working capital can be used if there is significant variation in working capital during the year.

Example
To illustrate, if sales are £4 million and working capital is £1.2 million, then the rate of turnover of working capital is 3.3 times.

Debtors and creditors days

Turning now to individual current assets, it is more usual to relate these to sales one by one rather than treat working capital as a total entity. If this is done on debtors, it is common practice to invert the ratio and multiply by 365 days. The ratio *debtors/sales x 365* tells us the number of days credit being taken by customers. Similarly, the ratio *creditors/purchases x 365* days denotes the period of credit taken from suppliers.

Example
When annual sales are £4 million per annum, and debtors at the year-end are £0.5 million then debtors days are £0.5 million/£4 million x 365 which equals 45 days. Assuming no marked seasonal variations in sales exist, customers are taking 45 days on average to settle their bills. If there are significant seasonal variations in sales, this ratio is inaccurate and sales ledger data would be needed for a more accurate figure.

Stock turnover

Similarly the ratio *stock/cost of sales x 365* days tells us the number of days' stock being carried.

Debtors, creditors and stocks are discussed again in Chapter 18 in relation to the management of working capital.

LIQUIDITY RATIOS (SHORT-TERM)

Previous ratios have examined the performance of a company from the viewpoints of efficiency, both in the control of costs and in the use of its assets, and of its profitability. In order to survive, companies must also watch their liquidity position, by which is meant keeping enough short-term assets to pay short-term debts. Companies go out of business compulsorily when they fail to pay money due to employees, bankers, or suppliers. There are two main ratios used to examine the liquidity position of a company, namely, the quick ratio and the current ratio.

Quick ratio (acid test)

The terms *acid test* or *quick* ratio are applied because this ratio is crucial to a company's survival. It takes the form of liquid assets: current liabilities, where a 1:1 ratio means a company has sufficient cash or near cash to pay its immediate debts. Liquid assets are defined here as all the current assets excluding stocks, which cannot quickly be converted into cash. In effect liquid assets are debtors, cash and any short-term investments, such as bank deposits or government securities.

Example
If a company's liquid assets are £380,000 and current liabilities are £300,000 then the resulting ratio of more than 1:1 seems satisfactory at that point in time. The exact quick ratio is calculated from:

$$\text{Quick ratio} = \frac{\text{Liquid assets}}{\text{Current liabilities}} = 1.3:1$$

A company can survive with a liquidity ratio of less than 1:1 if it has unused bank overdraft facilities. Any existing bank overdraft is classified as a current liability, but if not withdrawn or reduced by the bank it should not really count as a short-term debt. Converting an existing overdraft into a longer-term loan would also transform an adverse liquidity ratio.

In some industries it is not unusual for stocks and work-in-progress to be turned into cash before all creditors are due for payment. Building construction and food retailing are cases in point where seemingly adverse liquidity ratios pose no threat to the company.

Current ratio

This is another test of a company's liquidity and includes stocks and work-in progress in the current assets, on the grounds that stocks eventually turn into debtors, and then into cash itself. It is calculated by relating all current assets to current liabilities. A norm of 2:1 is regarded as satisfactory in most industries but this is a somewhat arbitrary figure and it may be a better guide to look at the norm for each particular industry. The above points about bank overdrafts also apply as do the ability of some firms to turn stocks into cash more quickly than others.

Example
Using the same figures as in the quick ratio but now including stocks of £350,000, the current assets become £730,000 and the current liabilities remain at £300,000. The current ratio of 2.4: 1 indicates this company has more than sufficient short-term assets to meet its short-term debts.

$$\text{Current ratio} = \frac{\text{Current assets £730,000}}{\text{Current liabilities £300,000}} = 2.4:1$$

A high ratio here may indicate solvency, but may also indicate poor management of one or more of the constituent items. Unless there are large unused cash resources in current assets, the answer to an apparent surplus of current assets may be found in other ratios, for example, a slow stock turnover or high debtors days. Also, it should be remembered that the absolute value of a particular ratio may not be as important as its trend.

LIQUIDITY RATIOS (LONG-TERM)

The distinguishing features of borrowed capital as opposed to shareholders' capital are that borrowings must be serviced by interest payments and repaid either in instalments, or at the end of a period of time. There is no such legal obligation to pay dividends to owners, nor is share capital repayable. From a long-term liquidity point of view, too much debt is risky, as the higher the proportion of capital raised by loans, the higher the proportion of profit going as interest.

A judicious amount of borrowed capital can be beneficial to the shareholders and this aspect is measured below and discussed in Chapter 16 under the heading of *capital gearing*. For the moment let us examine the ratios concerned with measuring the amount of debt a company can assume.

Debt ratio

The proportion of debt to total assets expressed as a percentage is used to quantify the amount of debt owed by a firm. In effect, this ratio measures the proportion of assets owned by a company which is owed to creditors of various kinds. In this context, debt includes all loans, overdrafts, trade creditors, tax and other liabilities. The higher the percentage, the less willing creditors will be to extend further credit.

Gearing ratio

This measures as a percentage the proportion of all borrowing, including long-term loans and bank overdrafts, to either the total capital employed or the amount of equity. In the latter case, the gearing ratio is sometimes also known as the *debt/equity ratio*.

Example
When total borrowings are £4 million and ordinary share capital plus reserves are £16 million, then total capital employed equals £20 million. Borrowings therefore represent either 25 per cent of equity or 20 per cent of total capital employed. This level of borrowing would not be regarded as excessive but the volatility of profits in the past must be considered before making a final judgement.

Income cover

This is a measure of the proportion of profit taken up by interest payments and can be found by dividing the annual interest payment into the annual profit before interest, tax and dividend payments. The greater the number, the less vulnerable the company will be to any setback in profits, or rise in interest rates on variable loans. The smaller the number, then the more risk that level of borrowing represents to the company. A value between five and 10 times might be considered reasonable, but a lot depends on how stable the profits are for a particular business.

Example
When annual interest is £70,000 and profit before interest is £100,000, then income cover of only 1.4 times means that most of the profit is going in interest payments. Any fall in profits or rise in interest rates will make this company vulnerable, apart from the fact that there is very little left for tax payments, shareholder dividends or reinvestment.

$$\text{Income cover} = \frac{\text{Profit before interest £100,000}}{\text{Interest charges £70,000}} = 1.4 \text{ times}$$

One must also look for peculiarities in any one industry. Property development is heavily dependent on borrowed capital and any dramatic change in market conditions for letting can pose severe problems for the companies concerned. Memories of the property boom and collapse which triggered off the secondary banking crisis of the 1970s were scarcely fading before the next property slump hit us in 1990, causing many company collapses.

FINANCIAL INVESTMENT RATIOS

An investor looking at company shares as potential investments or, if already a shareholder, wondering whether to continue to do so, has a range of financial ratios and statistics to consider. Most of these are discussed in detail in Chapter 19, but a brief summary is given here for completeness:

- market capitalization – the stock market valuation of all the company's shares.
- earnings per share (eps) – the amount of profit earned on one ordinary share.
- price/earnings ratio (p/e) – the number of years' earnings represented by the market price.
- dividend yield – the yearly dividend as a percentage of the market price of a share.
- dividend cover – the number of times the profit earned covers the dividend paid out.
- net asset value (nav) – the balance sheet value of assets owned by one share.

INTERFIRM COMPARISONS

Mention was made earlier that ratios can be used to compare aspects of one company's performance with competitors. It is possible to conduct such an exercise by using the information in the published annual accounts of similar firms. This information can be requested from the company or more usually extracted from a data base, some of which are found in many large libraries. Alternatively, a search can be instigated at Companies House, but this may prove expensive when a number of companies are involved.

Some firms use an organization called the Centre for Interfirm Comparisons and participate in a study of their industry. Financial information, including detailed costs, is submitted in confidence and comparative ratios produced. Ideally, data must be adjusted to a common basis for all firms so that, for instance, a firm which leased all its assets adjusts its costs and assets to align with other firms who own their assets. Trade organizations themselves sometimes promote interfirm comparisons as a service to their member companies.

PUBLIC SECTOR

Some of the above ratios have little meaning or application for many public sector organizations which are not profit-orientated, nor have owners seeking a return on investment. However, it is some years since the concept of return on capital employed found its way into the National Health Service and many of the above ratios are relevant to private healthcare. Ratios used to measure performance in the NHS and local government, for example, tend to concentrate on measures relating to inputs and outputs and are known as the three Es – economy, efficiency and effectiveness.

Where public sector organizations carry out trading activities that could be performed by private sector organizations, they may be obliged to prepare accounts and submit tenders on the same basis. This makes the profit margin and return on capital ratios used by private sector organizations just as relevant.

LIMITATIONS OF RATIO ANALYSIS

It should not be thought that performance ratios are a panacea for all ills. They are a relatively crude diagnostic tool which can help managers and investors identify the strengths and weaknesses of a company. They identify the areas to examine in more depth, but suffer from the limitations of the financial statements from which they are prepared. In particular, care must be taken when deciding whether to use historical cost or inflation adjusted data to calculate ratios.

The other main difficulty relates to goodwill. If internally generated, goodwill will not appear on the balance sheet as an asset or as part of the capital employed. If goodwill was purchased in the past, it most likely will have been written off against reserves and again not appear in the balance sheet as an asset or form part of the capital employed. However, in future when FRS 10 comes into effect, it may well appear as an asset and form part of capital employed.

Comparisons of some ratios over time, or with companies in other countries whose accounting standards differ from those in the UK, need to be interpreted with great care.

PREDICTING BUSINESS FAILURE

There are numerous reasons for business failures, most of which can be summed up as a shortage of cash. This may have been a problem from the start if the enterprise had insufficient capital, or it may have been a subsequent development due to unprofitable trading, too-fast expansion, excessive borrowing, slow-paying customers, difficult trading conditions or just plain bad management. The final demise of a business is when a creditor sues or applies to put it into receivership or liquidation This may be a trade creditor who has waited much longer than the agreed credit period, but is just as likely to be the taxman or the bank manager.

It is claimed that up to one in every three new companies set up will not survive five years. These are by nature predominantly small businesses. Other companies with a longer track record and a listing on the stock exchange have a much lower failure record. One reason may be their ability to raise new equity instead of having to rely on bank borrowing.

The financial ratios discussed in this chapter have been viewed with hindsight, based on information extracted from published financial statements. The trend of some key ratios may tell us a lot about the financial health of a company. Pointers to a poor financial state might include, in no particular order:

- increasing losses;
- falling profit margins;
- rising gearing ratio;
- increasing debtors days;
- increasing creditors days;
- falling stock turnover rate;
- reduced or passed dividend.

Z scores

The question might be posed as to which ratios could be used to predict a business failing in the future. A further question might be the relative importance to attach to each of the ratios identified as being useful in this context. A final question might ask if the above could all be wrapped up in a single score that could be used to predict failure or survival – a so called *Z score*.

A number of researchers in different countries have come up with their own models over the years, including Altman, Taffler and Robertson. Altman's early model (1968) was based on 33 failed American manufacturing companies, each paired off against a similar on-going company. His final selection of the following five financial ratios was from an original 22 in number, and the calculation of his Z score comprised:

$$Z = 1.2X_1 + 1.4X_2 + 3.3X_3 + 0.6X_4 + 1.0X_5$$

where Z is the combined total of the weighted ratios X1, X2....and

X1 = Net current assets/ total assets.
X2 = Retained earnings/total assets.
X3 = Profit before interest and tax/total assets.
X4 = Market value of equity/book value of total debt.
X5 = Sales/total assets.

Both on-going and failed companies are then ranked together by size of Z score and upper and lower limits identified. Above the upper limit no failed companies are misclassified as ongoing, whilst below the lower limit no ongoing companies are misclassified as failed. Altman described a grey area between the upper and lower limits where companies could be misclassified.

Z score models should be developed for specific industries and their use limited to such. This is because financial ratios have different values in different industries. Some industries are capital intensive (eg chemicals) and some are not (eg contractors). Some have large stocks and work-in-progress (manufacturing) and others have none (eg electricity distribution).

Information on Z scores can be obtained commercially and is likely to appeal to investment analysts and companies trying to check up on the durability of customers, suppliers and potential joint venture partners. Information on creditworthiness can be obtained from credit agencies like Dun & Bradstreet with a comparison of the time taken to pay invoices against industry norms. Any consistent deterioration in this payment performance could also be an early warning of possible business failure.

Further reading

Altman, EI (September 1968) Financial ratios, discriminant analysis and the prediction of corporate bankruptcy, *Journal of Finance*, September.
Holmes, G and Sugden, A (1997) *Interpreting Company Reports and Accounts*, Prentice Hall, Englewood Cliffs, New Jersey.
Jones, R and Pendlebury M (1996) *Public Sector Accounting*, FT/Pitman, London.
Walsh, C (1995) *Key Management Ratios*, FT/Pitman, London.

Self-check questions

1. What is an accounting ratio?
2. Complete the following equation:
   Return on capital = profit margin x ....?
3. Is there an ideal value for each ratio? If not, how are ratios used?
4. Which ratio would you use to examine whether a company was short of cash if you knew it could not borrow any more money?
5. Which company is more vulnerable? Company A, which pays annual interest of £50,000 and makes a profit of £100,000, or Company B, which pays £150,000 interest and makes £500,000 profit?
6. What ratios are used to measure performance in public-sector services?
7. What is the purpose of a Z score?

10

Other performance measures

INTRODUCTION

In the past, business performance has been interpreted as purely financial performance with overmuch attention paid to the financial ratios derived from the two financial accounting statements of profit and loss account and balance sheet. Nowadays, it is recognized that performance measurement should include non-financial indicators as well as financial indicators so that all business objectives can be monitored. The increasing use of non-financial indicators in business decision-making was evidenced in a study by Scapens *et al* (see Further reading).

PERFORMANCE MEASURES IN MANUFACTURING INDUSTRIES

Performance measures will vary widely according to industry, organization and reporting level, but in any organization they should be integrated with its business strategy and objectives. In manufacturing industry, non-financial indicators may relate to the following areas:

- Competitiveness
  - size of the order book
  - number of orders received in period
  - percentage market share achieved
  - number of customers lost
- Productivity
  - standard hours produced
  - volume of throughput achieved in period
  - volume of work backlog
  - downtime of equipment
  - lost production due to maintenance
- Quality
  - percentage defect rates of purchased materials/components

- percentage defect rates on own products
- time spent on rework
- number of warranty claims
- Service
  - adherence to delivery dates
  - after-sale response time
- Cash
  - stock turnover rate
  - customer invoices days outstanding
  - supplier invoices days outstanding
- Safety
  - number of injuries.

PERFORMANCE MEASURES IN SERVICE INDUSTRIES

The research publication by Fitzgerald *et al* (1991) mentioned in Further reading, synthesized ideas from various authors on performance measures in service businesses into the following six generic performance dimensions:

- competitiveness;
- financial performance;
- quality of service;
- flexibility;
- resource utilization;
- innovation.

The first two dimensions, competitiveness and financial performance, represent the *ends* or the results of what has been achieved. The remaining four dimensions, service quality, flexibility, resource utilization and innovation, represent the *means* by which the first two are achieved.

A number of types of performance measure were listed under each dimension. For example, quality of service measures included reliability; responsiveness; appearance; comfort; communication; courtesy; competence; access; availability; security.

Example
The manager of the creditors' section of a large company wished to bring in performance measures relating to the cost, productivity, efficiency and quality of the staff's effort. A meeting with the section's supervisors was held to brainstorm ideas for suitable performance indicators, both financial and non-financial. The following suggestions were put forward at the initial meeting:

Cost – average cost of processing one supplier invoice
Productivity – number of invoices processed per person during each week
Efficiency – time delay from receipt of invoice to ledger posting
Quality – percentage of transaction errors out of total transactions

BALANCED SCORECARD

The term *balanced scorecard* is attributed to Kaplan and Nolan (see Further reading) and results from a research project undertaken in 1990 in the United States. It describes a framework from which a set of performance measures can be developed. The framework consists of four key questions which an organization asks itself, looking from four different perspectives. Only one of these perspectives is financial, hence the inclusion of balanced in the title balanced scorecard. By looking at different perspectives, managers of a business can avoid making an improvement in one area that impacts adversely on another, or at least be aware of the consequences beforehand. The four perspectives are:

Perspective:	Question:
Organization learning perspective	Can innovation and change be sustained?
Business process perspective	What must we excel at and how do we rate?
Customer perspective	How do new and existing customers see us?
Financial perspective	How are we performing for our shareholders?

1. *Learning perspective.* This recognizes that an organization must change continuously just to hold its own. This is the age of new technology, international markets and international competition. Organizations must keep pace with the latest ideas leading to cost reduction, and with changing customer demand for new products and services.
2. *Business process perspective.* To meet customer expectations, an organization must do well in carrying out core business processes. To achieve this, it must focus on the key competencies and harness the latest technology.
3. *Customer perspective.* This looks at the business through customers' eyes and gets them to identify the factors that are critical to them. At a minimum, these are likely to include cost, quality, waiting time, and service level. Performance measures need to be developed to monitor each of these factors so these may include price, defect rates, on-time deliveries and service delays respectively.
4. *Financial perspective.* The above three perspectives all culminate in this perspective of how well the business has created shareholder value. Performance measures of key interest to shareholders are sales and profit growth, profit margin and return on equity, dividend and earnings per share.

BENCHMARKING

Although the term *benchmarking* has only come into vogue in recent years, its practice goes back 20 years or so. It is attributed to the Xerox Corporation of America who were looking for ways of competing with Japanese companies which were threatening their markets.

Benchmarking is concerned with seeking out best practices and implementing them in one's own business to enhance performance. A local example for the author is found at the Nissan car manufacturer in Tyne and Wear. They have set a European record for productivity in their industry and host hundreds of visitor groups in search of best practice ideas.

The process of benchmarking can be expressed in three simple words as illustrated in Figure 10.1.

First, the managers of a business must learn about their own practices and processes to know about how things are done at the moment. Next, benchmarking with others is conducted to see how it is done elsewhere. Finally, change is implemented to benefit from the findings when the first two steps are compared.

Learn
↓
Benchmark
↓
Change

Figure 10.1 *The benchmarking process*

Types of benchmarking

Benchmarking can range from the informal to the very formal. At an informal level is the collection of data and information from unplanned events, say, the result of discussions and observations arising from contact with business people outside the company. These may include technical representatives, buyers, suppliers and competitors.

Formal benchmarking can be broken down into a number of different types:

- internal benchmarking;
- external benchmarking (non-competitive);
- external benchmarking (competitive);
- best practice benchmarking.

1. *Internal benchmarking* is looking at ways things are done within the same organizations ie examining current practice. This is very appropriate in large organizations where there is a devolved and near-autonomous structure typified by divisions within a group of companies. Benchmarking with partners in other divisions is a good way to learn about how things are done in one's own business before approaching other companies. It can also lead to changing practices where different divisions have grown or inherited practices independently, resulting in different levels of performance.
2. *External benchmarking* (non-competitive) involves finding partners in other industries. The common thread is the similarity of the processes and practices rather than the similarity of the final product. An example here might be a residential home for the elderly benchmarking with a hotel group.
3. *External benchmarking* (competitive) needs to be approached with some care as certain information will be non-poolable for commercial or legal reasons. The sharing of information on how tasks are performed and processes carried out, however, poses no such problems and benefits can accrue to all

parties, particularly if the processes studied are unique to the industry such that no non-competitors can be found.

4. *Best practice benchmarking* is seeking out those organizations that are renowned for carrying out a particular process in the best way. Such organizations are identified by asking suppliers, customers, academics, business analysts and trade associations. The emphasis here is on collaboration rather than industrial espionage, although it is obvious that the potential benefits are not equal to all parties concerned. It may be that some organizations with a high reputation for best practice in one or more fields may have to put a limit on collaboration if demands on staff resources threaten the efficient running of the business. Once a process is identified, a team of people with different skills is assembled. As most of the work is to elicit information, team members need coaching in interview and questionnaire design skills.

Benchmarking will not succeed without the backing of senior management. They need to release the resources for a study to be carried out and, equally important, they need to be committed to change if it is shown to be beneficial from the findings.

Further reading

CIMA (1993) *Performance Measurement in the Manufacturing Sector,* CIMA, London.

Cook, S (1997) *Practical Benchmarking,* Kogan Page, London.

Fitzgerald, L *et al* (1991) *Performance Measurement in Service Businesses,* CIMA, London.

Kaplan, RS and Norton, S (1992) The balanced scorecard – measures that drive performance, *Harvard Business Review,* Jan/Feb.

Newing, R (1995) Wake up to the balanced scorecard, *Management Accounting,* March.

Scapens, R *et al* (1996) *External Reporting and Management Decisions,* CIMA, London.

Smith, M (1994) *New Tools for Management Accounting,* FT/Pitman, London.

Self-check questions

1. Suggest three performance measures suitable for measuring quality in a manufacturing industry.
2. What is meant by a balanced scorecard?
3. Define benchmarking.
4. Name three types of benchmarking.

Part 2
Management accounting

The financial statements discussed in Part 1 are used monthly by top management and biannually by external parties interested in the performance and financial position of the global enterprise. Functional managers within the firm may not be privy to the monthly statements nor will they find them of much help in the day-to-day running and management of resources under their control.

Their need is for much more detailed information to allow them to control costs; to price realistically; to plan and control future activities; to measure and evaluate performance; and make the best use of resources. Very many decisions which managers take are based on financial information. Knowing the jargon, what information to ask for and how to use it is an essential requirement for any business person. Management accounting can be seen, therefore, as a vital part of the wider management process.

The second part of this book is concerned with just these techniques, which assist managers in their everyday work of costing products and services, controlling those costs, fixing prices, managing budgets and communicating effectively.

11
Costing basics

INTRODUCTION

Cost is a word used to describe the money spent on a particular thing. In our private lives we talk about the cost of running a car or the cost of heating our home. In a business context we can talk about the cost of labour, or the cost of running a department, or the cost of a particular product or service sold to customers.

Every business organization incurs costs –whether we are self-employed, or work for local government, or are employed in a profit-seeking organization. Costs are incurred on the resources consumed by the organization when carrying out its business objective of satisfying customers. The resources that are consumed are materials, people's effort, bought-in services, wear and tear on equipment, and even money itself, which has an interest cost.

These running or operating costs are referred to by accountants as *revenue expenditure* to distinguish them from the initial cost of new physical assets, such as buildings, equipment and vehicles. The acquisition costs of these fixed assets is referred to as *capital expenditure*. This chapter is primarily concerned with the former, ie revenue expenditure incurred on the day-to-day running costs of the organization when doing work for its customers and clients.

Costing is the analysis of costs so that they can be allocated to products/services, activities, departments and specific time periods. This objective analysis of costs is typified when they are charged to the end product or department consuming such costs. There is also a need for a subjective analysis of costs. This looks at the nature and type of costs and describes them in various ways – for which we later need to learn a little jargon. Costing is therefore an in-house accountancy service to provide relevant information to managers in a timely and cost-effective way. We shall start our study of costing by considering where cost information comes from and how accountants deal with it.

SOURCES OF COST DATA

Accountants receive information about costs from the managers and supervisors in their organization. It is these managers and supervisors who consume resources and incur costs. They notify their financial colleagues about costs by forwarding documents describing the cost concerned. Typical costing document names are:

- timesheets;
- invoices;
- goods received notes;
- stores issue notes or requisitions.

If accountants receive thousands of these documents each week, how are they to cope with such masses of data? There are two likely answers. First, the information on any document is condensed by expressing it in a kind of shorthand known as a *cost code*. Second, computers are used to sort, store, process and retrieve the information in a more meaningful form. Let us examine these two solutions in turn.

Cost codes

A cost code is a numbering device that turns a written description of costs into a series of numbers, or numbers and letters combined in an alpha/numeric code. An example of a cost code outline is shown in Figure 11.1.

01	182	5002
Originating dept, cost centre, or location number	Number describing the type of expense, the work done, or source of income	Job, contract, batch, product, service, or project number

Figure 11.1 *Typical cost code structure*

Cost code numbers are the key to an information database and can be used to identify:

- in which department or cost centre the cost originated;
- what resource has been consumed and why;
- the end product or service to which the cost is charged.

The size and complexity of the cost code depends very much on the size and complexity of the organization and its products. No two organizations' cost code systems will be the same unless they deliberately use a uniform system. What is suitable for ICI plc, for example, would be way over the top for a small family firm of electrical contractors.

Apart from having cost codes for costs and income, accountants need further codes to describe all assets and liabilities. The term used in Chapter 2 to describe the whole accounting code system was the chart of accounts.

Example

Using this electrical contractor as an illustration, the following structure and sample codes would be appropriate:

Cost centre no	*Description no*	*Customer job no*
01 Installation	121 Wages – Electricians	5001 ABC Ltd
02 Stores	122 Wages – Storekeepers	5002 DCE Ltd
03 Administration	123 Wages – Cleaners	5003 XYZ Ltd,
04 Purchasing	124 Wages – Clerks	etc.
05 Accounts	181 Materials – Cable	
06 Estimating, etc	182 Materials – Boxes	
	183 Materials – Conduit	
	184 Materials – Cleaning	
	201 Rent	
	202 Rates	
	203 Electricity, etc	

Use of computers

Costing documents are passed to the accounting department at regular intervals. Some code numbers are entered by the senders, but others are added later by the accounting staff. This is often the case with numbers of a repetitive nature, as with, say, the cost centre number. The value of each transaction is entered into the computer along with the relevant codes to say which source it came from, what the cost is about and the job/product to which it should be charged. Most overhead costs cannot be charged to an end product directly. However, knowledge of the source department and the nature of the overhead cost from the first two series of codes will facilitate the sharing out of overheads to different products at a later stage. The wider use of computers to process financial data is shown in Figure 11.2.

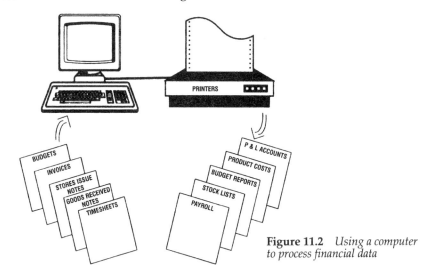

Figure 11.2 *Using a computer to process financial data*

TERMINOLOGY

Like lots of subject areas, costing has more than a little jargon of its own! Most of it we learn as we go but it is useful at this stage to concentrate on a few basic terms.

Cost centres

A cost centre is a physical location within an organization. It is usually a whole department or a section of a department but it could be an activity or even one expensive machine. Usually, each cost centre's budgeted costs and actual costs are compared monthly, to feed useful information back to the manager concerned. This is why each cost centre needs its own unique location code. We explore *budgetary control* later in Chapter 15.

Cost unit

A cost unit refers to something different than a cost centre. It is the product or service we either provide to others within our organization, or which we provide to outside customers. In a printing firm, for example, each bespoke print order from a customer will have its own unique job number and is a cost unit. In a mass-production industry, such as consumer durable goods, each washing machine or video player is a cost unit, although they may be costed in batches for convenience.

Direct and indirect costs

Costs can be split into two broad categories for costing and pricing purposes. These are known as direct and indirect costs. A direct cost is one that can readily be identified with and charged to a particular cost unit. In the printing firm just mentioned, direct costs will be the material costs of paper, card and ink, together with the cost of machine time and the cost of labour expended on the preparation, printing and finishing stages.

An indirect cost is more general in nature and cannot be specifically identified with any particular cost unit. These indirect costs, or overheads as we called them earlier, are first charged to cost centres and then shared out over the products and services produced. Indirect costs for the printing firm will include management and administration salaries, heating, lighting, rates, etc.

Fixed and variable costs

There is another way of looking at costs and classifying them into different categories. This analysis is concerned with how a cost behaves when there is a change in the level of activity. Some costs stay the same total amount regardless of activity levels from week to week. Such costs are known as fixed costs, of which rent and business rates are classic examples.

Other costs behave differently. If, say, the total cost of raw materials moves up or down in relation to the level of output, as one would expect, then this is called a variable cost. The analysis of costs into fixed and variable categories is most useful when making one-off decisions about the best course of action in circumstances where activity levels will change – say, the effect of cutting prices to increase sales volume. The main accounting technique that uses this analysis of costs into fixed and variable categories is called *marginal costing*, and is pursued in Chapter 13.

COSTING LABOUR, MATERIALS AND EXPENSES

The resources firms use consist of three basic elements:

- Labour – The cost of people employed by an organization in both direct and indirect capacities.
- Materials – The cost of physical raw materials used directly in operations and other materials used in service activities.
- Expenses – The cost of bought-in services. Some are directly chargeable to customer products, eg subcontract or outwork. Other expenses relate to the multitude of fixed overhead costs, eg rates, electricity, legal fees.

We now want to look at the costing of each of these resources in turn, before showing how they are used to help fix prices or prepare estimates.

LABOUR COSTS

In some industries, such as education and health, labour costs may form more than half of the total running costs of an organization. Other service industries, such as financial services, are also very labour intensive, but new technology is gradually reducing the manual tasks here as well as elsewhere.

Manufacturing industries used to be very labour intensive with control of direct labour costs justifiably getting a high profile. With the coming of automation and robotics, this is no longer the case, resulting in attention shifting to machine costs, material costs and indirect labour costs.

Nevertheless, labour costs are still significant in all organizations and need to be carefully costed and controlled. To do this we need documentation, which usually takes the form of timecards and/or timesheets.

A timecard is clocked into a time-recording machine to verify attendance and record the hours worked. A timesheet (as in the example shown in Figure 11.3) can be used for the same purpose and, in addition, records both work done and cost unit/ cost centre numbers. This would all need checking by a supervisor to maintain accuracy.

Other documents in use – in manufacturing particularly – are a piecework ticket (if remuneration is based on output) and a job card (if work is done by more than one operative or moves from one department to another).

All these documents – timecards, timesheets, job cards and piecework tickets – will be used by accounting staff to prepare the payroll and to charge labour costs to appropriate cost units and cost centres. Direct labour, including any

Weekly Time Sheet

Name						Clock no			
Dept or Cost centre						Week ending			
Job or code no	Description of work	Hours taken					Hours	Rate per hour	Cost £
		Mon	Tue	Wed	Thu	Fri			

Signed
(Worker)

Signed
(Supervisor)

Figure 11.3 *A typical timesheet*

bonuses and premium rates, can be directly charged to the products/ services worked on. Indirect labour, however, is first channelled to cost centres and then absorbed into product/service costs by using overhead recovery rates. There are a number of different payment systems to choose from when considering how to reward direct labour for their efforts.

Payment systems

The remuneration paid to employees can be based on the number of hours worked or on output achieved or some kind of combination of the two. The main types of payment systems are as follows:

1. *Time-based system.* Pays a basic hourly rate for normal hours but enhanced rates after that. An example would be £6 per hour up to 37 hours and £9 per hour (time and a half) for each hour in excess of 37 per week.
2. *Measured day work.* Pays high basic rates for high output and high-quality effort with agreed targets.
3. *Incentive scheme.* Relates pay directly to output with certain safeguards for workers when output is restricted for reasons beyond their control. Piecework is the name given to an incentive system where a set amount is paid for each unit of output.
4. *Premium bonus system.* Pays normal hourly or daily rates plus a bonus for any time saved relative to the time allowed.

Regardless of payment method, the cost of direct workers is charged directly to the products or services (cost units) on which they work. This cost will usually be enhanced by the employer's contributions to National Insurance, holidays, pensions and any other remuneration-related overhead. Similarly, the pay of indirect workers (enhanced by these employee-related overheads) can be charged to the cost centres where they work. Overheads accumulated in each cost centre are then charged out to cost units benefiting from its services. This overhead recovery process is described later.

MATERIAL COSTS

Some businesses hold stocks of materials or components in their stores for issue at a later date. The purchase and subsequent issue of these materials is also documented at various stages to ensure that volumes and values are known and charged to the right cost units and cost centres. In larger organizations some of these documents may not exist in paper form if the procedure is computerized. Nevertheless, it is helpful to appreciate the function of the following typical documents, irrespective of whether they exist as such, or not:

- *Purchase requisition.* This is raised internally as soon as the re-order point is triggered. A requisition specifies the quantity, quality, price and delivery requirements.
- *Purchase order.* This is sent out for the economic order quantity to the selected supplier who meets the requirement.
- *Goods received note.* Made out after materials are received and matched with purchase order and technical specifications.
- *Goods returned note.* Raised only if any materials need to be returned to suppliers.
- *Invoice from supplier.* Checked against goods received note and purchase order before payment is made.
- *Stores requisition.* When duly authorized, this is the only means of obtaining materials from store.
- *Stock record.* Kept manually by storekeeper and/or kept by computer recording all receipts and issues. The individual stock records are checked by a physical stocktaking on a continuous rotating basis.

All these documents and records have a part to play in the bookkeeping and costing systems for materials. If materials are ordered for a specific purpose, the invoice can be specifically charged to the cost unit and/or cost centre concerned. What is not quite so straightforward is what charge to make for materials that have been held in store for some time and are subsequently issued. The following are the alternatives available.

Bases for pricing stores issues

Two problems arise when purchase prices vary over time and a particular stocked item may comprise various amounts bought at different prices. The cost of the materials issued is a charge against income in the profit and loss account so that profit is affected if this cost can vary. The value that is placed on an issue from stock also affects the remaining stock value shown as a current asset in the balance sheet. The options for pricing stores issues are as below:

- *First in first out (FIFO)*. A popular method that issues oldest materials first at old prices. Remaining stock is therefore valued at recent prices for balance sheet purposes.
- *Last in first out (LIFO)*. More popular in the US, but not accepted as a valid basis by the Inland Revenue in the UK.
- *Standard price*. All similar materials are held in store at the one predetermined standard price specified and are issued at that value. Purchases at non-standard prices are still valued at this standard price but the cost variances are written off to the profit and loss account immediately.
- *Weighted average price*. This compromise between FIFO and LIFO values, prices stores issues and materials remaining in store at the same average price.

Example

A firm bought 200 units of material at 60p per unit in May and a further 400 units at 50p in August. The standard purchase price specified for this material is 60p. What is the cost of 300 units of this material issued in September under each of the different stores pricing systems?

Each pricing method gives a different answer, being £170, £150, £180, and £160 respectively. The calculations are:

FIFO	200	at 60p	+ 100 at 50p	=	£170
LIFO	300	at 50p		=	£150
Standard	300	at 60p		=	£180
Average	100	at 60p	+ 200 at 50p	=	£160

Over the whole life-span of any one company there will be no difference between these four methods of pricing stores issues. The total cost of all materials purchased is the same under all four methods and the profit made by the company over its whole life is therefore identical. However, this is not true when we consider a short period of one month or a year in the life of that same company. The profit made in any one period will differ according to which method of stores pricing was used.

The FIFO method of pricing stores issues flatters profit when the price of materials is rising. The weighted average method similarly flatters profit when material prices are rising, but less so. The standard cost basis is the most realistic, provided the specified price is updated for changes in market prices of each material.

Once materials have been valued, direct materials can be charged out to the cost units by using the relevant job or batch number. Indirect materials are charged to the cost centre incurring them, to be charged to cost units later as part of the total overhead recovery.

EXPENSES

We can dispense with direct expenses rapidly. These may occur if, say, a special piece of equipment is hired to do a job or if work is sent out on a sub-contract basis. The invoice for such expenses can be charged to the cost unit concerned in much the same way as direct labour and direct material costs are coded with the job number concerned.

Indirect expenses, however, have no such direct connection with cost units and are consequently charged to cost centres along with indirect labour and indirect materials. The treatment of all these three indirect costs is the story of overhead recovery, which we tackle next.

OVERHEAD RECOVERY

Overhead is just another word for *indirect cost*. Overheads are usually just as essential a cost as direct costs, but they sometimes get tagged as non-productive costs. This is patently untrue as all the production in the world is useless without a sales force to sell it, accounts staff to pay wages and suppliers and administrative staff to deal with other paperwork. All these costs are overheads.

From a costing viewpoint overheads are a challenge. Although there is no direct link with the end product going to customers, overheads still have to be charged to cost units if we want to know their total costs. Why do we need to know the total cost of a product?

- for stock valuation to enable the production of financial accounts;
- for pricing and preparing estimates of cost units;
- to know what profit we are making at a given selling price.

The question posed for managers and accountants is – how much overhead to charge to different product lines and to each cost unit? There are three broad approaches to this problem:

- use one single global overhead recovery rate;
- use multi-department overhead recovery rates;
- use activity-based overhead recovery rates.

Global overhead recovery rate

Consider how a local garage charges each customer with a share of its overheads for service or repair work. Normal practice is that it combines overheads with direct labour costs, and charges an enhanced hourly rate to recover the cost of mechanic's time and overheads – and an element of profit!

This obviously is an easy and cheap way to deal with the costing of overheads. At the beginning of a year the garage estimates the cost of all its overheads and the number of mechanics' hours it will normally be able to charge out. The hourly overhead charge is worked out by dividing the estimated overheads for the year by the number of mechanics' hours in that same time.

Example

A garage estimates that its total overheads for the coming year will amount to £200,000. It also estimates that chargeable time will amount to 20,000 hours. The overhead charge/recovery rate is £10 per hour.

If all customers were having similar work done then this system is likely to be as fair as any other. Most overheads accumulate with time as does rent, rates, office salaries, heating, etc, so to include overheads at £x per hour seems fair at first glance. However, in some circumstances this might not be regarded as a fair way to charge customers for different kinds of work. What this global overhead recovery system does not allow for is that some customers may need the use of special equipment for a certain kind of repair while other customers do not. If the overheads include charges for the depreciation and maintenance of this equipment then the first customers are being subsidized by other customers who are being overcharged.

Many small firms use the above approach of putting all overheads into one big pot and then charging them out to cost units at an hourly rate according to the direct labour hours going into each product. This approach is shown in Figure 11.4.

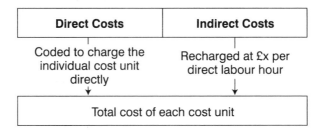

Figure 11.4 *Global method of overhead recovery*

Multi-department overhead recovery rates

Larger organizations with diversified products and more diverse production or operation systems find the global approach to overheads inappropriate due to its lack of discrimination. They cannot afford to undercharge some products, so gaining market share on less profitable lines, and then overcharge on other products, so losing market share on the more profitable lines.

For this reason they channel all overheads into their relevant cost centres wherever they arise. Cost centres providing a service to other operational cost centres have all their overheads recharged to them on the basis of the amount of service provided. All overheads are now in operational cost centres which charge them out to cost units, but *only* those passing through that cost centre. In this way equity is established between different products. This more equitable system is illustrated in Figure 11.5.

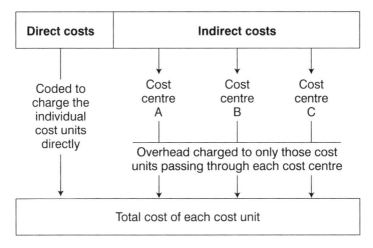

Figure 11.5 *Multi-department overhead recovery method*

Activity-based overhead recovery method

A subtly different means of overhead apportionment has appeared in recent years based on the principles of *activity-based costing* (ABC). The impetus for this approach derives from the need for manufacturing companies to have reliable valuations on their finished stocks and work-in-progress to prepare the financial accounts. Accounting standards decree that these stocks are valued on the basis of direct costs plus some appropriation of production overheads only.

The traditional method of absorbing production overheads into product costs (as in Figure 11.5 above) has been to relate those overheads to the direct labour cost or to the direct labour or machine time involved. As a result, production overhead charges of x per cent of direct labour cost or £y per direct labour hour or £z per machine hour have been used to calculate product costs and satisfy financial accounting needs for stock valuations.

In many cases, though, the direct labour cost is now a very small proportion of total production costs and production overheads are a much higher proportion because of the technology now being used. To base the overhead recovery of a large amount on a small base is fraught with danger. Added to this is the problem of variable sizes of production runs, where the time taken on actual production takes no account of the overheads incurred on pre-production set up and production scheduling. Direct labour cost reflects the volume of production, but not the complexity of the overhead functions supporting that production. The end result was that product costs in some manufacturing companies became discredited for pricing and profitability purposes and the search was on for a better method.

ABC analyses overhead costs into *activities*, which probably transcend departmental boundaries, and are collected in cost pools. Examples of activities might be:

- estimating;
- set-up;
- materials handling;
- invoicing.

The prime cause of demand for a particular activity is identified as a *cost driver*. If, say, quality inspections is an activity and the number of inspections is the cost driver, then the cost driver rate will be determined by dividing the cost pool for the inspection activity by the total number of inspections carried out in the period. The end result might seem little different to the traditional method of departmental/cost centre overhead recovery rates, but this is not the case. There are far more activities than there are cost centres/departments and ABC does a better job in identifying overhead costs with the products that incur them.

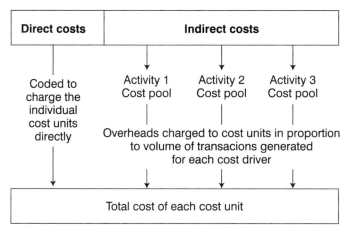

Figure 11.6 *ABC method of overhead recovery*

ABC is not limited to production overheads only and can be applied to administrative, selling and distribution functions where activity cost pools and cost drivers can be established. In fact, ABC is not limited to manufacturing companies and is now frequently applied to service organizations. Nor is its use limited to product costing, but extends to customer profitability analysis, activity-based budgeting and other management applications.

We can now see how the total cost of any product or service is built up. Direct labour, direct material and direct expenses can all be coded with a job number to identify a particular cost unit. Indirect labour, indirect materials and indirect expenses have to be shared out over cost units in a way that does not favour one product line at the expense of another. This may be by use of one global overhead recovery rate; or along traditional department/cost centre overhead recovery rate lines; or, in more complex situations, by use of activity cost pools and their associated cost drivers. The next chapter continues the costing story by examining the way businesses use cost information to help fix their prices.

Further reading

CIMA, (1996) *Management Accounting: Official Terminology*, CIMA, London.
Drury, C (1996) *Management and Cost Accounting*, ITP, London.
Innes, J and Mitchell, F (1998) *Activity-based Costing*, Kogan Page, London.
Lucey, T (1996) *Costing*, Letts, London.
Turney, PBB (1998) *Activity-based Costing: the Performance Breakthrough*, Kogan Page, London.

Self-check questions

1. Is costing primarily concerned with revenue or capital costs?
2. Which documents typically convey basic cost data to accountants in an organization?
3. Distinguish a cost unit from a cost centre.
4. Define indirect costs.
5. Give an example of a variable cost for:

   - a leisure centre;
   - a firm making cosmetics; and
   - an electricity supply company.

6. In what ways can direct labour be remunerated?
7. What bases can be used to price materials drawn from an internal store?
8. In what ways does an activity-based costing system differ from a departmental overhead recovery system?

12
Costing and pricing

INTRODUCTION

Organizations need to know the total cost of each product or service they provide to their customers for the following reasons:

- to value work-in-progress and completed work as current assets in the balance sheet;
- to determine the cost of sales to enter in the profit and loss account;
- to control product costs by comparing them with a predetermined target or standard cost;
- to know what profit is made at any particular selling price;
- to fix selling prices based on total cost, although it should always be borne in mind that there are other non-cost influences on prices.

When prices are cost based, this calculation usually takes place before the order is received from the customer. This is the case when an estimate or quotation is requested for one-off or purpose-built items. Where standardized products are concerned, the normal selling price is usually based on the total cost incurred on producing the product or providing the service. An element of profit is added in both cases for profit-seeking enterprises.

Sometimes work may be undertaken on a *cost plus* basis, meaning that the supplier will be reimbursed for all legitimate direct costs plus an agreed percentage for overheads plus a further agreed profit percentage. Some government contracts are let out on this basis. The selling price in these cases can only be worked out after the event. The costing procedure for working out the production cost of any product or service is the same, irrespective of whether it takes place before or after the work is completed. This procedure is called *absorption costing* by accountants and is a key step towards *full cost* or *total cost* pricing.

ABSORPTION COSTING

This term was chosen to describe the approach whereby products are charged with all the direct costs associated with each product and also absorb a share of the total production overheads. We can therefore say:

Total production cost	=	Direct costs	+	Share of production overheads

Example
A jobbing printer receives an enquiry for 100,000 leaflets of A5 size printed in black ink. The cost estimator has prepared the following estimate of resources required to do the job:

Direct costs:
   Paper – 204 reams of A4 at £3 per ream
   Ink – 2 litres at £9 per litre
   Labour time – 2 hours at £15 per hour

Indirect costs:
   Production overheads and machine utilization – 2 hours at £55 per hour.

The total production cost is as follows:

	£
Direct costs:	
Paper	612
Ink	18
Labour	30
Indirect costs:	
Production overheads	110
Total production cost	£770

The precise methods used, and overhead recovery rates charged, vary from one organization to another and depend on whether one global rate, multiple departmental rates or cost driver activity rates are employed.

FULL COST PRICING

The above example of a product absorbing production overheads is an important stage on the way to finding the total cost and then adding a profit margin to arrive at a selling price. Full cost pricing can be described as:

Direct costs	+	Share of overheads	+	Profit margin	=	Selling price
Direct materials		Production overheads				
Direct labour		Administrative overheads				
Direct expenses		Selling + distribution overheads				

Example

Returning to our earlier example, let us now assume that selling, distribution and administration overheads are recovered by charging £20 per hour and an extra 10 per cent of total costs is added for profit.

The quoted selling price can now be completed as follows:

Direct costs:	£
Paper	612
Ink	18
Labour	30
Indirect costs:	
Production overheads	110
Total production cost	770
Other overheads	40
Total cost	810
Profit	81
Selling price to quote	£891

In larger firms, a number of departmental overhead-recovery rates may be needed to determine total costs. This approach is used to channel overheads only to those products benefiting from the services provided by a particular department.

Example

The following details have been assembled to work out the price for a job in response to a customer's request:

Direct materials: 7.5 kilos at £10.50 per kilo

Direct labour:	Department	Hours	Rate per hour
	Machine shop	2.0	£8
	Assembly dept	1.0	£6
	Packing shop	0.2	£5

Production overheads: These are recovered by means of separate hourly recovery rates for each of the above departments.

Other overheads and profit: An oncost of 25 per cent to the total production cost to cover selling and administration costs, plus an element of profit.

The annual budgets for overheads for the above three departments are:

Department	Hours	Overheads	Hourly rate
Machine shop	1,000	£50,000	£50.00
Assembly dept	1,500	£22,500	£15.00
Packing shop	800	£26,000	£32.50

The price quotation can now be prepared as follows:

		£	£
Direct materials:	7.5 kilos at £10.50		78.75
Direct labour:	2 hours at £8	16.00	
	1 hour at £6	6.00	
	0.2 hours at £5	1.00	23.00
Overheads:	2 hours at £50	100.00	
	1 hour at £15	15.00	
	0.2 hours at £32.50	6.50	121.50
Total works cost			223.25
Oncost of 25% for selling and administration overheads plus profit			55.81
Selling price to quote to customer			£279.06

PROFIT MARGINS

Profit margins can vary very much between firms in the same industry and also from one industry to another. To understand why they vary we need to look again at the relationship of three key accounting ratios – return on capital, profit margin and turnover of capital which were first described in Chapter 9.

Most profit-seeking firms set financial objectives in the form of a return on capital. If a firm had £2 million capital invested in business assets then it might regard a pre-tax annual profit of £400,000 as reasonable. This equates to a 20 per cent return on capital.

If this annual profit of £400,000 was earned on sales of £4 million, this gives a profit margin of 10 per cent. These sales of £4 million, when related to the capital employed of £2 million, result in a turnover of capital of two times, ie each £1 of capital generates £2 of sales in the year.

These three ratios are related to each other as follows:

Return on capital	=	Profit margin	x	Turnover of capital
20%	=	10%	x	2

Not all firms earn a 20 per cent return on capital. Some earn more and some less, depending on the state of the economy and the quality of their management. In the long run, a reasonable return on capital is essential for a firm to remain independent and attract new capital to facilitate growth.

Firms also differ in the size of the other two ratios. Some industries have a high profit margin to compensate for a low rate of turnover of capital, as will be found with capital intensive activities, such as electricity generation and electricity distribution. Other industries have a low profit margin compensated by a high turnover of capital rate, as found in construction, civil engineering and food retailing.

The conclusion we can draw from this is that there is no one profit-margin percentage that applies to all firms. Each firm sets its own target in the light of what is achievable in its own industry and circumstances. The 10 per cent profit margin used in the estimating example may or may not be typical of the printing industry. We would have to look at the results of surveys carried out by their trade associations, or business monitoring organizations, to know what was the norm.

A survey of large manufacturing and service companies in 1986 by Mills and Sweeting showed that cost-related pricing methods were the most popular with approximately 70 per cent of respondents. A similar proportion also selected full/absorption costing as the primary cost method used. A later survey of UK manufacturing companies by Drury *et al* (1993) showed that 84 per cent used cost-plus pricing, but in a flexible manner.

This does not necessarily mean that profit-seeking companies stick rigidly to prices determined by total costs. Companies use absorption costing as a long-term guide to what they need to sell at to earn a reasonable rate of return. In the short term, companies often trim their prices to suit market conditions. This can be disguised by the use of discounts as opposed to an overt price cut. This angle is explored more in the following chapter on marginal costing where the concept of *contribution* is introduced.

Some industries are dominated by just one or only a few large suppliers. Small firms in these industries may have to be price followers rather than price determiners, unless they can differentiate their products on service or quality grounds.

COSTING METHODS

Working out the total cost of a product may not be quite as straightforward as it sounds in some industries where different methods of production or operations are used. There are a number of costing methods specifically designed to suit the way a particular product is made or service provided in varying industries and sectors. These costing methods go under various names:

- job costing;
- batch costing;
- contract costing;
- process costing;
- service costing.

Essentially, these five methods derive from only two main forms – *job costing* or *process costing*. We now look at the distinguishing features of each costing method.

Job costing

This applies where an individual job is carried out to a customer's specification, either at the supplier's premises or at the customer's premises. Jobbing printing and repairs to domestic appliances are relevant examples. The earlier examples (building up costs to quote a price) illustrated job costing.

Each job is costed as a separate entity and given its own unique *job number* in the cost coding system. This number is inserted on all prime documents –

timesheets, stores issue notes and invoices – so that all direct costs related to each particular job are specifically charged to it. Overheads are added later in line with the recovery methods and recovery rates used by that firm. In this way the total cost of each job is gradually built up until the job is physically completed. This information can all be recorded by computer, but in some firms a *job card* may accompany the work through its various stages and departments. Resources consumed are logged on to the job card as the work progresses, in the same way as it would be entered on a computer record of the same job number.

Batch costing

Where a number (batch) of identical products (cost units) are produced at one time they are often treated as one job in total and costed as such. The unit cost is therefore the total cost divided by the number of cost units in the batch.

Example
A batch of 1,000 washing machines was produced by a factory last week. Direct costs of labour and material parts charged to the job number for this batch amounted to £80,000. Overheads attributable to this production were a further £70,000.

$$\text{Unit cost} = \frac{\text{Total cost}}{\text{Number of units}} = \frac{£80,000 + £70,000}{1,000} = £150$$

Contract costing

This applies to any very large job, usually associated with the construction industry, and often carried out at the client's site or premises. This is another variant of job costing, so that each contract, or part of a contract, will have its own job number. However, there are a number of special features of contract costing that distinguish it from job and batch costing.

Direct costs of labour and materials still apply, but there may be additional direct costs for plant hire or work done by subcontractors. Site overhead charges can be specifically charged to an individual contract so the only overhead apportionments needed are those that relate to head office charges.

Example

                    Contract No 123

	£
Site wages	20,400
Site salaries	18,600
NI, pensions, etc	6,200
Subcontract work	17,000
Internal plant hire	3,500
External plant hire	7,000
Materials delivered to site	46,000
Site overheads	5,300
Head office charges	2,750
Total contract costs to date	£126,750

Progress payments, assessed on the value of work done, help to offset the amount of working capital needed to finance contract work. This system of payment allows contractors and civil engineering firms to carry out multi-million pound schemes with only a relatively small amount of capital.

Process costing

This system of costing applies to a continuous and ongoing process that never, or rarely, stops. In such circumstances the unit cost cannot be separately recorded as in job costing. The unit cost in process costing is found by dividing the total costs for a period of time by the output over that period.

Example
The total of all direct and indirect costs for running a coal mine for a week amounted to £6 million. Output during this time amounted to 200,000 tonnes.

$$\text{Cost per tonne} = \frac{£6m}{200,000 \text{ tonnes}} = £30 \text{ per tonne}$$

In some process industries there may be partially completed products at any moment in time so that at the end of an accounting period these need to be converted into *equivalent whole units* in order to calculate the average unit cost of each complete unit.

Example
A company started a process on 1 March and incurred total costs of £100,000 during the month. Output for the month was 2,000 complete products plus 200 that were 40 per cent partially completed.

$$\text{Cost per unit} = \frac{£100,000}{2,000 + (200 \times 40\%)} = \frac{£100,000}{2,080} = £48.07$$

Further situations in some process industries, for example oil refining, are when products are produced either *jointly* or as a *by-product* of the main process. The costing treatment of by-products, so called because they do not have significant value relative to the main product, is that their *net realizable value* goes to offset the costs of the main product.

However, when products are produced simultaneously in a process, with each product having a significant value on its own, these are referred to as *joint products*. The costing problem this throws up is how to split the common costs incurred up to the separation point. This can be done in one of two ways:

1. *By volume* – the common costs are apportioned *pro rata* to a physical measure of the quantity of each produced; or
2. *By market value* – the common costs are apportioned on the basis of the market value of each joint product at the time of separation.

Service costing

This system of costing applies to any service industry where a uniform or standard service is provided to customers. In theory it should be easier to cost services than, say, manufactured products, because there are no stocks and work-in-progress to be valued. In practice it may be hard to define some services and to draw boundaries to separate one service from another. Without such definition it will be impossible to cost separate services.

Service costing is similar to process costing in that the total costs of providing the service over a period of time is divided by the quantity of services provided to get a unit cost. Transport or electricity businesses could divide their total costs for a period of time by the activity taking place during that time to lead to the average *cost per passenger mile* or the *cost per kWh* respectively.

Example
The running costs of a local swimming-pool amount to £16,000 per week. Last week 8,000 people used the pool. The average cost per swim is therefore £2.

Where there is not a single homogeneous service provided, as with a swim, but a mixture of swims, saunas, exercise sessions and the like, then a detailed cost analysis not unlike product costing will be required. Activity-based costing techniques may be employed here to advantage.

The actual unit cost of a service is used to help fix prices or other charges, but can also be used as a basis for cost control. For example, comparisons can be made with past unit costs or with pre-set targets, or by benchmarking with similar organizations.

TARGET COSTING

This is not so much a costing technique as a management process to drive down costs to a level that will earn a satisfactory margin on the target selling price. This is the very reverse of cost-plus pricing which builds up direct and indirect costs to a total cost, then adds a profit margin to arrive at the selling price, as shown in Figure 12.1.

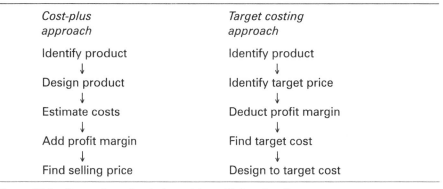

Figure 12.1   *Comparison of cost-plus pricing with target costing*

Target costing is attributed to the car manufacturer Toyota as far back as the

1960s and was widely copied by other Japanese manufacturers. More recently it has been adopted in other countries, not least those hosting Japanese-owned plants and their satellite suppliers. Whereas cost-plus pricing, if rigidly adhered to, ignores the customer and the state of the market, target costing is market driven and starts at the customer end. It addresses what the customer will be prepared to pay and what competition will allow to be charged.

The main thrust of target costing is in the design stage. Multi-discipline teams are formed to look at all aspects of product design, customer usage, value engineering and production processes. It is said that cost reduction is much more easily achieved at the pre-manufacturing stage than once the product is designed and into regular production.

INFLATION

When estimating future costs to establish an overhead recovery rate, full allowance for the anticipated rate of inflation should be made for the review period. Similarly, when actually quoting estimates or fixing selling prices, the up-to-date cost of materials and depreciation should be used. To do otherwise will not result in sufficient profit being made to replace the resources consumed at today's prices.

Further reading

Bhimani , A and Okano, H (June 1995) Targeting excellence: target cost management at Toyota in the UK, *Management Accounting*, June.
Drury, C *et al,* (1993) *A Survey of Management Accounting Practices in UK, Manufacturing Companies*, ACCA, London.
Drury, C (1996) *Management and Cost Accounting*, ITP, London.
Glautier, MWE and Underdown, B (1997) *Accounting Theory and Practice*, FT/Pitman, London.
Lucey, T (1997) *Management Accounting*, Letts, London.
Mills, RW and Sweeting, R (1988) *Pricing Decisions in Practice*, CIMA, London.

Self-check questions

1. Prepare a price quotation for the jobbing printer (mentioned early in the chapter) who has now received an order for 10,000 A5 menu cards. Direct materials are estimated at £180 and machine time will take three hours. All other cost and profit information is as before.
2. What size profit margin is required to give a return on capital of 30 per cent when the turnover of capital is two times?
3. What costing method is most suited to oil refining?
4. How would a local authority know if its unit cost for providing a particular service was high, low, or indifferent?
5. What two bases can be used to split the common costs of joint products up to the separation point?
6. What is the purpose of target costing?

13
Marginal costing

INTRODUCTION

The previous chapter described the full cost of a product or service as a combination of direct costs and a share of the indirect costs. Marginal costing is a technique which also divides costs into two categories, but of a somewhat different nature. In this case costs are identified as being either *fixed* or *variable*, relative to the quantity of output:

A fixed cost is so called because, in the short run, it does not vary in total when output fluctuates. Rent and rates for a factory, shop, or office are good examples of fixed costs. Variable costs are those whose total cost (not unit cost) varies pro rata with the volume of output. The value of direct materials used on the product or service sold to customers is a typical variable cost.

It is possible to express fixed and variable costs in the form of a diagram or graph as shown in Figure 13.1.

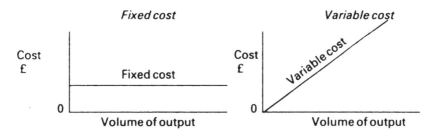

Figure 13.1 *Fixed and variable cost behaviour*

Purposes of marginal costing

There are a number of reasons why we analyse costs into fixed and variable categories. In general it is for the purpose of answering questions or making decisions as to the best course of action in the short term. These include:

- a choice between alternative cost structures;
- the volume required to break-even or make a specified profit;
- the consequences of a change in product mix;
- one-off pricing decisions;
- make-or-buy decisions.

The similarity of variable costs to direct costs, and fixed costs to indirect costs, is sometimes a source of confusion. They are not quite the same for a number of reasons. Direct costs usually include the cost of direct labour and materials used on the product itself. Direct material is a variable cost because its cost varies exactly in proportion to the number of products made. This is not always the case with direct labour, particularly in the short term. For example, if a direct labour force is on a guaranteed weekly wage, we cannot say the cost is variable when there is a contractual agreement to pay them a fixed sum irrespective of the level of output achieved.

Fixed costs will all be classified as overheads or indirect costs, but some overheads vary *pro rata* to output. Power, quality inspection and some distribution costs are examples of variable overheads.

We can often use simple graphs to express the relationship of costs to output and use the graphs as an aid to decision-making.

Example
You are comparing the charges of two car hire firms before you decide which one to use. Firm A offers a car at a fixed rate of £20 per day plus 20p for every mile. Firm B charges only £12 per day but 30p for every mile. The two alternatives can be drawn on one diagram as shown in Figure 13.2.

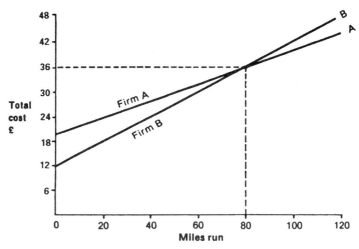

Figure 13.2 *Comparison of car hire costs*

The total cost of using either car comprises the daily fixed charge plus the mileage cost, which varies according to miles run.

We can conclude from the graph that firm B is the one to patronize if the daily mileage is expected to be less than 80 miles, while firm A should be chosen for a daily mileage in excess of 80. The total cost is equal where the two lines cross at £36 read off the vertical scale and is called the *break-even point*.

BREAK-EVEN ANALYSIS

This idea of break-even point is also used by firms to depict that level of output where sales revenue just equals total cost. To find this point on a graph we need to plot fixed costs, variable costs and sales revenue against output, when the break-even point is where neither a profit nor a loss is made – hence the use of the term *break-even*.

Example
A firm makes only one product, which sells for £10. The variable cost per unit is £5 and fixed costs total £75,000 pa. Maximum capacity is 25,000 units per annum, but the firm is presently operating at only 80 per cent capacity. Figure 13.3 shows the break-even chart drawn from this information.

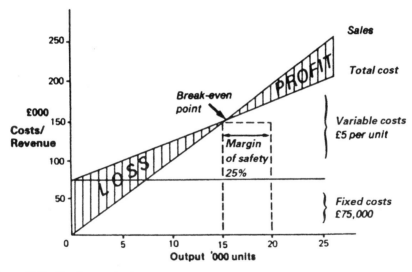

Figure 13.3   *Break-even chart*

Break-even is reached at 15,000 units when sales just equals total costs of £150,000. Output of less than this amount results in a loss, while greater output makes a profit. The size of profit or loss at any output can be read off the graph at a glance, being the vertical distance between the total cost line and sales line.

Margin of safety

Also represented on the graph is the *margin of safety* which represents the proportionate fall in output which can take place before a loss is incurred. In this example, the present level of output of 20,000 units can fall by 25 per cent to 15,000 units before a loss commences. Therefore the margin of safety is 25 per cent.

Separation of fixed and variable costs

Although the theoretical distinction between fixed and variable costs is easily understood, it is not so easy in practice to separate them. Some costs fall into an in-between category called *semi-fixed* or *semi-variable*, where there is a fixed amount of cost plus an element that varies with output.

One way to separate total costs into fixed and variable types is to graph total costs against the relevant levels of output. If the data covers a number of years, the total costs should be updated to today's prices using relevant cost indices. The scattergraph is obtained from plotting total costs against level of output and drawing a line of best fit through the plots. Where the line intersects the vertical line at the origin approximates to the level of fixed costs. Figure 13.4 shows this approach which identifies fixed costs at approximately £200,000.

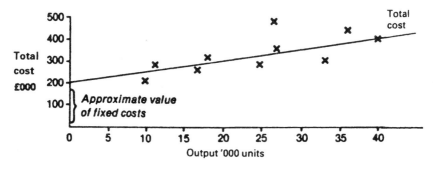

Figure 13.4 *Scattergraph used to separate fixed and variable costs*

Another reason for the practical difficulty in separating costs into fixed and variable categories is that such analysis varies with time. In the very long run all costs are variable because offices or plants can be closed down and then no further costs will be incurred. In the very short run of a few days, most costs are fixed, apart from direct materials, power and possibly some wages, depending on the contracted method of payment.

Although we represent fixed costs as a horizontal line on a break-even chart, it is not true to say that fixed costs will remain constant over a wide range of output levels. It could be that more supervisors or managers are required the higher the level of output, or more space or machinery is needed which result in increased rates or depreciation. Therefore fixed costs may increase in steps as output increases, corresponding more to the picture in Figure 13.5 than the horizontal line shown in previous diagrams.

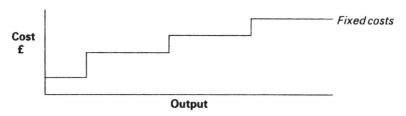

Figure 13.5 *Stepped fixed costs*

Break-even charts are a useful way of depicting profit or loss at varying levels of output. They can be drawn for a firm as a whole or for one product only. In the latter case the fixed costs are those specifically applicable to the product, together with a share of the total to be apportioned over all products.

Limitations of break-even charts

It is probably true that break-even charts are seen more often in textbooks than in real life. This is because the charts have some severe limitations. Clearly, costs do not move in a linear fashion across a wide range of activity levels. Nor does the product mix ratio stay constant in a multi-product firm. Any change in the mix will invalidate a chart as total sales value and total variable costs will vary with the mix. Finally, a chart cannot predict how many sales will be achieved at a certain price – that can only be attempted by market research. A break-even chart can only predict what profit will be made for a given selling price over a range of possible sales volumes.

CONTRIBUTION

The term *contribution* is used to describe the difference between sales value and variable costs only. It is therefore an intermediate level of profit before fixed costs have been charged.

We refer to different products making a contribution towards fixed costs and profit, by which we mean that they contribute to the common pool from which fixed costs are paid and profit remains.

Combining these two formulae, we get:

| Sales | – | Variable costs | = | Contribution | – | Fixed costs | = | Profit |

Contribution break-even chart

It is possible to draw a break-even chart in a slightly different manner. If the variable cost is drawn first and then the fixed cost on top, the resultant total cost is the same as if we had represented costs in the original reverse order. The reason for changing the order is to be able to show the value of contribution.

Example
Using the same basic data as for Figure 13.3, the break-even chart which identifies contribution as the shaded area is shown in Figure 13.6

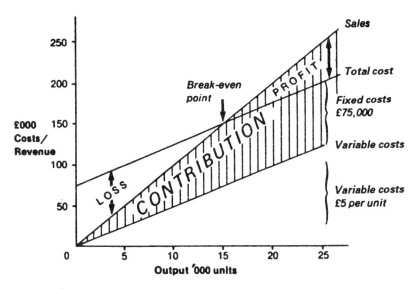

Figure 13.6 *Contribution break-even chart*

The profit and loss areas are still identifiable as such and the break-even point remains the same at 15,000 units.

Contribution analysis

A most important use of the concept of contribution occurs when decisions have to be made concerning product profitability. It might be thought that the size of the profit or loss would be the determining factor here, but this is not necessarily the case.

Example
Imet Ltd manufactures three products, A, B and C, of which the first two have

124

been making acceptable profits, but C has been losing money for some time and the directors are considering whether to drop it. The most recent results for last month are as follows:

Product	A	B	C	Total
	£000	£000	£000	£000
Sales	60	120	90	270
Less Total costs	42	99	93	234
Profit or (Loss)	18	21	(3)	36

The directors have considered a number of possible courses of future action, but meanwhile have no new products available. Nor can they sell more of products A or B without dropping the selling price. The immediate decision is whether to drop product C and apparently save £3,000 per month.

On investigation by the accountant, it is found that the total costs of the products includes £54,000 of fixed costs apportioned £12,000, £24,000, and £18,000 respectively. The fixed costs of £18,000 presently borne by product C will continue irrespective of whether that product is made or discontinued.

A more helpful analysis of the situation is to set out the contribution made by each product to the total fixed costs incurred by the firm and the overall profit achieved. This is shown in Figure 13.7.

Product	A	B	C	Total
	£000	£000	£000	£000
Sales	60	120	90	270
Less Variable costs	30	75	75	180
Contribution	30	45	15	90
Less Fixed costs				54
Profit				36

Figure 13.7 *Contribution analysis by products*

The directors of Imet Ltd can now conclude that it is better to continue selling product C for the moment because it is making a contribution of £15,000 towards fixed costs. If product C is discontinued, the contributions from the remaining two products will not change, neither will the fixed costs incurred by the firm. Profit will therefore fall by £15,000 to only £21,000. So discontinuing product C immediately is not advisable.

Contribution ratio

Another use of the concept of contribution is when measuring the profitability of products. If the profitability is measured by expressing the net profit as a percentage of sales, product managers may argue about the unfairness of the apportionment of fixed costs to their own product. Because of the general nature of most fixed costs, there is no direct link between them and individual products. One way around this endless debate is to express the contribution as a percentage of sales by calculating what is known as the *profit/volume ratio* or *contribution ratio*:

$$\text{Contribution ratio} \quad = \quad \frac{\text{Contribution} \times 100}{\text{Sales}} \quad \%$$

Example

Using the information in Figure 13.7, the contribution ratios for the three products are calculated and are now shown in Figure 13.8, where Product C is shown to be the least profitable product with the lowest contribution ratio.

Product	A	B	C	Total
	£000	£000	£000	£000
Sales	60	120	90	270
Contribution	30	45	15	90
Contribution ratio	50%	37.5%	16.7%	33.3%

Figure 13.8 *Assessing product profitability by contribution ratios*

OPTIMUM PRODUCT MIX

Sometimes firms need to know the particular mix of products that will make the best profit. This situation arises when there are capacity constraints that do not allow the firm to make all the products it can sell. The approach to this problem is to make those products that bring in the highest *contribution per unit of scarce resource*. Production is allocated to products in their descending order of profitability as measured by £ *contribution per unit of scarce resource* be that space, skilled labour, raw materials, or any other scarce resource.

Example

A firm makes only three products and has no space to expand further. Its management want to know which products are the most profitable so that they can plan their sales promotion activities accordingly. The following information is available:

Product		A	B	C	Total
		£000	£000	£000	£000
Sales		300	150	400	850
Less:	Direct labour	20	20	30	70
	Direct materials	100	60	100	260
	Variable overheads	30	10	30	70
	Allocated fixed overheads	75	25	155	255
Total costs		225	115	315	655
Profit		75	35	85	195
Space occupied (sq m)		3,000	1,000	6,000	10,000

In this situation the scarce resource is space and, therefore, the firm should make the most profitable use of that space. This will be achieved by ranking products according to their contribution (not profit) per square metre. The above information should therefore be represented in a marginal costing format to arrive at the *contribution per square metre* on each product as shown in Figure 13.9.

Product	A	B	C	Total
	£000	£000	£000	£000
Sales	300	150	400	850
Less: Variable costs	150	90	160	400
Contribution	150	60	240	450
Contribution ratio	50%	40%	60%	53%
Space occupied (sq m)	3,000	1,000	6,000	10,000
Contribution per sq m	£50	£60	£40	£45

Figure 13.9 *Contribution per unit of a scarce resource*

If we ignore the scarce resource aspect for a moment, we would normally have ranked the three products in order of their contribution ratio, CAB (60 per cent; 50 per cent; 40 per cent). When we take account of space being the scarce resource, the contribution per square metre ranks the products in a different order, BAC (£60; £50; £40). This firm should endeavour to switch production away from product C to product B or, failing that, from C to A.

PRICING

The previous chapter explained how firms can fix selling prices based on the total cost of a product plus the profit margin required to earn an acceptable rate of return on capital. An alternative approach is to set the profit/volume ratio required to recover both total fixed costs and leave the required profit.

Example
A company has fixed costs of £200,000 per annum, a profit target of £50,000 and budgeted sales of £600,000. The total contribution required is therefore £250,000 (£200,000 fixed costs + £50,000 profit). On budgeted sales of £600,000, a contribution of £250,000 amounts to a contribution ratio of 42 per cent. Selling prices can now be set for individual products at a level which leaves a 42 per cent contribution after the variable costs have been deducted. As with full cost pricing there is no guarantee that firms will be able to charge these prices, but they do indicate the level of prices needed to achieve a particular return.

Another situation arises in a recession where firms are not able to obtain orders at reasonable prices. Intense competition for scarce orders may result in firms quoting prices which do not fully cover costs. Ship-repairing is sometimes a case in point. Some repair jobs are very quickly completed so in this situation the only significant variable costs are those for direct materials and any direct labour needed on a short-term contract basis. Any price in excess of these variable costs will make a contribution towards fixed costs, which in this instance may even include direct wages of any permanent labour force that is temporarily not engaged on other work.

Obviously no firm can survive very long quoting prices below full cost, or obtaining work whose contribution does not recover fixed costs. In the short term, firms will price jobs well below full cost (ie at a loss) if the alternative is no work at all and even bigger losses!

CALCULATING CHANGES IN OUTPUT

When calculating product costs on a full cost basis, the fixed costs are apportioned over the budgeted volume of output at £x per unit. At higher or lower levels of output the fixed cost per unit is lower or higher respectively, even though fixed costs in total remain the same. It is therefore advisable, when considering changes in output, to leave fixed costs aside and use the contribution approach.

Example
Let us take as an example M Ltd whose directors are considering a 10 per cent reduction in the price of one of their products, to increase market share. They wish to maintain profit at the present level by offsetting the volume gain against the price reduction. The present situation is as follows:

Sales of 10,000 units at £20 each	200,000
Variable costs of £15 per unit	150,000
Fixed costs	40,000
Profit	10,000
	£200,000

The increased volume of sales required at the now lower price of £18 can be calculated from the number of unit contributions needed to make up the total contribution required, as follows:

Unit contribution	=	selling price – variable cost
	=	£18 – £15
	=	£3
Total contribution required	=	Fixed costs + Profit target
	=	£40,000 + £10,000
	=	£50,000
Required volume of sales	=	$\dfrac{\text{Total contribution £50,000}}{\text{Unit contribution £3}}$ = 16,667 units

Therefore to make the same total profit of £10,000, an increase from 10,000 units to 16,667 units in volume sales (ie 67 per cent) is needed to offset the proposed 10 per cent price reduction.

DIFFERENTIAL COSTING

In certain situations where we have to make a choice between two alternative courses of action, it can be useful to set the costs for each alternative side by side and look at the overall difference in total costs or profit. This technique is often termed *differential costing* because we are looking at the differences in costs/revenues between the alternatives.

Example
You plan to make a journey to Edinburgh city centre by yourself for fun and have a choice of going by train or by car. Cost is the only consideration in this case and the relevant costs for each alternative are:

	By train	By car	Difference
	£	£	£
Local travel to station	2.00	nil	+2.00
Train fare	25.00	nil	+25.00
Car travel (variable costs only)	nil	16.40	−16.40
Car parking fee	nil	3.00	−3.00
	27.00	19.40	+7.60

Ignoring all other aspects but cost, your decision will be to travel by car as it has the advantage of being £7.60 cheaper. This is the total difference in cost between the two alternatives. Notice that car travel is priced at marginal cost on the grounds that road fund licence, insurance and most depreciation are time-based fixed costs and are incurred regardless of this decision. The variable costs of this journey are fuel, servicing and tyre wear.

However, if you were negotiating with an employer for reimbursement of car expenses for journeys taken for work purposes, you would regard some, if not all, of these fixed costs as relevant and require reimbursement for them. Sometimes a compromise rate is agreed whereby the employer pays for all variable costs and makes some contribution towards the fixed costs; thereby both parties gain something.

Make or buy

Differential costing can be applied to so-called *make or buy* decisions where, ignoring non-cost considerations, buying-in can be justified by a company when the purchase price from outside is cheaper than the marginal cost of production. The term make or buy does not just refer to physical products but also to service activities, for example:

- employing own catering staff or franchising out;
- employing own cleaners or putting function out to tender;
- employing own legal staff or hiring professional firm.

Example
An organization's office cleaning is contracted out at present, for an annual fee of

£12,500. As an alternative, the organization could employ its own part-time cleaners at a cost of £9,000 excluding employer's NICs. Cover for sickness and holidays would add another 10 per cent to this figure. In either case the organization pays for the permanent hire of equipment at £80 per month and would have to buy cleaning materials costing £500 per annum if it used its own cleaning staff. The following differential cost analysis will assist us in making a decision.

	Own	Contract	Difference
	£	£	£
Cleaning materials	500	nil	-500
Contract fee	nil	12,500	+12,500
Cleaners' wages	9,000	nil	-9,000
Holiday/sickness cover	900	nil	-900
Hire of equipment	960	960	nil
Totals	11,360	13,460	+2,100

The conclusion from this differential cost analysis is that the organization should employ its own cleaners because using a contract cleaner has an additional annual cost of £2,100.

The above example may be criticized on the grounds that it does not take all costs into account when employing one's own cleaners. Staff have to be recruited and trained both initially and when someone leaves. This is a cost bearing on the personnel function. Staff also have to be paid and records maintained even if they are not eligible for income tax and national insurance. This is a cost bearing on the payroll section of the accounting function. There are also likely to be other costs relating to demands for supervision, purchasing, insurance and other functions. In this example these are likely to be small incremental additions to overheads and therefore difficult to cost. In a larger make or buy situation, we may have to cost incremental effects on overheads or we would not be making a valid comparison.

Where capital expenditure is involved in a make or buy decision, then investment appraisal techniques will have to be employed to allow for the capital expenditure and the time value of the money invested. These topics are discussed in Chapter 17.

Outsourcing

Throughout the 1990s there has been a marked increase in the divestment of support activities and facilities management to other organizations. This may not necessarily be on cost grounds alone, but to enable management to concentrate on core activities.

When manufactured items are concerned, the decision to outsource is of strategic importance, particularly if it is made before any investment takes place. The advantages of using a contract manufacturer for components or finished products include:

- reduced investment in fixed assets and working capital;

- no set-up, development and training costs;
- commercial risk reduced in uncertain markets;
- quality assurance to relevant British Standards where appropriate;
- management freedom to concentrate on marketing and strategic issues.

There can also be a downside. A company's ability to innovate and develop its product range may be weakened by outsourcing if the necessary know-how is retained by the contract manufacturers. The features of the traditional buyer-supplier relationship is a short-term adversarial one with each trying to get the best price with little sharing of ideas between the two parties.

More recently, the move has been towards *partnership sourcing* as an alternative to straightforward outsourcing, with a consequent big reduction in the number of suppliers. Key features of partnership sourcing are:

- long-term relationship;
- pooling of technical information;
- sharing of the risks and rewards.

THROUGHPUT ACCOUNTING

The term *throughput* originated with Goldratt in the early 1980s, although the term *throughput accounting* is attributed to Waldron and Galloway in the late 1980s. Goldratt's main interest was in production scheduling systems and he focused on the problems caused by production bottlenecks. From this he developed the concept of throughput and his *theory of constraints*. Throughput is the rate at which money is generated through sales. Goldratt's definition of throughput is very simple and somewhat akin to contribution:

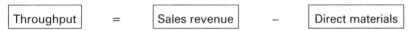

| Throughput | = | Sales revenue | – | Direct materials |

Goldratt observed that production capacity was not so much a limiting factor as production bottlenecks (for example a machine) which either reduced the effective capacity or led to a build-up of work-in-progress. His goal was to maximize the throughput of a factory and to focus attention on managing the bottlenecks.

This could be done by holding buffer stocks in front of the bottlenecks (to ensure continuity of work); to identify rejects before the bottleneck stage (to avoid wasted effort); to concentrate new investment on removing the bottleneck or lessening its impact. At a later stage, Goldratt widened his interest from bottlenecks to any constraint that limited the achievement of goals. He argued that any improvements other than on constraints or bottlenecks would not lead to increased throughput.

Throughput can be used to measure progress towards the removal of a bottleneck. It should be recognized that once one bottleneck is removed another scarce resource will likely take its place as the new bottleneck.

Goldratt took issue with cost accounting and thought it the enemy of productivity. His reasoning was that under absorption costing, overheads are borne by goods going into stock and work-in-progress just as much as they are borne by goods that are sold. Goldratt's emphasis on maximizing throughput is, by definition, concerned with sales as opposed to production. This point can be illustrated by looking at Figure 13.10a later where all overheads (and direct labour) are treated as operational expenses and charged against sales. Any stocks and work-in-progress carried over a period end are valued at material cost only under throughput accounting, so there is no incentive to boost stocks as they carry no overheads and, therefore, do not affect profit.

Another term used by Goldratt is *inventory*. This might appear somewhat misleading as the term is used to embrace both stocks and fixed assets. In other words, inventory here means the total capital investment. The concept of *return on inventory* is therefore akin to return on investment or return on capital employed.

Operational expense was the name he gave to the money spent on all non-material costs and includes all labour and production overheads. So we can say in Goldratt terminology that:

$$\boxed{\text{Net profit}} \quad = \quad \boxed{\text{Throughput}} \quad - \quad \boxed{\text{Operational expense}}$$

and also that:

$$\text{Return on investment} \quad = \quad \frac{\text{Throughput} - \text{Operational expense}}{\text{Inventory}} \quad \%$$

Goldratt again might seem at odds with cost accounting with his emphasis on increasing throughput rather than controlling costs, reducing operational expense and reducing stock levels. He is in tune though with the rationale of *just-in -time* and *total quality management* in that both these practices should also result in increased throughput.

Primary ratio

Apart from introducing us to the term throughput accounting, Galloway and Waldron produced a number of ratios used to measure factory performance, departmental performance and a means of placing products in rank order.

A primary measure of manufacturing performance relates throughput (sales less material costs) to total factory costs excluding materials costs. A ratio greater than unity is needed for the business to be profitable.

$$\text{Primary ratio} \quad = \quad \frac{\text{Throughput}}{\text{Total factory cost}}$$

Secondary measures are used to relate throughput to a scarce resource to identify the amount of *throughput per unit of resource* in a not dissimilar way to that described earlier when discussing *contribution per unit of scarce resource* for ranking purposes.

Comparison of throughput accounting with marginal costing

The similarity of throughput accounting and marginal costing is evident in other ways. If we compare their respective definitions, we find:

The difference between throughput and contribution definitions lies in the fact that material cost is a variable cost, but the latter may also include some labour and overhead costs. Throughput deducts only material costs from sales whereas contribution deducts all variable costs from sales. This is evident when we contrast a throughput profit and loss account with a marginal costing profit and loss account as shown in Figures 13.10a and 13.10b

	£000
Sales	4,000
Direct material cost of sales	1,500
Throughput	2,500
Operational expense (all treated as fixed costs)	1,800
Profit	700

Figure 13.10a *Throughput profit and loss account*

The difference is in the treatment of direct labour and variable overheads. In throughput accounting these are treated as fixed costs and included in operational expense. They are not deducted from sales to arrive at throughput. In marginal costing these items are treated as variable costs and are deducted from sales before calculating contribution.

	£000
Sales	4,000
Variable costs	2,200
Contribution	1,800
Fixed overheads	1,100
Profit	700

Figure 13.10b *Marginal costing profit and loss account*

There is no difference between the final profit in Figures 13.10a and 13.10b. In each case it amounts to £700,000. The two profit and loss accounts bring out the difference between throughput and contribution caused by the inclusion of £700,000 direct labour and variable overheads as variable costs in Figure 13.10b.

Further reading

Drury, C (1996) *Management and Cost Accounting*, ITP, London.
Dugdale, D and Jones, TC (1996) *Accounting for Throughput*, CIMA, London.
Lucey, T (1997) *Management Accounting*, Letts, London.

Self-check questions

1. Draw a break-even chart to decide from which firm you would hire a car. Firm A charges £25 per day plus 14p per mile while Firm B charges £18 per day plus 20p per mile.
2. Draw the break-even chart shown in Figure 13.3 and read off the amount of profit made when output equals 18,000 units.
3. Referring to the information in Figure 13.7, would you advise the directors of Imet Ltd to discontinue product C if they could use the same resources to produce 80 per cent more of product A? (Assume same cost and selling price per unit).
4. Your repair yard has been asked to tender for an immediate repair to a damaged ship, which will provide work for the next few weeks. The yard is short of work, with many workers idle, although being paid a guaranteed wage. You have heard that another firm has already tendered on the basis of direct costs only, without any contribution to overheads or profit. Will you still put in a bid? Give reasons for your answer.
5. A firm sells a product for £25 which has a variable cost of £14. Fixed overheads amount to £800,000 in total and the firm requires a return of 20 per cent on the £1.5 million capital employed. How many products need to be sold?
6. A firm has sales of £200,000, £300,000, and £400,000 for its three product lines X, Y, and Z and variable costs of £100,000, £180,000, and £280,000 respectively. Owing to a skilled labour shortage, production will have to be cut back next month to the 650 hours that will be available. The three product lines currently consume 350, 350, and 300 hours respectively. Advise the firm on the most profitable product mix to adopt until full production can be restored.
7. Assuming cost is the sole consideration, when is it preferable to buy-in rather than source internally?
8. What is meant by throughput?
9. What is the difference between throughput and contribution?
10. What performance indicator would you use to measure changes in throughput efficiency?

14

Standard costing

INTRODUCTION

Cost information can be used equally in a forward planning context as in an examination of past events. *Standard costing* is a control technique which compares standard costs and revenues with actual results to obtain variances which are used to stimulate improved performance (CIMA). The standard cost of a product (or service) is the total cost of labour, materials and overhead apportionment that should be incurred in the production process.

When production takes place the actual costs of the batch are compared with the predetermined standard cost for that quantity. Inevitably differences, now called variances, will occur and these are examined for their causes in order to improve future performance. Figure 14.1 illustrates this sequence of events as a control cycle.

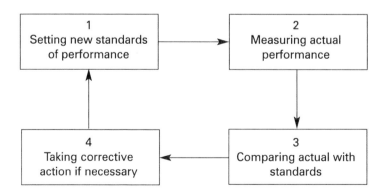

Figure l4.1 *The control cycle*

Firms use standard costing techniques for a variety of reasons:

1. The actual setting-up of the standard cost specification involves determining the most suitable materials and methods of operation from the viewpoints of both firm and consumer.
2. Once set, a standard becomes a yardstick against which performance can be measured.
3. Standard costing also engenders cost consciousness in employees who know that costs are being monitored, and, it is hoped, acts as a motivator if the standards are realistically set.
4. Top management can stand back from the day-to-day management which they can delegate and control by requiring explanations only of significant variances from standard.
5. Finally, a standard cost is a firm base from which to price products, set budgets and value stock.

RATIOS

Before going into the detailed analysis of variances, it is useful to look at some measures of company performance associated with the standard costing technique. Central to these measures is the concept of the *standard hour* which represents the amount of work which can be done in one hour under standard conditions. The standard hour is a useful common denominator with which to aggregate different operations and different products. With this definition we can measure the operating *efficiency* of a firm by relating the standard hours equivalent of the work produced to the actual hours taken:

$$\text{Efficiency ratio} = \frac{\text{Standard hours} \times 100}{\text{Actual hours}} \%$$

For example, last week a firm took 500 actual hours to produce goods equivalent to 450 standard hours. Its efficiency ratio for last week is therefore 90 per cent, which is adverse compared to the 100 per cent potential target.

Another ratio is used to measure the level of *activity* as opposed to the level of efficiency as above. The activity ratio relates the actual work produced to the budgeted work for that period, both being expressed in standard hours:

$$\text{Activity ratio} = \frac{\text{Actual standard hours} \times 100}{\text{Budgeted standard hours}} \%$$

Taking the same example where actual standard hours were 450, let us assume the budgeted standard hours were 475. The activity ratio is therefore 94.7 per cent which again is adverse when 100 per cent is achievable. A third ratio measures *capacity usage* by relating actual hours worked in a period to the budgeted standard hours:

$$\text{Capacity ratio} = \frac{\text{Actual hours} \times 100}{\text{Budgeted standard hours}} \%$$

Using the same figures from the previous illustrations, when 500 actual hours are expressed as a percentage of 475 budgeted standard hours, the capacity ratio is 105.3 per cent. This indicates a favourable variance achieved by somehow working more hours than planned.

STANDARD COST SPECIFICATION

When applying standard costing to any product, the starting point is to specify quantities and grades of the labour and material elements and include an apportionment of budgeted overheads to arrive at the total standard cost. The setting of labour and material standards involves determining the best layout, methods of operation and most suitable materials which may lead to economies over previous practice. Management science plays a part here with the application of such techniques as method study, work measurement, value analysis and value engineering. An example of a standard cost specification is given in Figure 14.2.

Product: AB Fittings			Batch size: 100
	Quantity	*Unit price*	*Standard cost*
Materials:			
Metal A	40kgs	£22.50 per kg	900.00
Packaging	1 carton	£2.50	2.50
			902.50
Labour:			
Operation 1	8 hours	£7.00 per hr	56.00
Operation 2	12 hours	£6.00 per hr	72.00
Packer	1 hour	£4.50 per hr	4.50
			132.50
Overheads: (std allowances)			
Variable overheads		45p per unit	45.00
Fixed overheads		£1.80 per unit	180.00
			225.00
Total standard cost			1,260.00
Standard profit			78.00
Standard selling price			£1,338.00

Figure 14.2 *Standard cost specification.*

VARIANCES

Periodically, the actual costs of production are compared with the predetermined standard as laid down in the specification. Variances will be disclosed where the actual cost of some, or all, elements differ from the standard cost for the quantity actually produced. These variances could be expressed as a (+) or a (–) representing an adverse or favourable result, or the symbol letters (A) or (F) used instead. The disadvantage of using (+) and (–) signs is that one has to get the formula the right way round. The advantage of using (F) and (A) signs is that one can use common sense regardless of which way round the formula is put.

Variances are capable of further analysis, as we shall see, to identify their cause and allow management to take remedial action if necessary. In practice the specification and actual costs are all computerized so that no laborious calculations are required in multi-product firms. Basically there are only two main types of variance:

- price variances – relating to purchase price of resources; and
- volume variances – relating to the volume of resources consumed or activity level.

Example

Referring back to the standard cost specification in Figure 14.2, let us assume a batch of 100 fittings was made recently using 45kg of metal which had just been purchased for £21.30 per kg.

The total material cost variance for metal is the difference between the actual cost and standard cost:

Actual cost	–	Standard cost	=	Material cost variance
45kg x £21.30 = £958.50		40kg x £22.50 = £900.00		£58.50 (A)

This £58.50 variance results from two causes and not just one. On the one hand extra costs are incurred through using 5kg more metal than specified, resulting in a material usage variance of 5kg x £22.50 = £112.50 (A). On the other hand the firm bought the metal more cheaply than it expected and thus saved £1.20p x 45kg = £54 (F) which is the material price variance. To summarize:

Total material cost variance		£58.50(A)
Material usage variance	£112.50(A)	
Material price variance	£54.00(F)	£58.50(A)

Variances for other costs and sales can be similarly divided into two main types and the full list is shown in Figure 14.3.

Price variances:	Volume variances:
Material price variance	Material usage variance
Labour rate variance	Labour efficiency variance
Variable overhead expenditure variance	–
Fixed overhead expenditure variance	Fixed overhead volume variance
Sales price variance	Sales volume variance

Figure 14.3 Price and volume variances

Before looking at a more comprehensive example, it is necessary to define each variance carefully and explain it in more general terms.

Material cost variances

Material price variance represents the difference in purchase cost caused by a variation in the unit price of the material. It is calculated from the difference between the actual and standard price per unit of material multiplied by the actual quantity purchased.

Formula: (AP – SP) AQ

Material usage variance represents the difference in the cost of material used caused by more or less efficient use of that material. It is calculated from the difference between the actual and standard quantity used evaluated at the standard price. In some situations it is possible to analyse this further into mix and yield variances. (Note that any variation from the standard price is contained in the price variance itself).

Formula: (AQ – SQ) SP

Labour cost variances

Labour rate variance represents the difference in labour cost caused by any variation from normal rates of pay. It is calculated from the difference between the actual and standard rate per hour multiplied by the actual number of hours paid.

Formula: (AP – SP) AQ

This is the same as the material price variance, the rate per hour being the price of labour.

Labour efficiency variance represents the difference in labour cost caused by the degree of efficiency in the use of labour compared with the specified standard. It is calculated from the difference between the actual hours taken and the standard hours allowed, evaluated at the standard rate per hour.

Formula: (AQ – SQ) SP

This is the same as the material usage variance.

Variable overhead variances

Variable overheads are those whose total cost varies *pro rata* with the level of production, as opposed to fixed overheads whose total cost does not vary with the production level.

Variable overhead expenditure variance represents the difference between the actual cost and the total amount recovered at the standard rate per unit of output. It is calculated from the difference between actual variable overheads and the quantity of output multiplied by the standard recovery rate per unit.

Formula: AC – (AQ x SR)

(Note that when variable overheads are recovered on a labour basis, as opposed to a product basis, then a variable overhead efficiency variance can arise, akin to a labour efficiency variance).

Fixed overhead variances

Fixed overhead expenditure variance represents the difference between the actual cost and the estimated or budgeted cost of those overheads.

Formula: AC – BC

Fixed overhead volume variance represents the under- or over-recovery of fixed overheads caused by the actual volume of production being different from the budgeted volume on which the recovery rate is based. It is calculated from the difference between actual and budgeted volume multiplied by the standard recovery rate per unit.

Formula: (AQ – BQ) SR

The survey of manufacturing companies by Drury *et al* mentioned in Further reading at the end of this chapter found that about 80 per cent of the responding organizations did *not* compute fixed overhead volume variances.

Sales variances

Sales price variance represents the profit lost or gained by selling at a non-standard price. It is calculated from the difference between standard and actual selling price multiplied by the actual quantity sold.

Formula: (SP – AP) AQ

Sales volume variance represents the profit margins on the difference between actual sales and budgeted sales. It is calculated from the standard profit margin multiplied by the difference between budgeted sales volume and actual sales volume.

Formula: (BQ – AQ) x standard profit per unit

A note of caution should be sounded here. It should not be assumed that all standard costing systems will use the same basis as that shown above. In certain industries using chemicals, the material cost variances are capable of further analysis, as are labour and overhead variances in many other industries. The basis of overhead recovery can also influence the precise method of overhead variance calculation.

It is also possible to base a standard costing system on marginal costing principles as briefly outlined at the end of this chapter. Notwithstanding these exceptions, the above analysis of variances provides a good grounding for most practical systems. The following example demonstrates the calculation of basic material and labour variances:

Example
The standard cost of an article comprises:

| Material X | 2 kg per article at £5 per kg |
| Labour | 6 hours per article at £7 per hour |

Last week 400 articles were produced and the actual costs were:

| Material X | 850 kg at £4.50 per kg |
| Labour | 2,300 hours at £7.00 per hour |

From this information we can calculate the material cost variance and the labour cost variance together with their respective price and volume variances.

Material cost variances:

| Actual material cost | Standard material cost | Material cost variance |
| 850 x £4.50 = £3,825 | 2 x 400 x £5.00 = £4,000 | £4,000 – £3,825 = £175(F) |

Material price variance = (AP £4.50 -SP £5.00) AQ 850 = £425 (F) ⎫
⎬ = £175(F)
Material usage variance = (AQ 850 – SQ 800) SP £5.00 = £250 (A) ⎭

The saving of £175 in material costs has two causes. Material X was bought more cheaply than standard, thus saving £425. Possibly because the cheap material was substandard, excessive waste occurred costing £250. Overall the company saved £175; therefore the precise reasons are worth investigating with the purchasing officer and production supervisor respectively.

Labour cost variances:

| Actual labour cost | Standard labour cost | Labour cost variance |
| 2,300 x £7 = £16,100 | 6 x 400 x £7 = £16,800 | £16,800 – £16,100 = £700(F) |

Labour rate variance = (AP £7.00 – SP £7.00) AQ 2,300 = nil ⎫
⎬ = £700(F)
Labour efficiency variance = (AQ 2,300 – SQ 2,400) SP £7.00 = £700(F) ⎭

There is no rate variance, so the saving in labour cost of £700 is all due to the workforce being more efficient than the standard set. Again this is worth investigation with production supervisors to see if lessons can be learned for future occasions.

The ratios and variances mentioned rely on the preparation of budgets detailing planned levels of output, costs and income. This also means that a firm operating a system of standard costing should be able to predict the profit that it will make in a future period from its trading operations. The actual profit it makes will be the same as the budgeted profit if there are no sales or cost variances. Any adverse variances will reduce the actual profit relative to that budgeted, while favourable variances will enhance the actual profit.

A profit and loss account can be prepared on standard costing lines. This does not show the absolute values of income and expenditure, but the detailed variances which affect the budgeted profit and reconcile it with the actual profit. A more comprehensive example now follows to illustrate this approach.

Example

Carr Chemicals Ltd is a one-product firm. The company uses a standard costing system and prepared the following budget for last week which was expected to result in a profit of £6,200:

Budget for one week

	£	units	£
Sales at £3.00 per unit		10,000	30,000
Direct materials – 10,000 kilos at £0.50 per kilo	5,000		
Direct labour – 2,000 hours at £6.40 per hour	12,800		
Variable overheads – 10,000 units at £0.25 each	2,500		
Fixed overheads – £3,500 per week (£0.35 per unit)	3,500		
Total costs	12,800	10,000	23,800
Budgeted profit at £0.62 per unit			£6,200

Unfortunately, they did not sell as many products as they had planned, as the actual results show, but yet a greater profit was achieved.

Actual result for one week

	£	units	£
Sales at £3.20 per unit		9,000	28,800
Direct materials – 9,500 kilos at £0.45 per kilo	4,275		
Direct labour – 2,000 hours at £6.00 per hour	12,000		
Variable overheads	2,000		
Fixed overheads	3,250		
Total costs	21,525	9,000	21,525
Actual profit			£7,275

We can now draw up a statement reconciling the actual profit with the budgeted profit by detailing the adverse or favourable variances for the week. This is shown in Figure 14.4 and shows in detail how the extra profit was achieved:

Profit and loss account for the week:

	£	£	£
Budgeted profit			6,200
Variances:	(F)	(A)	
Sales price variance (£3.20-£3.00)9,000	1,800		
Sales quantity variance (9,000–10,000)£0.62		620	
Material price variance (£0.45-£0.50)9,500	475		
Material usage variance (9,500–9,000)£0.50		250	
Labour rate variance (£6.00-£6.40)2,000	800		
Labour efficiency variance (2,000–1,800)£6.40		1,280	
Variable O/H expenditure variance 2,000-(9,000 x £0.25)	250		
Fixed O/H expenditure variance (£3,250-£3,500)	250		
Fixed O/H volume variance (9,000–10,000)£0.35		350	
Total variances	£3,575	£2,500	£1,075(F)
Actual profit			£7,275

Figure 14.4 *Standard costing profit and loss account*

(Note that the standard quantities used in the labour efficiency, material usage and variable overhead expenditure variances are based on the actual production level of 9,000 units).

STANDARD MARGINAL COSTING

It is possible to use a marginal costing approach to standard costing when a *standard contribution* is determined instead of the *standard profit* used in a full cost system. The contribution price variance will be identical with the sales price variance representing the profit lost or gained by selling at a non-standard price.

Contribution price variance = Sales price variance

Where the two systems differ is that the sales and fixed overhead volume variances are replaced by one contribution volume variance, being the contributions lost or gained on the difference between budgeted volume and the actual volume of activity.

Contribution volume variance = Sales volume variance + Fixed overhead volume variance

INFLATION

The standard cost specification should be based on current prices of the relevant costs. This may lead to periodic revisions of the standard cost and selling price. The survey by Drury *et al* published in 1993 showed that nearly 70 per cent of respondents formally reviewed standards annually, although not necessarily just because of inflation.

REVIEW

Various writers have forecast a decline in the use of standard costing due to changing manufacturing technology and new thinking on costing. The Drury survey found that only 11 per cent of respondent manufacturing companies had stopped using standard costing systems in the last 10 years and 76 per cent were still using such systems.

Further reading

Drury, C *et al* (1993) *A Survey of Management Accounting Practices in UK Manufacturing Companies,* ACCA, London.
Drury, C (1996) *Management and Cost Accounting,* ITP, London.
Lucey, T (1997) *Management Accounting,*Letts, London.

Self-check questions

1. What is a standard hour?
2. Define the activity ratio.

3. Name some management techniques, which may be used when setting a standard cost specification.
4. Variances are either favourable or ...?
5. Define and give the formula for the labour efficiency variance.
6. The standard cost specification for a product is as follows:

Selling price		£31
Less: Factory costs:		
Direct material – 12 kg at £0.50	£6	
Direct labour – 2 hours at £6.00	£12	
Variable overhead per product	£2	
Fixed overhead per product	£5	
		£25
Standard profit per product		£6

KKK Ltd budgeted to produce and sell 1,100 products last week. Actual production and sales was only 900 and other information is as follows:

Selling price – £32
Direct material – 12,600 kg at £0.55
Direct labour – 1,600 hours at £6
Variable overheads £2,100
Fixed overheads £5,700

Produce a statement reconciling the budgeted profit with the actual profit by disclosing all possible variances.

7. The standard material cost of fabric specified for a particular garment is £4.50, comprising three metres at £1.50 per metre. Last week, 1,000 garments were made using 3,200 metres of fabric bought in at £1.40 per metre. Calculate the total material cost variance and analyse further the material price variance and material usage variance.

15

Budgetary control

INTRODUCTION

We need to distinguish *revenue budgeting* from *capital budgeting*. Revenue budgets are concerned with forecasts of sales revenue and operating costs going into the budgeted profit and loss account. This applies to all organizations, of all sizes, in any sector, and is the focus of this chapter. A capital budget is concerned with plans for capital expenditure on individual projects or specific assets, which need to be included in the budgeted balance sheet. This budget is again applicable to all organizations, but may be inextensive in some, and is discussed in Chapter 17.

Similarity of budgeting with standard costing

There are many similarities between a system of budgetary control and the standard costing technique discussed in Chapter 14. They are both concerned with planning and control involving the setting of targets and the later comparison with actual results. Differences called *variances*, arising from comparisons of target with actual, are identified so that corrective action can be taken if necessary.

Much detailed preparatory work is common to both budgetary control and standard costing as they are both concerned with detailed operating costs and revenues. Where the two systems differ is in the unit and scale of application. A standard cost specifies the selling price and cost of a product while a budget is prepared for an organizational unit called a financial responsibility centre. Budgets and budgetary control are applicable in all organizations, whether manufacturing or service industries, whether profit-seeking or not.

Purpose of budgetary control

The main purpose of budgetary control is to plan and control the firm's activities. Corporate and strategic planning are concerned with the long-term broad objectives of the firm, possibly stretching five years ahead. Budgetary control, however, is an expression of short-term financial plans to meet objectives in the coming accounting year. The short-term objective may be to earn a specified rate of return on capital, or to achieve a certain level of turnover or market share. In some organizations the objective may simply be not to overspend, but to keep spending within a grant or budget allocation. Although budgets are plans for activity in the very near future, they must be compatible with what the firm is trying to achieve in the longer term.

Using a system of budgetary control, senior management can practise the principle of *management by exception*. They delegate responsibility for activities, functions and departments to middle managers, allowing themselves time to concentrate solely on deviations from plans and future strategy. This avoids them getting overwhelmed by involvement in day-to-day activities, the vast majority of which are probably running to plan. Put more formally, budgetary control is a classic example of a control cycle.

Control cycle

There are six sequential stages to the control cycle, as illustrated in Figure 15.1.

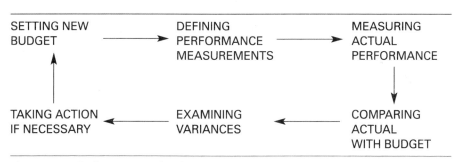

Figure 15.1 *Budgetary control cycle*

Stage 1. *Setting new budget* – this starts the control cycle off and is the original budget set in the manner described later, dependent on the size of the organization.

Stage 2. *Defining performance measurements* – these are the means by which the budget holder's performance is going to be measured. Typical performance measures include a set return on capital; a specified sales target or market share; a profit target; keeping costs within budget.

Stage 3. *Measuring actual performance* – once performance measurements have been set then actual performance can be recorded. This is made possible by the use of cost centre numbers (and capital job numbers) when inputting financial transactions to the financial database.

Stage 4. *Comparing actual with budget* – measuring actual performance is insufficient by itself without a yardstick with which to make comparison. The original budget, or a later revised budget, is that yardstick.

Stage 5. *Examining variances* – differences between actual and budget items are called variances and significant ones need to be identified and their causes investigated. Significance here may be defined as an absolute sum of money or a specified percentage variation from budget.

Stage 6. *Taking action if necessary* – there is no point to the previous stages if this does not happen. Information may be gleaned that helps avoid future mishaps or repeats a benefit that can be transferred elsewhere. Every attempt should be made to get back on target if this is realistically possible.

Stage 1. *Setting new budget again* – this starts the cycle off again but there is no point in setting a new budget after each monthly review as future comparisons may become meaningless. Some organizations keep the original budget fixed, get budget holders to forecast the outcome at the end of the budget year quarterly, and for the remainder of the year make comparisons against both original budget and latest forecast.

PREPARATION OF BUDGETS

There is no one method of budget preparation suitable for all organizations of all sizes. In a small organization the responsibility for budget preparation may rest with an owner/manager or accountant who liaises with other parties to collect the relevant information. The detailed items will reflect past performance, but more importantly take account of expected changes in prices and volume of activity in the near future. The budget is usually based on the accounting year of the organization and phased into shorter periods like monthly intervals. A typical example is shown in Figure 15.2.

	July	Aug	Sept	Oct	Nov	Dec	Jan	Feb	Mar	Apr	May	Jun	Year
SALES													
Cost of sales													
GROSS PROFIT													
Salaries													
NICs													
Travelling exps													
Rent													
Business rates													
Light, heat													
Insurance													
Repairs & mtnce													
Stationery													
Telephone													
Postage													
General exps													
Audit fees													
Depreciation													
Bank charges													
Interest paid													
TOTAL O'HEADS													
NET PROFIT													

Figure 15.2 *Phased budget format for small enterprise*

In medium-sized companies a more formal budgeting procedure will be required. Top management should specify broad objectives to a budget committee comprising representatives of both directors and functional managers. The committee then interprets these objectives into outline plans for each departmental head who in turn submit their detailed proposals. This process may continue a number of times to get the necessary integration and co-ordination of the individual budget proposals. Detailed instructions should be distributed to each budget holder including a timetable, budget formats and forecasts of price changes for the coming year.

Essentially, this is a bottom-up approach with managers retaining ownership of their budgets, as opposed to imposed or top-down budgets, where ownership and some motivation is lost. In practice, the iterative process usually adopted is a combination of top-down and bottom-up, with a few attempts made before a budget proposal is completed.

When finally accepted by the budget committee, the functional budgets are aggregated into a *master budget*. This consists of:

- a budgeted profit and loss account for the year, phased into months;
- a projected balance sheet at the year end;
- a budgeted cash flow statement for the year.

If approved by the board, this becomes the policy to be pursued for the coming year. In many firms this procedure, outlined in Figure 15.3, is assisted by an accountant or budget officer, who supplies information and advice to all concerned.

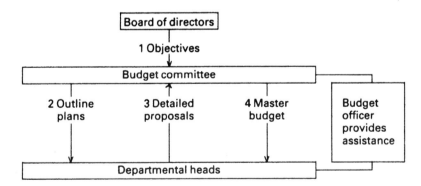

Figure 15.3 *Budget organization*

Identification of key factor

The starting point with budgeting is to identify the key factor which limits the firm's growth at this moment in time. In many firms this key factor will be sales volume but it could be a shortage of space, machinery, or materials. In many organizations, money itself will be the limiting factor, as is the case with local authorities and other grant-funded bodies.

1. *Sales budget.* Assuming sales is the key or limiting factor for a firm, this places the major responsibility for budgeting on the shoulders of the sales manager or director. The sales team will have to consider the present level of business, anticipate future trading conditions, obtain feedback from sales representatives and market research to come up with a sales budget. This budget is not just one total sales figure for the coming year, but must be analysed by customers, by markets, by sales area and by months.
2. *Production budget.* After specifying sales, the production budget comes next. The level of production must equate with budgeted sales except when stock levels change. Where stocks are not required, or are kept at a constant level, production and sales volumes will be identical. Therefore the starting point for budgeting production is the sales budget after taking into account possible changes in stock levels or the use of subcontractors. Production levels must fall within existing capacity as otherwise production would have been identified as the key or limiting factor rather than sales. The production budget specifies the products to be made, when production is to take place, which departments are to be used and the cost of labour, materials and machine time.
3. *Departmental overhead budgets.* These are prepared based on the level of service needed to allow the sales and production functions to meet their budgets. The production department overheads will be geared to the production levels specified for those departments. Similarly, the selling and distribution costs will be geared to the level of the sales budget while the various administrative departments' budgets will be determined by the overall level of activity. Research and development also has a budget, but this is more a long-term investment of funds not closely related to short-term needs and is very similar to the capital budget mentioned later in Chapter 17.

In this way the various functional and departmental budgets are prepared which facilitate the composition of subordinate budgets for material purchases and manpower planning. The functional budgets form the basis for a master budget in the form of a budgeted profit and loss account and projected balance sheet. It is this master budget which goes to the board for approval and, if not satisfactory, the marketing/production mix must be thought through again.

There is another budget which it is necessary for accountants to prepare using their professional skills and applying them to the vast store of financial information prepared in the budgeting process. The *cash budget* is quite literally a monthly budget of cash inflows and outflows which are expected to arise from the plans expressed in the functional budgets. Details of its preparation and uses are contained in Chapter 18 on the control of working capital. A *budgeted cash flow statement* is also prepared which is complementary to the cash budget in that it gives a summary of the reasons for all the cash inflows and outflows and any need for further financing in the budget period. This budgeted cash flow statement and the *capital budget* described in Chapter 17 are also part of the master budget going to the board for approval.

A schematic diagram of the budgeting process is shown in Figure 15.4.

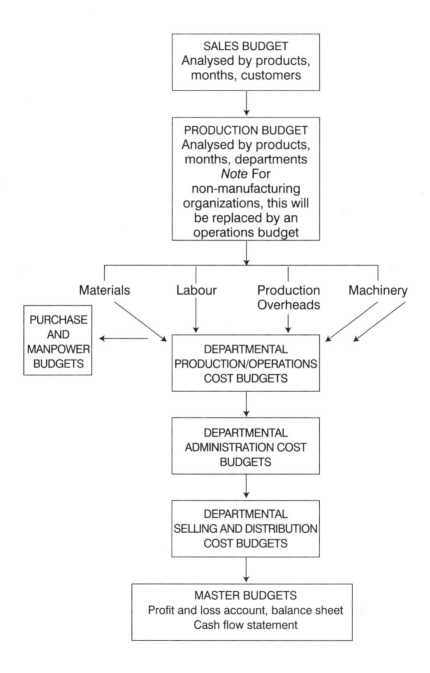

Figure 15.4 *The budgeting process*

Budget periods

Budgets are concerned with the planned income and expenditure for the coming year. The accounting year is the natural choice for the budgeting process, although it is broken down into months for regular comparison of actual with budgeted figures. These months may be of the calendar or lunar variety, or some other constant working period to avoid distorted comparisons due to the incidence of works and statutory holidays. Some firms work on a rolling year, adding a new month's budget as each month passes. Other firms extend the budget horizon by asking for detailed forecasts of out-turn up to two years ahead, with looser forecasts for a further few years. In this way, top management start to build a picture of what the next five years' results will look like and can adjust their strategic plans accordingly.

Budget reports

The comparison of actual results with budget takes place at two levels. Each functional manager is fed information about the costs (and income) under his or her control, comparing actual costs against budget for the month under review and for the cumulative months of the accounting year so far expired. An example of this is given in Figure 15.5. Sometimes a distinction is made between controllable costs and costs reallocated to a department although not wholly within the manager's control.

A line and subtotal may be drawn after controllable costs are listed. This indicates to the manager concerned his/her achievement against budget for items he or she has both responsibility, and authority over. If other overheads are then listed over which the manager has responsibility but no authority, care must be exercized in how this information is used to monitor that manager's performance.

Month.. Dept..							
Cost code	Description	Current month			Cumulative		
		Budget	Actual	Variance	Budget	Actual	Variance
320	Controllable Salaries etc	£ 3,600	£ 3,400	£ 200 F	£ 23,000	£ 24,300	£ 1,300 A
710	Non-controllable HO charges etc	1,000	1,100	100 A	7,000	7,700	700 A

Figure 15.5 *Monthly budget report*

At a higher level in the organization the actual profit achieved is compared with the budgeted profit and reasons for major differences reported to the board of directors. When a firm uses a standard costing system, the list of variances will link the budgeted profit with the actual profit achieved in the month. Where standard costing is inappropriate to the firm's products, the monthly profit and loss account will compare budgeted costs and revenues with the actual costs and revenues respectively, to disclose the variances.

There is no point in drawing trivial variances to the attention of departmental managers or directors. Limits may be set as to what counts as a significant variance, being either a percentage of the budgeted figure and/or a certain sum of money. In this way time is not wasted on insignificant events and explanations are only required when a variance is deemed to be important.

Packages are available, or dedicated software can be written, to produce monthly budget reports for each department which integrate with the total financial results. Much budgeting work can now be performed on standard spreadsheets, such as Lotus 1–2–3 without having to go to additional expense. A particular advantage of using spreadsheets occurs at budget-setting time when *what if* questioning or *financial modelling* can produce budgeted financial statements under a number of different assumptions. These might relate to activity levels, selling prices, wage and other cost changes and changes in the economic environment, for example, exchange rates or interest rates.

BEHAVIOURAL IMPLICATIONS

Motivation to achieve targets is a key feature of budgetary control. This is why ownership of a budget by the budget holder is most important, and motivation is not forthcoming when budgets are imposed from on high without consultation. Ownership of a budget is also enhanced when authority and responsibility go hand in hand. Managers are not going to be motivated if held accountable for costs totally outside their control. This was the purpose of dividing costs into controllable and non-controllable categories in the budget report shown in Figure 15.5.

Budget padding is often cited as a disadvantage of the bottom-up approach to budget preparation. Human nature, being what it is, may lead managers to *pad* their budgets or leave in *budget slack* so that budget variances are always favourable. Therefore, budgets must be realistic targets to aim at, being neither too optimistic to please the boss, nor too tight to be attainable. Any manager that consistently underspends his/her budget may warrant closer attention at budget-setting time!

The time consumed in budget preparation can be a turn-off. Most large organizations start budgeting for the following year some months before the previous year has expired. This means that experience of the current year is far from complete before managers have to commit themselves to the next year's costs and income.

Although run by accountants because of their access to the information required, budgets should not be seen as an accountant's tool. Budgetary control is a management tool and its motivating appeal will be diminished if it does not have the support of the chief executive and fellow directors.

Budget reports must be timely and contain information relevant to the recipient. If too much time elapses after the period end before issuing a budget report, then interest in variances and their causes will suffer.

INCREMENTAL OR ZERO-BASED BUDGETS?

Thought must also be given when setting budgets whether to base them on previous years' experience or start afresh with a clean sheet. The former approach is referred to as *incremental* budgeting, but it should not merely be the addition of inflation to last year's figures. The previous year's figures are taken as a base and then adjusted for expected changes in prices, costs and activity levels. A frequent criticism of this approach is that it does not encourage fresh thinking and may perpetuate existing inefficiencies.

A more recent approach is to start with a clean sheet – referred to as *zero base*. This ignores previous experience and requires a manager to justify all the resource requirements expressed as costs in his or her budget. Each item of expense is therefore questioned, first, as to whether it should exist at all and, only then, as to its precise level.

Zero-base philosophy may be restricted to certain administrative functions where it is particularly relevant in questioning redundant clerical procedures. It is, however, applicable in all functional areas. A major objection may be the time and effort needed to run a zero-based system compared to the quicker incremental budgeting approach. For this reason, some organizations require a zero-based budget from each department every few years, using an incremental approach in the intervening years. In this way only some departmental budgets are given the closest of scrutinies in any one year.

FINANCIAL RESPONSIBILITY CENTRES

In a very large organization or a group of companies, financial responsibility may be applied at multiple levels of authority to gain the advantages of better motivation, communication and decision-making. If we think of a pyramid with the parent company at the top of the tree, the successively lower levels of financial responsibility are shown in Figure 15.6.

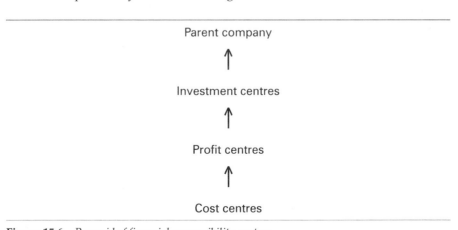

Figure 15.6 *Pyramid of financial responsibility centres*

Investment centre

This is the most autonomous unit with responsibility for managing and controlling its own assets, selling prices and costs. Typically it may be a separate business unit (a subsidiary company) or a division of a very large company. It will have its own profit and loss account, balance sheet and cash flow statement from which comparisons can be made with targets set by the group.

A key measure of performance is likely to be the *return on capital employed*, although a full financial ratio analysis could also be employed. This performance measure of return on capital is not without problems, largely brought about by the effects of depreciation on both the profit and asset values. Performance could also be affected by investment decisions that are influenced by short-term considerations even if worthwhile in the long run.

For these reasons another measure is sometimes adopted for divisions controlling their own investment. This is known as *residual income*. Basically it is an absolute profit target after deducting notional interest on the capital employed. The notional interest rate is taken as the company's cost of capital (see Chapter 16). If residual income turns out to be a positive figure then the division can be thought of as paying its way.

Example
Division A has a capital employed of £100 million, a pre-tax and interest profit of £15 million, and a cost of capital of 12 per cent. Its return on capital is 15 per cent and its residual income is £3 million (ie £15 million – £12 million notional interest).

A problem encountered with devolved financial responsibility is that of *goal congruence* by which is meant that the financial objectives and performance measures used for one unit are compatible with those of the whole organization. If financial autonomy allows a unit manager to pursue a path that is financially beneficial to that unit but not to the organization as a whole, then goal congruence has not been achieved.

Another problem that sometimes bedevils autonomous divisions within a company is where one division sells its goods and services to another division within the same ownership. The financial performance of both divisions will patently be affected by the price at which these transfers are made. This is the problem of *transfer pricing* which is discussed more in Chapter 22 in the context of international transfers and the taxing of profits in the country where the profit is deemed to arise.

Profit centre

This responsibility centre may form part of an investment centre and has control of all costs and revenues. It fixes its own selling prices and finds its own customers. Performance is measured in profit terms and by sales and cost variances from agreed budgets.

Cost centre

This is the lowest level of financial responsibility centre and there may be a number of them for each profit centre. CIMA defines a cost centre as a 'production or service location, function, activity or item of equipment for which costs are accumulated'. A cost centre manager has responsibility for expenditure only and his/her performance is judged by cost variances against an agreed budget.

It is a moot point whether budget performance is measured at the total budget level or line by line on the monthly budget report. Some organizations allow *virement* by which is meant that a saving under one cost heading can be transferred to another heading that is overspent.

ACTIVITY-BASED BUDGETING

Activity-based costing first had its application in the field of product costing in manufacturing industries, but is now widely used in the service sector for that same purpose. Another application of ABC is in the field of budgeting. This requires the identification of the *activities* and their *cost drivers* in each functional department. In the case of say, a purchasing department, cost drivers may include the number of suppliers; the number of orders placed; the number of deliveries.

Budgeted departmental running costs are allocated across these activities. The total cost for an activity is divided by the budgeted volume of activities to arrive at a budgeted unit cost for an activity.

This information helps in the decision of how much resource to allocate to each activity and to identify the resource changes that stem from a change in the level of a particular activity. The comparison of actual costs per activity with its budgeted cost is also likely to assist in the management of the overall budget. This is in marked contrast with the traditional budget approach of detailing cost headings, eg salaries, stationery, IT costs etc, with no correlation to what the money will be spent on.

FLEXIBLE BUDGETING

The system of budgeting discussed so far implied *fixed budgets* which remain unchanged irrespective of the actual level of activity achieved. If the actual level is significantly different from the budgeted level there will be significant *volume variances*. When standard costing is used, the difference in profit caused by the different level of activity is particularly quantified in the sales volume variance and fixed overhead volume variance.

In the absence of a standard costing system, the solution to the problem of variable levels of activity lies in the use of a flexible budget. This is defined by CIMA as a 'budget which, by recognizing different cost behaviour patterns, is designed to change as volume of activity changes'. Essentially the flexible budget consists of not one budget, but a series of budgets, each being based on a different level of activity within the expected range. For example, if a firm never expects activity to fall below 70 per cent it can prepare four budgets of income and expenditure at 70 per cent, 80 per cent, 90 per cent, and 100 per cent levels of the maximum capacity. Should the actual level turn out to be, say, 83 per cent, then the budget for that level can be derived by interpolating the 80 per cent and 90 per cent budgets. Comparison of actual results can then be made with the budget for the same level of activity. Any resulting variances are of a controllable nature as the change in volume has been eliminated.

Flexible budgeting obviously entails the analysis of costs into fixed and variable categories to forecast expenditure at different levels of activity. This is not the same analysis as indirect and direct costs because some indirects vary with the level of activity and some directs, possibly wages, are fixed.

The example in Figure 15.7 contrasts the variances arising under a fixed budget system with those applying in a flexible budget system. Under the fixed budget system, variances arising from a drop in the level of activity appear as favourable variances. When the budget is *flexed* to the actual level of activity, actual costs are compared with budgeted costs for the same level of activity. The variances resulting from this comparison are of a controllable nature because, by definition, a flexible budget obviates volume or uncontrollable variances.

In a survey of management accounting practices in UK manufacturing companies by Drury *et al* (1993), it was found that 42 per cent of the respondents used flexible budgets to compare budgeted with actual costs.

1. Illustration of a fixed budget report

	Fixed budget for month	Actual results for month	Variances
Activity	100%	85%	15% (A)
	£	£	£
Direct labour	33,000	31,000	2,000(F)
Direct materials	27,000	23,700	3,300(F)
Overheads	36,000	34,100	1,900(F)
Total	£96,000	£88,800	£7,200(F)

2. Flexible budget for the same month

Activity	70%	80%	90%	100%
	£	£	£	£
Direct labour	27,000	29,000	31,000	33,000
Direct materials	18,900	21,600	24,300	27,000
Variable overheads	10,500	12,000	13,500	15,000
Fixed overheads	21,000	21,000	21,000	21,000
Total	£77,400	£83,600	£89,800	£96,000

3. Flexible budget report for the same month

	Flexed budget 85% £	Actual results 85% £	Variances — £
Direct labour	30,000	31,000	1,000(A)
Direct materials	22,950	23,700	750(A)
Variable overheads	12,750	12,600	150(F)
Fixed overheads	21,000	21,500	500(A)
Total	£86,700	£88,800	£2,100(A)

Figure 15.7   *Comparison of fixed and flexible budget system*

Firms may use a mixture of fixed and flexible budgets for different departments. Essentially, the choice is that of fixed budgets fully integrated with a standard costing system to disclose volume variances, or flexible budgets where standard costing is inappropriate.

PLANNING, PROGRAMMING AND BUDGETING SYSTEMS (PPBS)

This form of budgeting applies to public service organizations, such as local authorities and hospitals. These organizations will run short-term, departmentally based budgeting systems to control expenditure within a financial year, in the same way as profit-seeking enterprises.

PPBS, however, differs from ordinary budgeting. First, it plans further than just one year ahead. Second, it transcends departments. PPBS is about how resources are going to be allocated to achieve the various objectives of the organization, for example, the care of the elderly. Once the objectives have been established, programmes are identified to meet those objectives and the costs/benefits of alternative programmes are assessed.

The chosen programmes form, in effect, a long-term plan to be pursued over a number of years. Each programme budget will disclose the cost of providing a service to satisfy an objective, broken down into time periods. It therefore informs management in a manner allowing them to make judgements about such effectiveness that would not be possible if programmes were fragmented in the departmental budgets concerned.

Further reading

Connolly, T and Ashworth, G (1994), An integrated activity-based approach to budgeting, *Management Accounting*, March.
Drury, C *et al*, (1993) A Survey of Management Accounting Practices in UK Manufacturing Companies, ACCA), London.
Drury, C (1996) *Management and Cost Accounting*, ITP, London.
Lucey, T (1997) *Management Accounting*, Letts, London.

Prendergast, P (1997) Budget padding: Is it a job for the finance police?, *Management Accounting*, November.
Secrett, M (1996) *Mastering Spreadsheet Budgets and Forecasts*, IM/Pitman, London.

Self-check questions

1. What is a key or limiting factor in budgeting?
2. What factors would you consider when fixing the sales budget for the coming year?
3. What is a cash budget?
4. What is a flexible budget?
5. What have budgetary control and standard costing systems got in common?
6. A firm has 350 kg of a raw material in stock at the beginning of a budget period. Production will use 10,000 kg of the material during the period and the firm wants the stock level to increase to 750 kg at the end of that time. What quantity must be purchased?
7. How does PPBS differ from budgetary control?
8. How does activity-based budgeting differ from traditional methods of budgeting?

Part 3

Financial management

The way in which a company finances its assets has an effect on the return on owners' capital and the overall cost of capital. Gearing up the capital structure, together with tax allowances on interest payments, can enhance the return on equity funds, but carries risks if taken too far. Many companies, including some household names, went bust in the 1989–92 recession as a result of overgearing. As we near the end of the 1990s, high *real* interest rates are keeping the sterling exchange rate high, relative to our EC competitors. This has led to an unbalanced economy with growth in retail and manufacturing faltering when the service sector is still growing strongly.

Capital is invested either in fixed assets or in working capital. This part of the book examines the techniques of investment appraisal which assist in the decision of whether, when and where to deploy scarce resources. Some research findings on the appraisal methods actually used by firms are also briefly discussed. The management of stocks, debtors and cash which make up working capital is also explored, together with newer developments such as factoring.

Both the raising of capital and its use affect the share price of a private-sector company through the impact on reported profit. Different ways of valuing company shares are discussed before examining their role in merger and acquisition situations, and the growing interest in management buy-outs.

Finally, the taxation of business profits is outlined under the system of corporation tax for limited companies and income tax for self-employed persons. The UK is a predominant trader with other countries and the accounting peculiarities of overseas, as opposed to home, trade are reviewed.

16
The cost of capital

INTRODUCTION

Capital is not free. Individual investors and financial institutions require a return on their investment in any company. In turn the company must earn a return on assets at least equal to the cost of capital employed in the business. To do otherwise will not satisfy the providers of that capital and will make the raising of future capital more difficult, if not impossible. Firms need to set a minimum required rate of return against which the profitability of proposed new investments is measured. This required rate must at least be equal to the cost of the different types of capital used in the business.

There are two main sources of new capital for new investments:

- borrowings; and
- share issues.

Firms can either borrow the money, usually from a financial institution, or they can obtain it from the owners. In this latter case new equity capital can be obtained in one of two ways. Companies occasionally sell new shares to existing shareholders on a *rights issue* or *open offer*. This may be unpopular as it tends to depress the existing share price on the Stock Exchange. The other way companies obtain new capital from the owners is by not paying out all the profits earned as dividends. By this means companies are assured of the extra capital they need and they save the expense of issuing new shares.

CAPITAL GEARING

Most firms use a mix of borrowed and owners' capital and the relationship between the two is known as *capital gearing*. A company is said to be highly geared when it has a large amount of borrowed capital relative to owners' capital. It is lowly geared when the proportion of borrowed capital is small. The calculation of a gearing ratio was first discussed in Chapter 9. Strictly speaking, gearing is the use of any prior charge capital, including preference shares. Prior charge in this context means a prior charge against profits before equity.

The relationship between these two sources of capital is also expressed by calculating each source as a proportion of the total capital. The two situations in Figure 16.1 illustrate different levels of gearing:

	(a) Low gearing	(b) High gearing
Equity (share capital + retained profits)	90%	50%
Borrowed capital	10%	50%
Total capital	100%	100%

Figure 16.1   *Example of high and low capital gearing*

There is no one particular level of capital gearing that is regarded as satisfactory for all companies. Each firm is examined on its past record, future prospects and the security of the interest and capital repayments. In most industries the 50 per cent borrowed capital indicated in Figure 16.1(b) would be regarded as very high, although much higher rates are not uncommon in the rather special case of property development. Even here, after the slump in property in the early 1990s, financial institutions may be more wary in future of lending too high a proportion of development capital.

It is possible to find examples of companies with no borrowed capital, resulting from a policy decision by management to finance growth internally from retained profits. Such companies eliminate the risks of defaulting on the loan or interest repayments, or having to reduce dividends to make interest payments when profits fall. On the other hand, they miss the opportunity of increasing the return to ordinary shareholders by investing borrowed capital to earn more than the cost of the interest, as Figure 16.2 shows.

When a company has no gearing the change in the profit results in the same proportionate change in the return on shareholders' funds. In the nil gearing example, doubled profits also double the return to the owners from 10.77 per cent to 21.54 per cent. The doubling of the same profit in the high gearing example more than doubles the return on ordinary shareholders' funds from 13.12 per cent to 30.62 per cent.

Most firms decide that a judicious amount of borrowed capital is beneficial and try to adhere to a target level of gearing over the years. It may be that in any one year the target is exceeded because conditions in the capital markets do not allow a particular kind of funding to take place. This can be redressed as soon as market conditions allow.

New projects must be financed by new capital, as opposed to existing capital which has already been spent on existing projects. We therefore need to look at the cost and the mix of new capital to calculate the minimum required

	Nil gearing £000	High gearing £000
Capital structures		
Ordinary shares of £1	2,900	1,400
Retained profits	1,000	1,000
10% loan stock	nil	1,500
	3,900	3,900
Profit of £600,000:		
Profit	600	600
Interest	nil	150
	600	450
Corporation tax at 30%	180	135
Earned for ordinary shareholders	420	315
Return on ordinary shareholders' funds	10.77%	13.12%
Profit of £1,200,000:		
Profit	1,200	1,200
Interest	nil	150
	1,200	1,050
Corporation tax at 30%	360	315
Earned for ordinary shareholders	840	735
Return on ordinary shareholders' funds	21.54%	30.62%

Figure 16.2 *Illustration of the effects of capital gearing*

rate of return on new investments. Also we must bear in mind the effects of taxation and inflation on each type of capital as they differ in certain respects. We will first examine the cost of borrowed capital, then the cost of equity, and take account of the different proportions to get an overall weighted average cost.

THE COST OF BORROWED CAPITAL

This can be very straightforward. If a company takes out a bank loan at a fixed rate of interest of say, 9 per cent, then this is the cost before any tax relief. In the case of a public offer, the rate of interest which has to be paid on new loans to get them taken up by investors at par can be regarded as the cost of borrowed capital. Such rates of interest vary over time in sympathy with interest rates obtainable on alternative investments. They also vary slightly according to the size of the loan and the degree of risk attached to the particular firm.

A different approach can be used to find the current cost of borrowing for a firm which has existing loans or debentures quoted on a stock exchange. If the fixed rate of interest on such loans is less than the current going rate, these securities will have a market price of less than the par value of the stock. This means investors will obtain a return from two sources – the interest payments and a capital gain on the eventual repayment of the stock at par.

Example

Suppose X Ltd has a 10 per cent loan stock standing at £83 per £100 nominal value, repayable at par in five years' time. An investor today is therefore willing to pay £83 for the right to receive £10 yearly interest for the next five years and £100 back at the end of that time. We can approach this in the way we calculate the internal rate of return (IRR) on industrial investments as explained in the next chapter. Figure 16.3 shows this to be 15 per cent, which will be the solution rate of interest which equates the purchase cost of £83 with the present value of the stream of future receipts.

Year	Cash flow £	PV factors at 15%	Present value £
0	−83	1.000	−83.00
1	+10	.870	+8.70
2	+10	.756	+7.56
3	+10	.658	+6.58
4	+10	.572	+5.72
5	+110	.497	+54.67
			+£0.23

Figure 16.3 *Calculation of the IRR as the effective rate of interest*

The IRR of 15 per cent obtained by an investor buying the company's existing loan stock can be regarded as the current cost of interest on new loans issued at par. It represents the money or nominal cost of new loans, which is used to calculate a weighted average cost of capital. The real cost of loan capital will be significantly less as investors are not compensated for the fall in the value of their capital caused by inflation. This is the reason for the gearing adjustment in the inflation-adjusted profit and loss account (see Chapter 7). In the 1970s this real cost of loan capital was negative after allowing for both inflation and the tax relief next mentioned. In the later 1980s and the early 1990s, the real cost of capital turned positive again, due to high interest rates relative to lower inflation rates. An 8 per cent base rate, for example, coupled with a 3 per cent inflation rate equates to a 5 per cent real cost of borrowing for firms with the best credit rating. Very small firms could expect to pay another 3–5 per cent.

Tax relief

Interest paid on loans, debentures and overdrafts is deductible from profits before calculating the corporation tax charge, whereas dividends are not. In effect tax relief is granted on interest payments which, with corporation tax at 30 per cent, reduces the rate of interest by nearly one-third. Figure 16.4 illustrates this point.

	Company A Nil gearing £000		Company B 50% gearing £000
Share capital and reserves	10,000		5,000
10% loan	nil		5,000
Total capital employed	10,000		10,000
Profit before interest and tax	2,000		2,000
Interest on loan	nil		500
Profit before tax	2,000		1,500
Corporation tax at 30%	600		450
Tax saved		£150,000	

Figure 16.4   *Illustration of tax relief on interest payments*

It can be seen that two companies with identical total capitals and annual profits do not pay the same tax charge. Company B which financed half of its capital requirement from a 10 per cent loan saves £150,000 of the £500,000 interest cost through tax relief. The effective rate of interest on the loan is therefore only 7 per cent.

$$\text{After-tax rate of interest} \quad = \quad \frac{\text{£0.5m} - \text{£0.15m}}{\text{£5m}} \quad \text{x 100\%} \quad = \quad 7\%$$

It is not surprising that firms find gearing attractive when they compare the after-tax cost of loans with the cost of equity capital!

THE COST OF EQUITY CAPITAL

The equity of a company is its risk capital, embracing ordinary share capital and retained profits which can be regarded as having the same cost. Companies retain profits to short-circuit paying out all profits with one hand while asking shareholders to buy new shares with the other. There is clearly a saving in administrative costs and professional fees by retaining profits, so this alternative will be slightly cheaper in practice.

Put simply, the cost of equity is the return shareholders expect the company to earn on their money. It is their estimation, often not scientifically calculated, of the rate of return which will be obtained both from future dividends and an increased share value. Unfortunately, simple concepts are not always so easy to apply in practice and the cost of capital is a favourite battlefield for academics with no one agreed practical solution.

Dividend valuation model

One approach to finding the cost of equity is to take the current gross dividend yield for a company and add the expected annual growth.

Example

For example, Gemmy plc has forecast payment of a gross equivalent dividend of

10p on each ordinary share in the coming year. The company's shares are quoted on the Stock Exchange and currently trade at £2.00. Growth of profits and dividends has averaged 15 per cent over the last few years. The cost of equity for Gemmy plc can be calculated as:

$$\text{Cost of equity capital} = \frac{\text{Current dividend (gross)}}{\text{Current market price}}\% + \text{Growth rate \%}$$

$$= \frac{(£0.10 \times 100)}{£2}\% + 15\% = 20\%$$

With this method, dividends are assumed to grow in the future at the constant rate achieved by averaging the last few years' performance. No residual share price is included as it is assumed that dividend payments continue to perpetuity. The 20 per cent cost of equity capital above is a nominal rate rather than a real rate of return to investors. It is an after-tax return as dividends are paid from taxed profits, unlike interest payments, which are allowed against tax.

Risk

Before turning to the next method, we need to clarify some aspects of risk. There are two broad types of risk:

- specific or unsystematic risk; and
- systematic risk.

Specific risk is of a kind that only applies to one particular business. It includes, for example, the risk of losing the chief executive; the risk of someone else bringing out a similar or better product; or the risk of labour problems. Shareholders are expected not to want compensation for this type of risk as it can be diversified away by holding a sufficient number of investments in their portfolios.

Systematic risk, however, derives from global or macro-economic events which can damage all investments to some extent and therefore holders require compensation for this risk to their wealth. This compensation takes the form of a higher required rate of return.

Capital asset pricing model

A slightly more complicated approach to the cost of equity tries to take the systematic risk element into account. It is known as the *capital asset pricing model* or CAPM for short. Put simply, CAPM states that investors' required rate of return on a share is composed of two parts:

- a risk-free rate similar to that obtainable on a risk-free investment in short-term government securities; and
- an additional premium to compensate for the systematic risk involved in investing in shares.

This systematic risk for a company's shares is measured by the size of its beta factor. A beta the size of 1.0 for a company means that its shares have the same systematic risk as the average for the whole market. If the beta is 1.4 then systematic risk for the share is 40 per cent higher than the market average. A company's share beta is applied to the market premium which is obtained from the excess of the return on a market portfolio of shares over the risk-free rate of return. In terms of a formula:

$$Ke = Rf + B(Rm - Rf)$$

where: Ke = cost of equity
 Rf = risk-free return
 Rm = return on market portfolio of shares
 B = beta factor

Example
Assume the risk-free rate of return is 5.5 per cent and the return on a market portfolio is 12 per cent. A company has a beta of 0.7 for its ordinary shares. What is its cost of equity?

$$Ke = Rf + B(Rm-Rf)$$
$$10.05\% = 5.5\% + 0.7(12\%-5.5\%)$$

Of the two methods described for finding the cost of equity for a company, the latter CAPM method is the more scientific. Ideally, the risk-free and market rates of return should reflect the future but current rates of return are used as substitutes. Beta factors measure how sensitive each company's share price movements are relative to market movements over a period of a few years. This information is available from commercial sources and companies do not have to work out their own beta.

WEIGHTED AVERAGE COST OF CAPITAL (WACC)

Having identified the cost of equity and the cost of borrowed capital (and that of any other long-term source of finance), we need to combine them into one overall cost of capital. This is primarily for use in project appraisals as justification of those that yield a return in excess of their cost of capital.

An average cost is required because we do not usually identify each individual project with one particular source of finance. Because equity and debt capital have very different costs, we would make illogical decisions and accept a project financed by debt capital only to reject a similar project next time round when it was financed by equity capital. To avoid this, all projects are deemed to be financed from a common pool of finance except for the relatively rare case when project specific finance is raised. This pool is composed primarily of borrowed and owners' capital together with depreciation and other retained profits. We can think of depreciation as retained profit for the specific purpose of helping to replace any assets that have worn out during the year.

Calculation of a weighted average cost of capital takes account of the different after-tax costs of debt and equity and of their significance in the make up of the total capital. The weightings used in the calculations should be based on the *market value* of the securities and not on their book or balance sheet values.

Example

Assume your company attempts to keep the gearing ratio of borrowed capital to equity in the proportion of 20:80. The nominal cost of new capital from these sources has been assessed, say, at 10 per cent and 15 per cent respectively and corporation tax is 30 per cent. Figure 16.5 shows the calculation of the overall weighted average cost.

Type of capital	Proportion	After-tax cost	Weighted cost
10% loan capital	0.20	7.0%	1.4%
Equity	0.80	15.0%	12.0%
	1.00		13.4%

Figure 16.5 *Calculation of the nominal weighted average cost of capital*

The resulting weighted average cost of 13.4 per cent is the minimum rate which this company should accept on proposed investments. Any investment which is not expected to achieve this return is not a viable proposition. Risk has been allowed for in the calculation of the beta factor used in the CAPM method of identifying the cost of equity. This relates to the risk of the existing whole business. If a company embarks on a project of significantly different risk, or has a divisional structure of activities of varying risk levels, then a single cost of equity for the whole company is inappropriate. In this situation, the average beta of proxy companies operating in the same field as a division can be used.

Further reading

McLaney, EJ (1997) *Business Finance,* FT/Pitman, London.
Mott, G (1997) *Investment Appraisal,* FT/Pitman, London.
Samuels, JM Wilkes, FM and Brayshaw, RE (1995) *Management of Company Finance,* ITP, London.
Watson, D and Head, T (1998), *Corporate Finance,* FT/Pitman, London.

Self-check questions

1. What is meant by a high level of gearing?
2. Using the illustration in Figure 16.2, calculate the return on equity in the high gearing case when the profit is £1,000,000 and the tax rate is 50 per cent.
3. What is the current cost of interest on a new loan if a firm has an existing 8 per cent loan repayable in three years' time and is quoted at £75 per £100 nominal value?
4. What is the after-tax cost of interest for a company paying 35 per cent rate of corporation tax if it pays 12 per cent interest on a bank loan?
5. Canny plc ordinary shares sell at £1.50 at the present time and the growth of profits and dividends has averaged 10 per cent pa in recent years. What is its cost of equity capital if the latest dividend was 8p net and the notional tax on dividends is 20 per cent?
6. Calculate the nominal weighted average cost of capital in Figure 16.5 when the proportion of loan capital to equity is 40:60.

17

Capital investment appraisal

INTRODUCTION

Investment appraisal is concerned with decisions about whether, when and how to spend money on capital projects. Such decisions are important ones for the companies involved because often large sums of money are committed in an irreversible decision, with no certain knowledge of the size of future benefits.

Example
Suppose a printing firm is considering buying a binding machine for £10,000, which will reduce labour costs on this activity by £3,000 every year for each of the five years the machine is expected to last. What the management of this firm have to consider – and this is no easy task – is whether a return of £3,000 every year for five years justifies the initial investment of £l0,000.

The essence of all investment appraisals is to measure the worthwhile nature of proposals to spend money, by comparing the benefits with the costs. If this measurement is done badly, it can hamper a firm's growth and employment prospects for years to come, and may lead to an inability to attract new investors. Financial institutions and individuals provide firms with capital in the expectation of a reasonable rate of return. If a firm invests that money in projects which do not yield a reasonable return then investors will be wary of that company in the future. The minimum return required on new investments will be the cost of capital as calculated in the previous chapter.

FINANCIAL MODEL

We measure the worthwhile nature of investment proposals by building simple financial models of the expected events. The model sets out the individual years on one axis and the cash flows on the other axis. A standard spreadsheet is ideally suited to this purpose. Using the binding machine example above, we can set out manually the expected events as cash inflows (+) or outflows (-) for each year of the machine's life, as in Figure 17.1. These cash flows start at year 0, which is the beginning of the first year when the project is initiated:

Year 0 –	10,000
Year 1 +	3,000
Year 2 +	3,000
Year 3 +	3,000
Year 4 +	3,000
Year 5 +	3,000
Total profit +	£5,000

Figure 17.1 *Financial model of the binding-machine project*

Types of investment situation

There are a number of basic situations where an appraisal takes place:

- *Expansion* – assessing the worthwhileness of expanding existing product lines requiring additional investment in buildings, plant, stocks, debtors, etc.
- *New product/diversification* – assessing the viability of the more risky investment in totally new products.
- *Cost saving* – assessing the profitability of a cost-saving scheme; for example, when an investment in a new machine automates an existing manual process.
- *Replacement* – deciding whether and when to replace an old machine with a new one to save operating costs or reduce wastage.
- *Alternative choice* – deciding between alternative investments to achieve the same ends; for example, choosing between two or more machines with different financial characteristics.
- *Financing* – comparing the cost of purchasing an asset outright with the alternative cost of leasing.

All the above investment situations have the same common approach. In each case we must decide whether the benefits we get from the initial investment are sufficient to justify the original capital outlay.

There may be some investment situations where no benefits are quantifiable in money terms. For example, the government may require firms to invest in fire detection and alarm systems in all their premises. In this case firms have no choice and, although there will be benefits in employee welfare, these are not readily quantifiable in cash terms. Even in this kind of situation, an appraisal technique could be used to help us make the choice between competing systems which have different financial characteristics.

Example
In the case of the fire detection and alarm system, one supplier's equipment may have a high capital cost, but a low maintenance cost over a long life. An alternative supplier's equipment may have a low capital cost, but high maintenance costs over a short life. We would need to formalize this information to make a rational judgement.

All appraisal methods require an estimate of the yearly cash flows attributable solely to the project under review. Typically there will be an initial cash outflow on a project, being the cash spent on the physical assets, such as buildings, plant, vehicles, machinery and the like. If any of these items need replacing before the project ends, then a cash outflow will also occur in that later year. Other cash outflows may occur through the firm building up stocks or giving credit to its customers. These working capital items will be cash outflows at the beginning of the project or at some subsequent date if increased in amount. At the end of a project the working capital is released and becomes a cash inflow at that time.

Cash inflows occur, for example, from sales revenue less their wage and material costs. No deduction from such income is made for depreciation as the total asset cost is shown as a cash outflow and, more important, depreciation is not a cash transaction. Where cost-saving projects are concerned, the cash inflow each year is the value of these cost savings, again without charging any depreciation. The cost of the investment will be shown in full as a cash outflow at the time of acquisition. It is worth emphasizing at this point that profits which accrue from cost-saving investments are just as valuable as profits from investments extending the firm's output.

At this stage all cash flows are expressed in £s of Year 0 purchasing power and inflation is ignored. A brief description of how to cope with inflation follows later, but first a review is needed of the four main methods used to appraise investment projects.

INVESTMENT APPRAISAL METHODS

Two of the methods are relatively crude measures of the worthwhile nature of an investment and this sums up their weakness. The remaining methods are much more precise as they are both based on yearly interest calculations. They are easy techniques to understand and, with the help of computers or calculators, are not difficult to implement. It should be appreciated later that only these latter methods can adequately incorporate taxation, inflation and uncertain future events.

Payback method

Simplicity is the keynote of this investment appraisal method. Payback measures the number of years it is expected to take to recover the cost of the original investment.

Example

Let us return to the printing firm mentioned in Figure 17.1. Using the same data, Figure 17.2 now sets out both the yearly and cumulative cash flows. Payback is completed where indicated at three and one-third years when the cumulative cash flows change from a negative to a positive figure:

	Yearly cash flows	Cumulative cash flows
Year 0	− 10,000	− 10,000
Year 1	+ 3,000	− 7,000
Year 2	+ 3,000	− 4,000
Year 3	+ 3,000	− 1,000 payback $3\frac{1}{3}$ years
Year 4	+ 3,000	+ 2,000
Year 5	+ 3,000	+ 5,000
Total profit	+ £5,000	+£5,000

Figure 17.2 *Payback period on the binding-machine project*

One disadvantage of this method is that cash received after payback is completed is totally ignored. Another disadvantage is that no attempt is made to relate the total cash earned on the investment to the amount invested. The payback method does not attempt to measure this total profitability over the whole life of the investment and other methods have to be introduced to do this. However, payback is still used and can yield useful information as an indicator of risk, but is best used in conjunction with other methods.

Accounting rate of return method

The rate of return purports to measure exactly what is required, namely, the profitability of the investment being the annual profit expressed as a percentage of the capital invested.

$$\text{Accounting rate of return} = \frac{\text{Average annual profit}}{\text{Average investment}}$$

Both these figures need some further explanation.

An *average annual profit* is used to allow for cases where profit fluctuates from year to year. This average is calculated by taking the total profits earned on the investment over the whole of its life and dividing by the expected life of the project in years. Profit in this context is after charging the total cost of the investment or wholly depreciating it in accountants' terminology. This total profit is more easily understood as the total cash inflows less the total cash outflows. The *average investment* is normally regarded as half the original investment on the grounds that it will be wholly depreciated down to zero by the end of its useful life.

Example

We refer back to the data illustrated in Figure 17.1 when the total profit over a five-year life was £5,000 and the initial investment was £10,000. This gives an accounting rate of return of 20 per cent in each of the five years.

$$\text{Average annual profit} \ = \ \frac{\text{Total profit over life £5,000}}{\text{Length of life 5 years}} \ = \ \text{£1,000 pa}$$

$$\text{Accounting rate of return} \ = \ \frac{\text{Average annual profit £1,000}}{\text{Average investment £5,000}} \ = \ 20\%$$

A disadvantage of this method is that the calculation can give misleading results. Provided total profits were £5,000 over the five years, the return will remain at 20 per cent irrespective of whether the pattern of cash flows increased, decreased or stayed constant as in the example used. Also, the method does not take timing into account. Nor will it help rank projects whose lives vary, as the rates of return cannot be directly compared in this event.

Ask any business person if they are indifferent about getting paid earlier or later, and you will find that time is important. Money received today is worth more than money received later, if only because of its ability to earn interest in the meantime. This is the reasoning behind the appraisal methods that are based on discounted cash flows. At a later stage it will also become apparent that the average investment is a statistical illusion. One reason is that the cost of the investment can be quickly reduced by the early receipt of tax allowances. If these benefits are averaged out over the life of the investment, they will not be shown at their true worth to the firm.

The true rate of return

The profitability of an investment should be measured by the size of the profit earned on the capital invested. This is what the accounting rate of return method attempts to do, but not with perfect success. An ideal method will not rely on averages, but will relate these two factors of profit and capital employed to each other in every individual year of the investment's life.

A useful analogy can be made with a repayment mortgage. In this situation the borrower pays to the bank a sum of money each year, usually divided into 12 monthly instalments for convenience. Part of this yearly sum is taken as interest to service the capital outstanding at the beginning of the accounting year, leaving the remainder as a capital repayment to reduce the capital balance. The profitability of the investment from the lender's viewpoint can be measured by the rate of the interest payment, assuming that the yearly capital repayments have paid off all the mortgage by the end of the agreed term.

Example
Figure 17.3 sets out the yearly cash flows of a building society mortgage of £60,000 repaid over 10 years with interest at 7 per cent pa on the reducing balance. The small balance outstanding at the end of 10 years is negligible given the size of the annual cash flows.

	Annual cash flow	Interest payment at 7% pa	Capital repayment	Capital balance outstanding
	£	£	£	£
Year 0	−60,000			−60,000
1	+ 8,542	4,200	4,342	55,658
2	+ 8,542	3,896	4,646	51,012
3	+ 8,542	3,571	4,971	46,041
4	+ 8,542	3,223	5,319	40,722
5	+ 8,542	2,850	5,692	35,030
6	+ 8,542	2,452	6,090	28,940
7	+ 8,542	2,026	6,516	22,424
8	+ 8,542	1,569	6,973	15,451
9	+ 8,542	1,081	7,461	7,990
10	+ 8,542	559	7,983	7 (outstanding)

Figure 17.3 *Repayment mortgage of £60,000 at 7 per cent interest over 10 years*

This building society is getting a *true* return of 7 per cent pa on the reducing capital balance of the mortgage. In fact, it would get slightly more if repayments are made monthly, but the interest calculation was done yearly. This is why it pays to shop around for a lender that will give credit for monthly payments by levying interest on the falling capital balance month by month. At the present time most banks and building societies charge interest on the capital outstanding at the start of their accounting year.

Compound interest

The calculations involved in proving the building society's return on investment to be 7 per cent are somewhat laborious. A simpler method is used in practice, based on the principles of compound interest.

Suppose £1 was invested one year ago at interest of 10 per cent pa. After one year the sum has grown to £1.10. If the £1 was invested two years ago it would have grown to £1.21 with the first year's interest reinvested or compounded. You will find this value on the Year 2 line of the compound interest table in Appendix 4, which gives the future value of £1 at various rates of interest over the next 20 years. Compound interest measures the future value of money invested sometime in the past.

Present value

It is equally possible to look at money in the reverse direction, namely, the present value of money receivable at a future point in time. The present value of a future sum of money is the equivalent sum now that would leave the recipient indifferent between the two amounts. The present value or equivalent sum to £1 receivable in one year's time is that amount which, if invested for one year, would accumulate to £1 in one year's time.

Example
Using a 10 per cent rate of interest, £1 receivable in one year's time has an equivalent value now of £0.909 because £0.909 invested for one year at 10 per cent will
accumulate to £1.

Figure 17.4 is an extract from the present value table shown in Appendix 5
compared with the compound interest factors at the same rate of interest
shown in Appendix 4. The relationship between the two tables is that in any
one year at the same rate of interest, one factor is the reciprocal of the other. For
example, for year 4 1/.683 = 1.464.

	Present value of £1 receivable in a future year with interest at 10%	Future value of £1 with compound interest at 10%
Year 0 (now)	1.000	1.000
1	.909	1.100
2	.826	1.210
3	.751	1.331
4	.683	1.464

Figure 17.4 *Comparison of present value and compound interest factors*

Returning to the building-society mortgage illustrated in Figure 17.3, this was
shown to have a true rate of profitability of 7 per cent. This can now be proved
using the simpler present value approach as in Figure 17.5. To do this, the cash
flows are tabulated yearly and brought back (discounted) to their present
value by the use of present value factors. In effect, interest is deducted for the
waiting time involved. The remaining cash is therefore available to repay the
original investment. The rate of profitability of the investment is measured by
the maximum rate of interest which can be deducted, while leaving just
enough cash to repay the capital invested. This rate of interest is the same 7 per
cent as found in Figure 17.3 and is called the *internal rate of return* or IRR for
short. The negative balance outstanding of £10 is negligible given the size of
the annual cash flows.

The effect of using present value (PV) factors on future cash flows is to take
compound interest off for the waiting time involved. If a higher rate of interest
than 7 per cent were applied in Figure 17.5 then not all the capital would be
repaid over the 10-year life. If a lower rate of interest than 7 per cent was used,
the capital repayments would be larger each year as the present values would
be larger. This would result in the mortgage being repaid in less than the 10
years stipulated.

Both the methods of calculation explained above in Figures 17.3 and 17.5
arrive at the same conclusion, although at first sight they may not appear
related. That they are related can be seen by comparing the capital repayments
in Figure 17.3 with the inverted present values in Figure 17.5 which are almost
identical apart from rounding-off differences. This will always be the case in

	Annual cash flow	Present value factors at 7%	Present value
	£		£
Year 0	–60,000	1.000	–60,000
1	+8,542	.935	+7,987
2	+8,542	.873	+7,457
3	+8,542	.816	+6,970
4	+8,542	.763	+6,518
5	+8,542	.713	+6,090
6	+8,542	.666	+5,689
7	+8,542	.623	+5,322
8	+8,542	.582	+4,971
9	+8,542	.544	+4,647
10	+8,542	.508	+4,339
			NPV – £10

Figure 17.5 *Calculating the rate of profitability on a £60,000 mortgage repayable over 10 years at 7 per cent using present value factors*

examples with constant annual cash flows. The present value approach will also give correct results with any fluctuating pattern of annual cash flows.

Net present value method

We can use this present value approach to assess the profitability of all investment projects. If the net present value is positive, the project is viable. If it is negative, the project is not viable. All we need to know is:

- the initial amount invested;
- the cost of capital for use as the discount rate;
- estimates of yearly cash flows;
- expected life;
- any residual values.

Example
The directors of E Ltd are considering investing £150,000 on a press to make and sell an industrial fastener. Profits before charging depreciation (ie cash inflows) are expected to be £60,000 for each of the first four years tapering off to £40,000 in Year 5 and only £20,000 in Year 6 when the press will be scrapped. E Ltd normally require a minimum rate of return of 20 per cent. The cash flows can be set out and multiplied by the present value factors at 20 per cent to demonstrate whether this project meets the 20 per cent required rate as in Figure 17.6.

The net present value (NPV) surplus of £28,060 means that the project is viable. The word 'net' in net present value means the sum of the negative and positive present values and this method of investment appraisal is widely known as the net present value method or NPV method for short.

	Annual cash flow	PV factors at 20%	PV
	£		£
Year 0	−150,000	1.000	−150,000
1	+60,000	.833	+49,980
2	+60,000	.694	+41,640
3	+60,000	.579	+34,740
4	+60,000	.482	+28,920
5	+40,000	.402	+16,080
6	+20,000	.335	+ 6,700
			NPV +£28,060

Figure 17.6 *Calculation of the net present value at 20 per cent*

Internal rate of return method (IRR)

The NPV method answers the question of a project's viability when tested against the required rate of return of that particular company. This required rate is alternatively referred to as the criterion rate, or cut-off rate – 20 per cent in the above example for E Ltd. Sometimes managers want to know not just whether a project is viable, but what rate of return they can expect on a project. To answer this question the NPV method is taken a stage further.

The annual cash flows in E Ltd above are big enough to allow much more interest to be deducted and still repay the original investment. These cash flows are discounted again at a higher trial rate of interest. Such trial is an educated guess, but a higher rather than a lower rate is chosen because of the NPV surplus that previously occurred. Now assuming a trial rate of 30 per cent was chosen, the annual cash flows are discounted by the present value factors at 30 per cent as in Figure 17.7.

	Annual cash flow	PV factors at 30%	PV
	£		£
Year 0	−150,000	1.000	−150,000
1	+60,000	.769	+46,140
2	+60,000	.592	+35,520
3	+60,000	.455	+27,300
4	+60,000	.350	+21,000
5	+40,000	.269	+10,760
6	+20,000	.207	+ 4,140
			NPV − £5,140

Figure 17.7 *Calculation of the net present value at 30 per cent*

As there is a deficit net present value of £5,140, the IRR is less than 30 per cent. This is because too much interest has been deducted to allow all the capital to be repaid. If instead of going to an estimated trial rate of 30 per cent the annual cash flows had been repeatedly discounted at 1 per cent intervals from the 20 per cent required rate then a zero net present value would have been found at about 28 per cent. This is the true rate of return on the project and is known as its internal rate of return. In other words, the IRR is the solution rate of interest which, when used to discount annual cash flows on a project, gives an NPV of zero. The IRR is also known as the *discounted cash flow yield*.

Interpolation

It would be a tedious task to adopt the above method of successive discounting at 1 per cent intervals but fortunately this is not required. The NPV calculation at 20 per cent and 30 per cent yielded a surplus of £28,060 and a deficit of £5,140 respectively. This provides sufficient information to estimate the IRR reasonably accurately by interpolation, which can then be proved by calculation. The interpolation shows:

$$20\% \ + \left\{ \frac{28{,}060}{28{,}060 + 5{,}140} \times (30\%{-}20\%) \right\} \ = \ 28.5\%$$

Another interpolation method takes the form of a simple graph with the rate of interest on the vertical axis and the net present value on the horizontal axis. The NPVs from the trial at the company's required rate and the further 'guesstimate' are then plotted against their respective interest rates and the two plots joined by a straight line. The approximate IRR is where the straight line intersects the vertical axis at a zero NPV. If the two plots are far removed from the actual rate of return, the interpolation may not be quite accurate and it should be proved by a final calculation.

It is possible to calculate the IRR to one or more decimal places. Although one decimal place may be justifiable, there is usually no case for further precision. This is because the basic data on which the calculations are performed are only estimates of future events. To calculate the IRR to, say, three decimal places, gives an impression of precision which is illusory.

Other short cuts

The interpolation techniques described earlier are obvious short cuts in the search for the solution rate of interest. Some managers may have access to calculators or computers which can rapidly answer the question of a project's rate of profitability. Another short cut is applicable where there is a constant annual cash flow in every year of the project's life. This method is based on the principle that if a constant cash flow is multiplied by individual PV factors the total present value will be the same as if the constant annual cash flow had been multiplied by the sum of the individual PV factors.

If the sum of the individual PV factors had to be arrived at by literally adding up the individual factors, this might be thought to be a long short cut! Fortunately a table exists with all the adding up done for the reader and the total of any number of individual year factors can be read off at a glance. Such a table is shown in full in Appendix 6 as the present value of £1 receivable annually or, put more simply, a cumulative PV table.

Such cumulative PV tables can be used as short cuts to both the NPV and IRR. Because the cumulative table applies only to constant annual cash flows, this technique is usually used for rule-of-thumb calculations on a project's profitability. Very often managers or industrial engineers want a quick guide as to whether it is profitable to pursue a certain course of action. This can easily be done using a cumulative PV table when the cash flows are relatively constant. A more precise evaluation incorporating taxation, grants, working capital changes, etc, can be done later.

Example

Consider the proposal to introduce a fork-lift truck to handle palletized stock in a warehouse at a cost of £50,000. This can be expected to yield an annual saving in labour costs less truck running costs of £18,500. The equipment is expected to last six years and the company regards a 25 per cent return before tax as a minimum requirement and this is shown to be achieved in Figure 17.8.

	Annual cash flow	Cumulative PV factors at 25%	PV
	£		£
Year 0	− 50,000	1.000	− 50,000
1–6	+ 18,500	2.951	+ 54,594
			NPV + £4,594

Figure 17.8 *Calculation of the NPV on a fork-lift truck project*

The above method quickly solves the NPV, but can be used to even greater effect in finding the IRR on a project. Here we require the cumulative PV factor to be first calculated and then looked up on the line of the relevant year of the cumulative PV table, in this case Year 6. Continuing with the fork-lift truck example, the cumulative PV factor which gives an NPV of zero must be equal to £50,000/£18,500. This is the cost of the investment divided by the constant annual return which is equal to 2.703. On the Year 6 line of the cumulative PV table, 2.703 almost exactly equates with the cumulative factor of 2.700 at 29 per cent, which is therefore the size of the IRR.

COMPARISON OF APPRAISAL METHODS

Four methods of investment appraisal have been discussed so far and useful conclusions can be drawn by comparing these four methods on the same projects. Figure 17.9 sets out three projects (A, B and C) with different lives and different patterns of cash flow and appraises them by payback, rate of return, NPV and IRR methods.

	Project A £	Project B £	Project C £
Year 0	− 200,000	− 200,000	− 200,000
1	+ 20,000	+ 80,000	+ 60,000
2	+ 40,000	+ 60,000	+ 60,000
3	+ 60,000	+ 60,000	+ 60,000
4	+ 60,000	+ 40,000	+ 60,000
5	+ 60,000		+ 40,000
6	+ 68,000		+ 20,000
Total profit	£108,000	£40,000	+£100,000
Payback period (ranking BCA)	$4^1/_3$ years	3 years	$3^1/_3$ years
Accounting rate of return (ranking ACB)	18%	10%	16.7%
NPV at 12% (ranking CAB)	− £884	− £12,580	+ £15,100
IRR (ranking CAB)	12%	8.5%	15%

Figure 17.9 *Appraisal methods compared*

The payback method selects project B as the most attractive investment, but ignores the short life remaining after payback is completed. This is taken into account, however, by the IRR method which shows up project B in its true light as the least profitable of all three projects.

The rate of return method selects project A as the most profitable simply because the average profit per year is more than in the other two projects. When the timing of those profits is taken into account then project A is shown to give an IRR, or true return, of only 12 per cent compared with its accounting rate of return of 18 per cent.

When project A is compared with project C on the IRR method the extra £8,000 profit on project A does not compensate for the slow build-up of the project. Even though total profit is £8,000 less on project C, the project is more profitable than project A because discounting emphasizes the value of the earlier high returns.

In short, payback can yield useful information but must not be used by itself. Either discounting method will give more accurate results than the rate of return method when assessing the profitability of an investment over its whole life. Firms may sometimes calculate the rate of return expected in the first year of operation and compare this with the actual return earned for monitoring purposes. This monitoring or post-audit appraisal is an important part of project investment. However, the complexities of taxation, grants, working capital and other items reduce the validity of the accounting rate of return method in many cases.

RANKING OF PROJECTS

There are two ways to rank projects in order of attractiveness when using discounting techniques. The simplest is to rank them by the size of their IRRs subject to the rules governing the two special situations mentioned below.

When firms use the NPV method, the size of the NPV surplus is not related to the amount of capital invested to earn that surplus. To compare the relative profitability of projects on the NPV method we go a step further and calculate a *profitability index* by dividing the NPV of the inflows by the original investment.

$$\text{Profitability index} \quad = \quad \frac{\text{NPV of inflows}}{\text{Capital invested}}$$

Example
Taking project C in Figure 17.9 as illustration, the NPV inflows totalled £215,100 and the capital invested £200,000, giving a profitability index of 1.0755. Any project is viable when the profitability index exceeds 1.000, but its relative profitability against other projects can be measured by the size of the index number.

Care must be taken when ranking in two special situations:

- capital rationing; and
- choice between mutually exclusive projects.

The selection of projects when capital is insufficient to finance all projects immediately should be based on the profitability index of the projects competing for those scarce funds. This allocates the capital available to those projects which return the most NPV. When a choice has to be made between alternative projects which are mutually exclusive, it should be based on the size of the NPV – either the highest NPV surplus, or the least NPV deficit, as appropriate.

TAXATION

When appraising the worthwhile nature of any investment, the effects of tax must be taken into account. The payment of tax on profits is offset to some extent by tax allowances on certain new assets acquired. These tax transactions must be incorporated into the yearly cash flows after allowing for any time lag on the payment of tax as explained in Chapter 21. Tax allowances reduce the tax liability of the company as a whole, and are therefore subject to the same time lag as tax payments.

Example
A medium-sized company is proposing to buy a machine for £100,000 at the beginning of its accounting year. Based on past experience, the machine is expected to last four years. Taxable profits are estimated at £45,000 each year comprising sales less operating costs ignoring depreciation. The firm pays tax at

30 per cent and gets 25 per cent pa capital allowances on the machine on a reducing balance basis. Assume a one-year time lag for tax payments and a two-year lag for tax savings. The cash flows for this project can be set out as in Figure 17.10 and would then be discounted in the normal way at the company's target rate.

Year	Investment	Taxable profit	Tax paid at 30%	Capital allowance (memo only)	Tax saved on allowance	Net cash flow
	£	£	£		£	£
0	− 100,000					− 100,000
1		+ 45,000		25,000		+ 45,000
2		+ 45,000	− 13,500	18,750	+ 7,500	+ 39,000
3		+ 45,000	− 13,500	14,063	+ 5,625	+ 37,125
4		+ 45,000	− 13,500	42,187	+ 4,219	+ 35,719
5			− 13,500		*+12,656	− 844

Note: *all remaining allowances claimed on short-life asset

Figure 17.10 *Cash flows incorporating 30 per cent corporation tax*

INFLATION

Up to this point the investment appraisal techniques discussed have implicitly ignored the existence of inflation and its effects on the future cash flows of projects being appraised. Inflation brings additional problems to project appraisals. It increases the uncertainty and makes more difficult the estimation of the future cash flows of sales revenue, operating costs and working capital requirements. It also influences the required rate of return through its effects on the nominal cost of capital.

In the context of investment appraisals it means that two aspects of the value of money must be considered. The time value of money has already been catered for by the use of present value factors which deduct interest for the time elapsed when waiting for future cash receipts. The other aspect is the change in the value of money itself, not because of the time lapse, but because the inflationary process decreases its purchasing power.

Real and nominal rates of return

When describing how to allow for inflation in investment appraisals, and cope with both these aspects, it is useful first to distinguish between the real rate of return on a project and its nominal rate of return. A simple example may clarify this difference between real and nominal rates of return.

Example
Suppose investors receive an income of £50 pa on an investment of £1,000. Their nominal rate of return is 5 per cent. If inflation is zero then the real rate of return will also be 5 per cent. If, however, inflation is running at 3 per cent pa then the

real rate of return is approximately the nominal rate minus the rate of inflation which leaves only 2 per cent:

$$\text{Real rate of return } 0.02\ (2\%) = \left\{ \frac{\text{Nominal rate of return } 1.05}{\text{Rate of inflation } 1.03} \right\} - 1$$

or

$$\text{Nominal rate of return } 0.05\ (5\%) = \left\{ \frac{\text{Real rate of return} \times \text{Rate of inflation}}{1.02 \qquad\qquad 1.03} \right\} - 1$$

Again, if inflation is running at 7 per cent pa then the nominal rate of return of 5 per cent is swamped by inflation and the investors get a negative real rate of return of about 2 per cent. This experience was all too painful for small investors way back in the 1970s, and some of the 1980s, when the rate of inflation frequently exceeded the rate of interest received on bank or building-society deposits and other similar investments.

Turning to an industrial context, a company's return on capital is the annual pre-tax and pre-interest profit expressed as a percentage of the capital employed in the business. This is a nominal rate of return. The real return on investment will be this nominal return less the rate of inflation.

The real and nominal rates of return referred to here for the whole company are not strictly correct because the concept of profit is not identical with that of cash flow. This is because profit ignores the timing of cash receipts and payments and can arise when cash is not even received. It is important to recognize that the company's one-year return on investment is conceptually different from the whole life project return based on the timing of cash flows.

It is far from uncommon for a wholly satisfactory project with a high estimated return to have an adverse effect on the company profit and loss account, particularly in the first year or two. This is because the initial investment costs show as depreciation and interest charges before revenue and profits start to flow at their full rate.

In the case of individual project appraisals, the nominal rate of return is the IRR found when discounting future cash flows that have been inflated to take account of anticipated inflation. The real rate of return on such a project, however, is this nominal rate of return minus the rate of inflation. If future cash flows on a project have been expressed in the constant value of Year 0 purchasing power, then the solution IRR is the real rate of return.

At appraisal time we are, therefore, faced with a choice whether to express future cash flows at their inflated values and find the nominal rate of return, or alternatively to express them in the constant purchasing power as at Year 0 and find the real rate of return. What influences us as to which choice to make depends on how top management express the target rate of return, and whether we see the future cash flows keeping pace with inflation or not.

Most firms will probably express the target rate of return in nominal rather than real terms. This is because the target rate is often based on the nominal costs of borrowing or the opportunity cost of alternative financial investments. If tax is incorporated in appraisals, no allowance is made for inflation so this is another argument for using nominal terms. What is important is that we do not mismatch targets with the way cash flows are expressed. Figure 17.11 summarizes the rules:

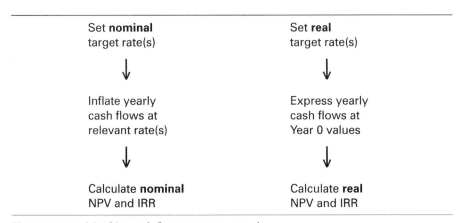

Set **nominal** target rate(s)	Set **real** target rate(s)
↓	↓
Inflate yearly cash flows at relevant rate(s)	Express yearly cash flows at Year 0 values
↓	↓
Calculate **nominal** NPV and IRR	Calculate **real** NPV and IRR

Figure 17.11 *Matching cash flows to target rates of return*

Calculating nominal cash flows

If the cash flow model is expressed in nominal terms to be discounted at a nominal target rate of return, a good starting point is to express the model initially in real terms at today's prices. These real cash flows can then be converted to nominal cash flows in two ways:

- by using the compound interest table found in Appendix 4; and
- by using a built-in function on a computer spreadsheet.

When a compound interest table is used, the present-day value of a cash flow is multiplied by the appropriate compound interest factor for the future year in question at the estimated rate of inflation for that period. Different rates of inflation can be applied to different future years if inflation is not expected to occur at a constant rate. In this case, inflation is cumulated year by year at different rates.

Example
A company makes a sales estimate for each of the next two years of £850,000, all at today's prices. Inflation is expected to be 2 per cent in the first year and 4 per cent in the second year. Find the nominal values for each year.

Year 1: £850,000 x 1.020 = £867,000

Year 2: £867,000 x 1.040 = £901,680

The same result can be achieved on a spreadsheet by applying the *series growth rate* for a specified number of years and repeating the process when that rate changes for a subsequent period of time.

UNCERTAINTY

In most industrial investment appraisals there is no certainty that the eventual outcome will be exactly as predicted at the time of the appraisal. Any one of a number of variables can turn out to have been incorrectly estimated. Variables in this context include capital cost; estimated life; yearly savings/profit; inflation rate; tax rate; residual values. There are a number of methods that can be used to reduce the inevitable risk and uncertainty. These include:

- set a short payback period;
- produce two further sets of cash flows based on optimistic and pessimistic assumptions;
- use a spreadsheet to perform sensitivity analysis on key variables;
- draw up a decision tree incorporating probability theory and present values;
- vary the discount rate with the risk category of the project under review.

In terms of application in the real world, *sensitivity analysis* is widely adopted in practice. Spreadsheets allow the value of one variable to be changed independently to the extent of its perceived range of inaccuracy from the original estimate. This could be caused by either inflation or a different level of activity. This process is repeated for each variable in turn and helps to identify the key variables that most affect the NPV or IRR of the project. Once they are found, more time can be spent on refining the value of key variables, or in redesigning the project to be less dependent on the key variables.

CAPITAL BUDGET

Capital expenditure on individual projects often entails the spending of relatively large sums of money which would not be possible unless the financing had been carefully planned. Sources of funds include:

- *depreciation* – which in effect allows some profit to be retained for asset replacements;
- *retained profit* – most companies do not distribute all profit as dividends;
- *new borrowing* – loans, debentures, mortgages etc, provided gearing is not excessive;
- *share issues* – a rights issue or open offer may be needed if other avenues are closed.

In medium- to large-sized companies, a capital budget is prepared at the same time that revenue and cash budgets are considered. Very often, more projects are put forward for inclusion in the coming year's capital budget than the funds available. One way forward may be to allocate funds to main programme areas before getting down to the selection of individual projects.

Example
A company has budgeted a maximum of £7.7 million funds available for capital investment in the coming year. Outline requests for authorization amount to £8.7

million, being £1 million more than the total budget. Top management decide to allocate the available funds as shown in Figure 17.12.

Investment category	Amount requested £	Amount allocated £	%
Legal/safety requirements	0.2m	0.2m	100.0
Replacements	1.0m	0.8m	80.0
Cost saving/efficiency	2.5m	1.7m	68.0
New products	5.0m	5.0m	100.0
Total	8.7m	7.7m	88.5

Figure 17.12 *Allocation of capital budget across categories*

The implications of this budget are that top management remain committed to meeting safety and legal requirements in full and to implementing new products as part of their corporate strategy. This leaves insufficient funds for the remaining two categories and they have had to be trimmed back. Selection of specific projects here will be based on the size of their profitability index in line with earlier ideas on capital rationing.

USE OF COMPUTERS

Any manager having to carry out investment appraisals on a regular basis will find a personal computer indispensable. Either a dedicated program to a specific company application or a general spreadsheet will perform the required calculations of NPV and IRR in next to no time. The hardest task will be to enter the basic cash flow information. When repeated runs on varied assumptions of cash flows are required (financial modelling, as it is termed), a computer can recalculate NPVs and IRRs almost instantly, so saving hours of manual effort.

Spreadsheets lend themselves to the matrix layout needed to set out cash flows over the life of an investment. Years go along one axis and the various cash flow items down the other axis. This forms a grid in which the values are entered in relevant cells. In this way, information in any cell can be subjected to arithmetical and discount calculations, which are built-in functions on most spreadsheets, without having to key in present value factors.

RESEARCH FINDINGS

Drury *et al* (1993), in their survey of management accounting practices in UK manufacturing companies, found that 63 per cent of respondents often/always used the undiscounted payback period, 57 per cent the IRR method and 43 per cent the NPV method, with some using multiple appraisal techniques. The relative attractiveness of payback is its ease of calculation and communication to other managers. It is also useful for risk-averse companies to see the capital investment returned within a year or two. One worrying feature of the survey was the high level (44 per cent) of respondents mismatching real cash flows with a nominal discount rate, thereby underestimating the profitability of a project.

Further reading

Drury, C *et al* (1993) *A Survey of Management Accounting Practices in UK Manufacturing Companies,* ACCA, London.
Drury, C (1996) *Management and Cost Accounting,* ITP, London.
Mott, G (1997) *Investment Appraisal,* FT/Pitman, London.
Samuels, M, Wilkes, FM and Brayshaw, RE (1995) *Management of Company Finance,* ITP, London.

Self-check questions

1. What are the situations where an investment appraisal is relevant?
2. What is the payback period for the annual cash flows contained in Figure 17.3?
3. What is the present value of £4,000 receivable in three years' time if the cost of capital is 12 per cent?
4. What is the net present value of an investment of £20,000 now, with an annual cash return of £5,000 for each of 10 years, if the cost of capital is 15 per cent?
5. What is the IRR on the example in Question 4?
6. Interpolate the IRR when the NPV surplus is £45,000 at 15 per cent and the NPV deficit is £25,000 at 20 per cent.
7. Is it worth buying a new machine costing £10,000 if it is expected to save £3,000 each year over a five-year life? The cost of capital is 14 per cent and the organization is not subject to corporation tax.
8. Differentiate between a real rate of return and a nominal rate of return.
9. What is the real IRR on an investment of £30,000, expected to produce an annual return of £8,000, rising in line with inflation, over its six-year life?

18

Managing working capital

INTRODUCTION

The capital of a company is employed in two distinct areas. Some of it goes to provide the permanent or fixed assets, such as buildings, plant and vehicles. The remainder goes to provide the working capital necessitated by having to pay for the cost of goods and services before recovering that money from customers.

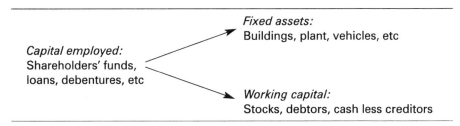

Figure 18.1   *The employment of capital*

A variation on the funding of working capital described in Figure 18.1 is to use short-term debt to finance stocks and debtors for the excess not covered by trade creditors. This may be the cheapest and most flexible method, but carries higher risk because renewal of bank overdraft facilities is never guaranteed.

Working capital is the value of all the current assets less the value of the current liabilities. It therefore includes the cost of stocks of raw materials, work-in-progress and finished goods, together with the amount owed by customers, less the amount owed to suppliers and other creditors:

$$\boxed{\text{Working capital}} = \boxed{\text{Stocks}} + \boxed{\text{Debtors}} + \boxed{\text{Cash}} - \boxed{\text{Creditors}}$$

The key to managing working capital successfully is to find the right balance between liquidity and profitability. A firm needs to be liquid enough to pay the wages and other bills when required, but on the other hand it needs to carry sufficient stocks so that production is not unduly disrupted nor customers dissatisfied with 'stock-outs'. Both these requirements can be met given unlimited working capital, but much of the stock would be idle for long periods of time. This means that profit would be lost due to the extra holding costs of large stocks and the interest costs of the capital involved. Therefore, we have to strike a balance between profitability and liquidity, recognizing that they pull in opposite directions.

How much working capital is needed is obviously related to the volume of business, namely, the level of sales. If we divide the annual sales by the amount of working capital, we find out how many times the working capital went round or circulated during the year.

Example
A company had sales last year of £2 million and average working capital of £0.5 million so working capital circulated four times during the year.

This circulation process is shown in Figure 18.2.

Figure 18.2 *The working capital cycle of a manufacturing firm*

For an existing company we can find the working capital requirement from the relationship of working capital to sales. In the example mentioned above, working capital represented 25 per cent of annual sales. Put another way, the firm needed £0.25 working capital for every £1 of sales. If this is typical of that firm's experience during the year and not an atypical year-end situation, we can say that for every £1 change in sales there will be a £0.25 change in working capital requirement. This may seem a crude relationship, but it will give accurate enough results for some practical purposes.

Another way the working capital requirement can be determined is from the length of the operating cycle. This term refers to the length of time between the company first paying out cash on materials, wages and overheads and the eventual receipt of cash from the sale of the goods or services produced. In basic terms, the longer the operating cycle, the more working capital that will be required and the lower the return on capital achieved. Conversely, the shorter the cycle, the less working capital will be required and the return on capital enhanced. The calculation of the operating cycle is shown in Figure 18.3 using hypothetical figures as an illustration.

	Weeks
Average time raw materials stay in stock	7
(–) Credit period granted by suppliers	(6)
	1
(+) Average time taken to produce the goods/services	3
(+) Average time finished goods stay in stock	2
(+) Average time customers take to pay	7
= Total length of operating cycle	13

Figure 18.3 *Length of the operating cycle*

Having determined the length of the operating cycle, a firm can calculate the maximum working capital requirement from the sales forecast for that length of time. Using the above example of a 13-week cycle, if sales are forecast at £2 million for the coming year, then £0.5 million (ie 13/52 x £2m) working capital will be required. This ignores the possibility of seasonal fluctuations when the £2 million sales would not be evenly spread over the year. Similarly the working capital required will also fluctuate in advance of the fluctuation in the level of sales. Also ignored is the possibility of a strategic change in stock levels.

The above calculation exaggerates due to the profit element in sales. Strictly speaking, the proportion should be applied to the cost of sales and not the full selling price.

A guide as to whether a firm has sufficient working capital and a viable mix of constituent items can be obtained from a look at two ratios previously met in Chapter 9. The *current ratio* of current assets to current liabilities looks for a norm of 2:1 or slightly less, ie there should be £2 of current assets for every £1 of current liabilities. It may appear that this is an arbitrary figure but it has long been regarded by business people as reasonable. The premise is that half of the current assets are stocks and therefore not quickly turned into cash to pay the current liabilities.

Excluding stocks from current assets leaves us with liquid assets and here we look for the obvious 1:1 ratio. Notwithstanding, it is quite easy to find examples of companies operating quite happily on ratios below this or below the 2:1 current ratio. One reason is that bank overdrafts are included in current liabilities, but unless they are called in they are not a current liability in the normal sense of the word. Also firms may have unused overdraft facilities with which to counter an apparently unsatisfactory liquidity position.

In some industries it is quite usual to meet adverse current ratios of less than 2:1 and this may be due to their individual circumstances. An example of this occurs in both food retailing and construction if stocks or work-in-progress are turned into cash before trade creditors have to be paid. In the past, supermarket operators have financed the acquisition of new premises from the credit obtained from food manufacturers, whose produce they have sold for cash before the manufacturers' invoices were due to be paid.

There are other reasons why the long-standing norms for current and acid-test ratios may not be so relevant. This relates to the moves to just-in-time with regard to purchasing stocks, and the increasing use of factoring customer debts. Both these topics are discussed later in this chapter. Having looked at working capital requirements in total, let us now examine how each constituent part is best managed.

THE MANAGEMENT OF CASH

There are a number of factors that have a bearing on the amount of cash a company needs to hold at any one time. Foremost will be its forecast of future cash inflows and outflows compiled in a cash budget. Another factor is the amount of liquid resources (if any) that can be converted quickly back into cash or the existence of agreed overdraft facilities. A budgeted cash flow statement can alternatively be used to predict future cash requirements. These two financial statements are now discussed.

Cash budget

This is the more detailed statement showing all the cash receipts and payments for the coming year broken down into monthly intervals. A typical example appears in Figure 18.4 containing the cash transactions we might expect to find in a manufacturing business. The layout illustrated makes it easier to compile and ensures rapid assimilation of the information.

When compiling the cash budget it is essential to allow for the time lags on transactions. If a firm finds that credit customers take an average of eight weeks to settle their account, then sales that take place in month one will appear as a cash inflow in month three. Similarly, purchases will not be paid for in the month of purchase but in a later month, depending on the credit period obtained from suppliers. Note also the absence of depreciation from a cash budget. The reasoning here is that depreciation is a *notional* expense, not one that is paid in cash terms.

Month	1	2	3	4	5	6	7	8	9	10	11	12	Total
Cash inflows:													
Sales													
Grant													
Total inflows													
Cash outflows:													
Wages													
Purchases													
Salaries													
Services													
Capital exp.													
Tax													
Dividends													
Total outflows													
Monthly +/–													
Cumulative +/–													

Figure 18.4 *A detailed cash budget*

Budgeted cash flow statement

The other instrument which helps to manage cash is the budgeted cash flow statement. It might be thought that this is similar to the cash budget, but there are important distinctions. If we refer back to Figure 5.2 in Chapter 5, the cash flow statement is a summary of the detailed cash transactions.

The first entry, for example, shows the cash flow from operating activities, of which profit is the main constituent item. The cash budget, on the other hand, details the individual items of income and expenditure making up that profit. The cash flow statement also shows items when they are paid for, and not when they were initially incurred and entered in the profit and loss account. The cash flow statement is therefore very useful in identifying the causes of the change in the liquid position. It highlights changes in stocks and debtors and in the level of investing activities, or new financing, for example, which are not obvious from the cash budget which simply records in detail the planned receipts and payments of cash.

Surpluses and deficits

Armed with these two statements, we should now know the size, duration and causes of potential surpluses or deficits of cash. Short-term cash surpluses of a few months' duration should be invested short-term to earn more profit while being capable of being turned back into cash when required. Examples are the purchase of tax reserve certificates, Treasury bills or other short-dated government stocks or investment on the London money market.

The taking of cash discounts for early payment to suppliers may be advisable if the annual rate of interest so earned exceeds that available on financial investments. If a surplus is disclosed that is expected to continue in later years, thought must be given to using this in the expansion or diversification of the existing business or in the acquisition of new businesses.

Forecast cash deficits obviously pose more of a problem than cash surpluses. A short-term deficit lasting only a few months will be disclosed in a cash budget and explained in the forecast sources and applications of funds. If the cause is a seasonal increase in stocks and debtors then the evidence of these statements will usually persuade the bank manager to extend overdraft facilities. Failing this, the firm may have to trim stocks, renegotiate credit terms, defer capital expenditure and somehow level out the peak cash outflows.

Long-term cash deficits are caused by a move to an increased volume of business, large capital expenditure programmes, or simply the effects of inflation which require more cash to finance the same activities. Such events have to be met by introducing new long-term capital. This may take the form of a rights issue of new shares, or a loan or debenture repayable over a number of years, or in full on redemption. Sale and leaseback of valuable premises may be a 'one-off' way of releasing funds for other uses but the rent will reduce profits in much the same way as would interest on a loan.

THE MANAGEMENT OF DEBTORS

Apart from retail shops, most UK companies sell on credit, so their managers must decide whom to sell to, on what terms and how to follow up late payments. Credit management is yet another balancing act where the gain from allowing credit to customers (profit on sale) is offset by the costs of interest, discounts, administration and bad debts.

Creditworthiness

When another firm applies for credit as a potential customer it would be rash indeed to agree credit without checking on creditworthiness. This can be done by employing a suitable credit agency like Dun & Bradstreet, or it can be carried out by the firm's own staff. Checks should include talking to other suppliers who have been quoted as trade references and checking bank references. Unfortunately, the latter may say little more than the length of time the account has been operated.

Sales representatives may form an opinion by calling at the potential client's premises and they may also hear valuable information on the informal grapevine. A copy of the client's annual accounts can be requested and perused using ratio analysis techniques to look at the profitability, liquidity and debt capacity. If an existing customer requests a higher credit limit, then his or her track record on prompt payment, or otherwise, can easily be checked.

193

Terms of sale

Having decided whom to sell to, a firm must now decide the terms of sale, being the length of the credit period and whether to offer cash discounts for early payment. The length of credit period is often settled by the normal terms for that particular industry. Firms compete with one another for custom and it would be difficult for one firm to impose a shorter credit period than its competitors, unless it had some compensating advantages. Typical credit terms demand payment by the end of the following month to that invoiced, which means a period of between four and eight weeks' credit.

Cash discounts are a way of stimulating early payment, thereby reducing the amount of working capital required. The disadvantages lie in the cost and administrative burden.

Example

If a cash discount of 2 per cent is offered for payment of invoice within two weeks, this may persuade customers to accept instead of taking a further four weeks' credit. A discount of 2 per cent for four weeks is equivalent to an annual rate of 26 per cent. If credit customers would have taken a further six weeks to pay after the expiry of the discount period then the 2 per cent discount is equivalent to an annual rate of 17 per cent.

Early payment induced by cash discounts will reduce profits, but it may be largely compensated by not having to borrow so much capital. The effective annual rate of cash discounts can therefore be compared with the cost of bank overdrafts or loans, which would be needed to finance the longer credit period taken when discounts are not offered.

The other factor to consider is administration and the loss of goodwill when disputes arise. Customers may claim cash discounts even though the cash is received after the end of the discount period. Sorting out this kind of problem can negate some of the advantages of early payment. Some firms offer a tapering discount/penalty scheme where the cash discount reduces in steps as the normal credit period shortens, but after that a stepped penalty is added to the invoice value according to the lateness of payment. An example of this approach is shown in Figure 18.5.

Payment within 2 weeks of invoice 3% discount
Payment within 4 weeks of invoice 2% discount
Payment within 6 weeks of invoice 1% discount
Payment after 6 weeks of invoice 1% penalty
Payment after 8 weeks of invoice 2% penalty

Figure 18.5 *Discount/ penalty scheme*

Follow-up procedure

Having sold to credit customers and specified the payment terms, we must consider what follow-up procedure to adopt with late payers. A suitable sequence might include:

- monthly statement;
- reminder letter;
- threatening letter;
- stop on further supplies;
- legal action.

Many firms use a monthly statement, both as a reminder and for the customer to check the balance on his or her account. If payment is not forthcoming in the stipulated time, a reminder letter should be sent followed by a more strongly worded letter about a fortnight later. Should payment still not be received, consideration should be given to terminating supplies and instituting legal action, and the customer informed accordingly.

Legal action for the recovery of the debt is appropriate where the debt is small or where the sale was subject to an unresolved dispute and the client's ability to pay is not in doubt. Where the debt is large and the customer's ability to pay is now in doubt, it may be more appropriate to bring matters to a head by applying to have the company wound up. Outstanding debtors' invoices are normally classed as unsecured creditors in a liquidation and therefore come nearly last in the order of payment. A *retention of title clause* in the contract of sale may help to recover goods for which payment has not been received. Consideration can also be given to taking out some kind of trade indemnity insurance against bad debts as a matter of policy.

Legislation is being considered which may allow small businesses to claim interest on overdue accounts. This may seem a helpful move, but is subject to criticism on the grounds that it may sour the trading relationship and also not necessarily bring in the value of the invoice that may be needed to keep the supplier afloat.

Use of computers

In this era of information technology, firms should have all the necessary information about customers' debts to hand. The overall debtor's position can be judged by the age analysis of invoices shown in Figure 18.6.

It can be seen that 14 per cent of total debtors have exceeded the stipulated time allowed. Not all of this will be deliberate slow payment or potential bad debts, but will be partly caused by inflexible payment procedures in the client firms. This overdue proportion (14 per cent) can be monitored against previous experience to identify trend movements and indicate a change in follow-up policy.

Apart from the overall debtors' picture, a print-out of individual overdue accounts for each customer is essential, with indicators of the follow-up stage reached in each case. Of particular concern will be the seven accounts which are more than three months' old. If an age analysis is not available, a rough guide to the credit period can be found by using the debtors days ratio

Duration from invoice date	% of total debtors	Cumulative total %	Number of accounts
0–14 days	28%	28%	264
15–28 "	25%	53%	205
29–42 "	19%	72%	147
43–56 " Due date	14%	86%	82 Due date
57–70 "	7%	93%	38
71–84 "	4%	97%	16
85–98 "	2%	99%	20
99+"	1%	100%	7

Figure 18.6 *Age analysis of debtors' invoices*

discussed in Chapter 9, which will indicate the efficiency of credit control when compared with the period allowed.

Before accounts become seriously overdue, there are a number of possible warning signals that might be observed. These include:

- bounced cheque;
- part-payment;
- post-dated cheque;
- lost in the post.

Factoring and invoice discounting

These are specialist finance services that provide working capital secured against the client's customers' invoices. The practice has been growing at an annual rate of some 20 per cent in recent years and long lost its tag as a 'last resort' source of finance. Its growth has come at the expense of short-term bank facilities which often caused problems for smaller enterprises at times of recession and weakened their chances of survival when support was withdrawn.

Factors will typically pay up to 85 per cent of invoice value immediately, with the balance, less fees and interest charges, after the customer settles the invoice in due course.

The main advantages of entering into a factoring/discounting arrangement are:

- to ease cash flow by substantially reducing the working capital requirement for credit sales;
- to finance the expansion of the business without *overtrading;*
- to ease the administration and management of customers' accounts and debts;
- to provide cover against possible bad debts.

Factoring is the term used when the service provided embraces full management of customer accounts and sales ledger as well as the provision of finance. It can be either *recourse* or *non-recourse factoring* depending on whether the bad debt risk is borne by the client or by the factor. Service charges are a small percentage of turnover, say 1–3 per cent plus interest charges of maybe 3 per cent, on the money advanced. Savings in the time saved by the client's accountancy staff will offset the service charge to some extent.

Invoice discounting is a more limited service than factoring, concentrated on the provision of finance against customer invoices, often without the client's customers' knowledge – hence the term confidential invoice discounting. Fees for this service may be less than 0.5 per cent of invoice value plus interest charges on the money advanced, somewhat similar to bank overdraft rates. The client remains responsible for bad debts. Invoice discounting is proving more popular even than factoring.

THE MANAGEMENT OF CREDITORS

Trade creditors are debts owed to suppliers of goods and services in whose books they appear as debtors. The policy for dealing with creditors is very straightforward and mirrors that of debtors. If no cash discounts are offered then the full credit period should be taken. To do otherwise, by making an earlier payment, would reduce the profit by increasing the amount of working capital which had to be financed by borrowed capital with consequent interest payments.

If cash discounts are offered then the decision, like with debtors, is whether the effective *annual* rate of interest earned by the discount exceeds the cost of capital used up by the early payment.

Example
When a 2 per cent cash discount is allowed for payment one month earlier than normal, this equates to an annual rate of 24 per cent. Provided the cost of available overdrafts, loans, or other sources of capital is less than 24 per cent, it will be beneficial to take the cash discount.

An overall check on the period of credit taken can be found from the ratio that calculates *creditors days*. This relates trade creditors to purchases in the following way:

$$\text{Creditors days} = \frac{\text{Trade creditors} \times 365}{\text{Purchases}}$$

Example
If creditors were £80,000 and the year's purchases £320,000, this equates to 91 days' credit taken from suppliers.

Creditors days will serve as a reasonable guide provided the creditors figure is not abnormally high or low at the time it is observed. Problems arise when examining other companies' published accounts with a view to calculating this creditor's payment period. First, the figure of trade creditors has to be found in the appropriate note to the accounts relating to all creditors due for payment within one year. This trade creditors figure should now be divided by 1.175 to eliminate VAT, which will apply to all but the smallest of businesses. The next step is to derive a purchases figure as this is unlikely to be disclosed, even in the most detailed notes accompanying the accounts. An approximation of the cost of buying-in materials and services can be calculated by subtracting value added from sales. Both these figures would usually exclude VAT in the published accounts, so no adjustment is necessary. See Chapter 8 if you need to recapitulate on value added!

THE MANAGEMENT OF STOCKS

When looking at the current ratio we saw that the assumption is made that stocks represent half of current assets in the case of manufacturing companies. The management and control of stocks is therefore crucial to the level of working capital at all times. There are three possible kinds of stocks in manufacturing industries:

- raw materials;
- work-in-progress;
- finished goods.

All three are likely to be present unless the product is made to a customer's one-off specification, which virtually eliminates finished goods stock. Rather surprisingly, the longest production cycles do not always involve a build-up of working capital. This happens when progress payments are received at frequent intervals, so utilizing the customer's capital instead.

In service industries physical stocks are not so prevalent, but work-in-progress in the form of wages, salaries and overheads may be very significant. Architect firms, for example, are paid *pro rata* to the value of building work done, but many months of work are put in at the design stage when no money may be received from clients.

In an ideal situation firms would need no stocks. Raw materials would be delivered daily; production would be completed the same day; and the finished goods would immediately be sold and delivered to customers. This situation is not usual in practice (but see JIT later) because firms buy in bulk to reduce the unit cost of purchases and to hold some stock as an insurance against non-delivery.

Production is not completed the same day in some industries. In many cases work-in-progress may consist of a number of stages when the need for buffer stocks and economical production runs leads to an abundance of components. Diverse product ranges result in larger stocks of work-in-progress and finished goods than found in a single-product company.

To ensure that production is never halted for lack of materials or component parts, and that customers are never dissatisfied, might entail holding very large stocks. The working capital tied up in this way ensures that firms produce and sell efficiently, but profits are offset by the costs of warehousing, possible deterioration and, most significantly, the interest on the capital tied up in stocks.

Economic order quantity (EOQ)

Managing stocks requires balancing these conflicting factors. It means setting stock levels to allow for nominal delivery times plus a small buffer stock for safety. This is achieved by calculating the re-order level which, on normal usage, will reduce the buffer stock level by the time delivery has been achieved.

Example
A company uses 200 kg of material X per week and delivery takes three weeks. The re-order level will be the buffer stock plus 600 kg.

The other balancing act occurs when setting the economic order quantity (EOQ). When buying in large quantities, extra discounts and reduced ordering and handling costs will be achieved, but these advantages are offset by the increased interest and storage costs. Conversely, if frequent orders are placed, interest and storage costs will be reduced, but ordering, handling and the unit purchase cost will increase. A formula is available for solving EOQ, where:

A = annual usage in units
S = ordering/handling cost per order
i   = cost of carrying stock as a %
C = unit cost of the stock item.

$$EOQ = \sqrt{(2AS/iC)}$$

Just-in-time (JIT)

Long-term contracts can be negotiated with suppliers whereby very frequent deliveries of small quantities are made, just sufficient to meet immediate production requirements. In some instances a number of deliveries are made daily. Both parties can benefit from this. Suppliers can plan ahead with greater certainty when they possess a long-term contract. They are also likely to receive payment on time, when the transfer of funds may be linked to delivery dates plus an agreed credit period.

The buyer also gains from introducing just-in-time systems of procurement. Safety stocks can be reduced or eliminated; stockholding costs are reduced if delivery is made directly to the point of production; savings also arise if the onus is placed on the supplier to meet specified quality standards, hence eliminating inspection and testing costs for the buyer.

The old adversarial relationship between customer and supplier is less appropriate in a JIT environment where shared goals are crucial to the avoidance of disruption caused by lack of parts. The emphasis now is one of long-term partnership, with as reduced a number of suppliers as possible conducive to efficiency.

Japanese-owned firms in the UK, like Nissan, for example, have perfected JIT techniques and achieved some of the highest productivity rates in Europe.

Material requirements purchasing (MRP)

The above formula for EOQ assumes demand is reasonably constant whereas in fact it may fluctuate considerably. This means that stock levels are much higher than they need be for considerable periods of time. Instead of estimating demand from past experience, *material requirements purchasing* is based on what needs to be purchased or manufactured to fulfil the planned level of production, to meet actual or expected orders from customers.

The demand for components to satisfy production needs is reduced by the stock-in-hand, and the net balance, when compared with the supply picture, determines when to initiate the order. Unwanted stock is not kept for long periods under this MRP system and the reduction in finance, storage and obsolescence costs can be considerable. Computers make the operation of this system feasible even when large numbers of components are involved.

Manufacturing resource planning (MRP II)

Manufacturing resource planning (MRP II) is a development of MRP and generates a master production schedule based on actual or expected orders in a forward period of time. Subject to adjustment for capacity constraints, MRP is then run to produce a *bill of materials* which leads to material orders from suppliers and a production plan for when to start jobs.

Darlington and Moar writing in CIMA's *Management Accounting* (October 1996) offer a critique of MRP II and its use in a market significantly changed since its introduction 20 years ago. One possible alternative system mentioned here is *optimized production technology* (OPT) which has been in use by manufacturing companies during the last 10 years.

Further reading

Brealey, RA and Myers, SC (1996) *Principles of Corporate Finance*, McGraw-Hill, New York
Darlington, J and Moar, C (1996) MRP rest in peace, *Management Accounting*, June.
Samuels, JM, Wilkes, FM and Brayshaw, RE (1995) *Management of Company Finance*, ITP, London.
Pike, R (1998) Managing trade credit to sustain competitive advantage, *Management Accounting*, June.

Self-check questions

1. Define working capital.
2. How can a firm determine the extra working capital required if sales are expected to increase by £100,000 next month and stay at that level?

3. Draw a pro-forma cash budget for the firm of your choice using the layout in Figure 18.4.
4. What checks would you undertake before granting credit to a new trade customer?
5. What is the annual cost of granting cash discounts of 2 per cent if it results in payment five weeks earlier?
6. How many days' credit are being taken by customers when debtors are £57,000 and annual sales are £250,000? Ignore seasonal fluctuations.
7. Name the three possible kinds of stock.
8. What decisions do firms have to take to ensure they do not run out of stocks of materials?
9. What benefits might a buyer expect from moving to just-in-time arrangements with its suppliers?

19

Share values

INTRODUCTION

Share capital is provided by the owners of limited companies, namely the shareholders. We saw in Chapter 4 that there are two main types of shares – *preference shares* and *ordinary shares*. Preference shares carry the right to a fixed rate of dividend before ordinary shareholders receive any dividend. Usually preference shareholders have no further right to an increased dividend, irrespective of the level of profit attained by their company. In a liquidation, preference shareholders receive their capital back before ordinary shareholders get the remainder, always providing that there is any money left for shareholders who are last in this particular queue.

VALUE OF PREFERENCE SHARES

The value of preference shares is therefore dependent on the fixed rate of dividend attached to their particular company's shares, and the relationship of that fixed rate with the current rate offered on new preference shares of a similar risk. If there is a perceived risk of non-payment of dividend, it will depress the market price of the shares. This will be very marked if the situation is expected to last some years and the arrears of dividend are not allowed to be accumulated over this period as is the case with non-cumulative preference shares.

Example
Ignoring the possibility of non-payment, let us consider the 7 per cent £1 preference shares in XYZ Ltd when the current rate of dividend being offered on similar new shares is 10 per cent. Obviously no one will pay £1 for existing shares giving them a 7 per cent return when they can buy new shares offering a 10 per cent return. The price of the 7 per cent shares will fall to a level where the holder receives a 10 per cent return.

$$\text{Preference share value} = £1 \times \frac{7\%}{10\%} = 70\text{p}$$

Where special voting rights attach to preference shares or where repayment is drawing close then the share price will reflect these factors. For tax reasons, new issues of preference shares are now uncommon and our main concern is with the value of a company's ordinary shares.

Convertible preference shares

A special form of preference share came to prominence in the 1980s called a *convertible preference share*. Such shares start their life as conventional preference shares but carry the right to be converted into a specified number of ordinary shares at a later date(s). Convertible preference shares provide an element of gearing into the capital structure and are often used to reduce the dilution of earnings for ordinary shareholders after a takeover of another company.

Unlike normal preference shares, the value of convertible preference shares is not just determined by the fixed rate of dividend it carries. It will also be influenced by the conversion terms; the share price of the ordinary shares; the prospects for the company's profits; and the length of time until the conversion rights expire.

VALUE OF ORDINARY SHARES

There are a number of possible reasons why ordinary shares need to be valued. When a public limited company first offers its shares to the general public it fixes a price at a small discount to what the shares are thought to be worth so as to be fairly sure of selling them all. If a company is taken over, its shares are bought by another company, or an individual, and those shares have to be valued to fix the cash purchase price or the value of any shares issued in exchange.

There are two taxes relating to the wealth owned by individuals subject to certain exemptions that apply. Capital gains tax applies to profits on the sale of shares, while inheritance tax applies to the value of shares given or bequeathed to another person. Normally the relevant value is the stock market price at the time of sale or transfer. In the case of private limited companies which are debarred from a stock market quotation, some other means of valuing shares has to be found.

There are two main approaches to valuing ordinary shares. We can either value them according to the assets backing each share or according to the profits earned by those assets through their use in the business.

Assets basis of valuation

Example
Consider the following balance sheet of EZ Engineering Ltd from which we will calculate the value per share on three different premises – book value, current value and break-up value.

	£000	£000
Fixed assets:		
Land and buildings		350
Machinery, vehicles		700
		1050
Current assets:		
Stocks, work-in-progress	400	
Debtors	250	
	650	
Creditors due within a year:		
Trade creditors	150	
Bank overdraft	200	
	350	
Net current assets		300
Total assets less current liabilities		1350
Creditors due after one year:		
11% Secured loan		400
Net assets		**950**
Capital and reserves:		
Called-up £1 share capital		500
Profit and loss account		450
		950

1. *Book value* – the value of the net assets owned by ordinary shareholders comprises the £1.7 million of fixed and current assets (£1.05 million + £0.65 million) less the £0.75 million total debts to outsiders (£0.35 million + £0.40 million) making £0.95 million. This is of course the same as the value of shareholders' funds which represent the net worth or equity. The net asset value (NAV) per share is the book value of shareholders' funds or assets belonging to shareholders divided by the number of shares issued:

$$\text{Net asset value} = \frac{\text{Share capital} + \text{reserves £950,000}}{\text{Number of shares 500,000}} = \text{£1.90 per share}$$

2. *Current value* – if the assets are valued at their current value to the company on a going concern basis, this will lead to a different value of the shares than that found above. The reason for this is to be found in historic cost accounting. (Refer back to Chapter 7 if you need a refresher!). Suppose the land and buildings in EZ Engineering's balance sheet have just been professionally valued at £550,000, an increase in value of £200,000. If fixed assets are increased by this amount, shareholders' funds also need to be increased by this amount to keep the double entry principle going. Consequently the individual share value increases £0.40 to £2.30 on this current value basis.

3. Break-up value is the third approach to an asset value, as when the assets are sold off one by one when a company stops trading and goes into voluntary liquidation. In this case, book values may not even be realized for some assets, for example, stocks and work-in-progress, but may be exceeded for others, as may be the case with land and buildings.

Using a balance sheet to calculate a share value poses some difficulties, of which the accounting treatment of goodwill in the UK is a case in point. This is dealt with after the other methods of valuing shares have been discussed.

Earnings basis of valuation

The second main approach to valuing ordinary shares is based on the profit after tax attributable to each share. Such profit is referred to as the *earnings per share* (EPS) and represents the total profit (after charging interest, tax, and preference dividends) divided by the number of ordinary shares:

$$\text{Earnings per share} \quad = \quad \frac{\text{Profit attributable to ordinary shareholders}}{\text{Number of ordinary shares}}$$

Example
In the balance sheet of EZ Engineering Ltd earlier, there were 500,000 £1 ordinary shares in existence. Let us now assume that the profit after tax was £150,000, in which case:

$$\text{Earnings per share} \quad = \quad \frac{£150,000}{500,000} \quad = \quad 30\text{p per share}$$

An earnings per share calculated from last year's profit may not be a good guide to the future maintainable profit if last year's performance was in any way abnormal. Companies do occasionally make an annual loss in which case the earnings per share is negative. In both situations an estimate is needed of the future profit and prospective earnings per share for the coming year(s). These are provided by stockbrokers to their clients and a summary is published, for example, in *The Estimate Directory*.

Assuming we know the earnings per share, this is translated into a share value by using a comparative price/earnings (p/e) ratio for other companies in the same field. A p/e ratio relates the earnings per share to the market value of the share as follows:

$$\text{Price/earnings ratio} \quad = \quad \frac{\text{Market price of the share}}{\text{Earnings per share}}$$

In the case of plcs with a stock exchange quotation, these p/e ratios can be found in the financial press or calculated from the company's accounts using the current market price. With unlisted or private companies this market price is non-existent. A merchant bank or trade association can sometimes be approached to advise on a comparative p/e ratio for companies in the same industry with a similar profit record and prospects.

Example

Referring back to EZ Engineering Ltd, we assumed that its earnings per share was 30p. If we now assume that similar small engineering companies have a p/e ratio of about 9 we can derive the share value for EZ Engineering by multiplying the earnings per share by this comparative ratio:

Share value = 30p x 9 = £2.70

This is a higher value than that obtained on the assets basis (£2.30) for the same company, but it would be sheer coincidence if they were identical. This is because share prices tend to fluctuate from day to day, so, therefore, must the p/e ratios as the earnings per share is a constant figure until the next year's profit is known. Companies' share prices tend to be valued more on the basis of future profit and dividend expectations than on the value of the assets they possess. Exceptions to this generalization include property and investment trust companies. Share prices based on earnings are often higher than net asset value, particularly in service industries where profits are more related to the skills of employees than the use of assets.

An examination of p/e ratios in, say, *The Financial Times*, will reveal wide disparities between apparently similar companies operating in the same industry. A favourite example of mine is to compare Marks & Spencer with other stores groups. Generally speaking, Marks & Spencer command a higher p/e ratio than most other store groups (ignoring special recovery situations) because of their proven management skills and track record. Consequently its shares are more highly regarded by investors who are willing to buy at a market price reflecting a much higher p/e ratio than they are prepared to pay for other stores' shares. Investors clearly expect that increased profits in future years will soon bring the p/e ratio down if calculated on the market price at the time of their original purchase.

Another reason why a p/e ratio may appear abnormal in comparison with other companies is when it is calculated on historic earnings per share, which are not expected to be maintained. A company can experience internal problems peculiar to itself, for example, a strike. On the other hand, a company about to launch a new product, for example, a drug manufacturer, will find its share price and p/e ratio very sensitive to new product announcements. This may also be the case even though the new product may take some years to produce actual earnings.

Rumours of an impending takeover may be another reason for an apparently high p/e ratio if earnings on assets are poor and the asset value per share considerably higher than the value based on earnings alone. After a prolonged recession, high p/e ratios may simply be discounting that recovery in profits is about to take place. Conversely, as the economy slips into recession, low p/e ratios reflect that the market price is up to date with events, but the historic earnings per share is not.

Discounted earnings basis of valuation

A theoretically sound approach to valuing ordinary shares is to calculate the present value of the stream of future earnings to perpetuity. This present value approach progressively reduces the worth of future earnings by deducting compound interest for the waiting time, as explained in Chapter 17. The sum of the present value for each year represents the current value of the shares.

For any one firm the discount rate used will be its cost of capital, while for an individual it will be the opportunity cost of the return available on alternative investments. Although useful for valuing securities with a fixed rate of return, it is not so easy in practice for an outsider to estimate future earnings on ordinary shares for most companies.

This discounting approach to share values is at the heart of the concept known as *shareholder value analysis* (SVA), taking a company's true value as the present value of its future cash flows. The use of this approach was enhanced by Rappaport in a publication back in 1986. This pointed to seven key drivers used to calculate the cash inflows and outflows needed in the model. The seven drivers are:

- sales growth rate;
- operating profit margin;
- cash tax rate;
- fixed capital requirements;
- working capital requirements;
- cost of capital;
- planning period.

Operating cash flows for future years are derived from the current year's sales figure by applying growth rates, profit margins and tax rates. Fixed asset and working capital requirements are based on the incremental sales each year. The resultant free cashflows are discounted at the company's cost of capital for the duration of the planning period.

SVA concentrates management's attention on closing the gap between the current share price and its true value by identifying areas to improve operating efficiency. Such measures to enhance shareholder value can be just as effective as either expansion or an increase in the level of gearing.

Goodwill

This topic was briefly mentioned earlier in the context of the asset value of a company's shares, and is now examined in more depth. When a company buys out another company, it takes over the physical assets and debts of that other company. In addition, it takes over the established name of the company which has been built up over a long period of time. The value of that name and reputation is an intangible asset and is known as *goodwill*. Most companies have their own internally generated goodwill, built up over a number of years. It is, however, a difficult thing to value as we cannot say what specific amount has been spent on its creation.

Goodwill will only appear in a balance sheet when it literally has been bought off another company. Usually this is done by taking over another company and paying more for the shares than the fair value of the physical assets acquired, less any debts assumed. The excess represents the payment for goodwill.

Example
In the earlier example of EZ Engineering, £2.30 per share represents the current value of assets owned by shareholders. Assuming EZ's shareholders were paid £2.50 on a takeover, then the purchaser has paid £100,000 (ie 20p x 500,000 shares) for goodwill.

If a company has gone into liquidation it may be possible to buy only the trade name from the liquidator, without taking over any physical assets. In this situation the whole payment represents the cost of goodwill. Sometimes goodwill is calculated as a certain number of years' purchase of profits. This is not a scientific calculation so much as an attempt to measure the purchase cost of goodwill against recent annual profits. In the final analysis, goodwill is worth only the discounted future benefits accruing to the name and reputation acquired.

Accounting standards FRS 10 and 11 specify the accounting treatment of acquired goodwill. In essence it is treated as an intangible fixed asset and written off over its expected useful life. This is similar to the depreciation process when an asset is reduced in value in the balance sheet by transferring some of its cost to the profit and loss account. Exceptionally, if there has been no impairment of the value of goodwill, it is not depreciated in that year.

STOCK EXCHANGE

The stock exchange is a market where financial securities are bought and sold and where, like any other market, the forces of supply and demand determine prices. There are markets in government stocks, major foreign stocks and shares, in addition to the UK company stocks and shares which are our main concern.

The existence of a stock exchange allows companies to tap a wide body of investors. It also allows those investors the means to realize their capital at any time by selling their shares to someone else through the market. The company whose shares are involved is not a party to these dealings other than needing to register the new owner of the shares for future dividend and annual report purposes. These transactions in second-hand shares form the bulk of the activity in the stock market.

Another function of the stock exchange is as a barometer of business confidence, obtained by measuring the movement of share prices of larger companies. Various indices of share prices are available, the most famous being the FTSE 100 index of share prices of 100 large companies and the FTSE All Share index.

Market-makers quote two prices for each company's share in which they are willing to deal. The higher is their selling price and the lower is their buying price with the difference representing their profit margin or *turn*. They adjust these prices according to how many shares they already hold as well as by anticipating market movements. Small investors cannot approach a marketmaker directly, but must deal through a broker who acts as their agent and tries to negotiate the best deal by comparing competitive quotes from the various marketmakers in that share. Information technology makes this a relatively easy task.

Fluctuations in share prices

It should be noted that share prices reflect future expectations, rather than current or past performance, with many investors looking up to a year ahead or more. Many factors influence share prices by working on the levels of supply and demand. General factors which affect share prices across the board are announcements of economic indicators, possible changes in government, wars, strikes and even international events. More specific factors affecting the share price of only one company are announcements (or rumours) regarding profits, dividends, orders, changes in management, new share issues and other happenings.

When a company announces its interim or final profits and dividend, there may not be any change in the share price, even when the figures are significantly different from the previous year. Only if the announcement is different from that *expected*, and already discounted by the share price, will there be any further price movement.

Efficient market hypothesis

The current market price of a share is often used in calculating a company's cost of capital. This raises the question as to the degree of efficiency with which the stock market operates in setting prices. An efficient market is one where prices immediately reflect all information that could influence current prices. Market efficiency refers to the degree to which relevant information is reflected in the price of stocks and shares and is defined in three forms:

- *weak form efficiency* – no investor should make a better return by using information on *past* movements in share prices and returns achieved.
- *semi-strong form efficiency* – asserts that share prices fully reflect all *published* information relevant to each company.
- *strong form efficiency* – implies that share prices reflect *all relevant information*, whether generally available or privy to only a few parties.

If a stock market operated in a state of strong form efficiency, investors and institutions might just as well track the market by investing in an appropriate tracker fund as they would not be able to achieve superior performance. This suggests that the market operates nearer a state of semi-strong form efficiency where business decisions are reflected in a company's share price once those decisions have been released to the stock market for public consumption.

NEW ISSUES

Invariably, limited companies start off as private companies and gradually grow in size. A company goes public and gets a listing on the stock exchange when its capital needs are no longer met internally or by bankers. Sometimes venture capitalists, or other owners, wish to realize some of their investment by getting a listing and parting with some of their shares. Often family-owned businesses may have no further capital of their own to fund expansion, or need to get a value of the business for tax purposes.

Both a merchant bank (issuing house) and a stockbroker are appointed to the company to help guide it through the lengthy process and value the shares at a realistic level. The price is fixed at the last possible minute to take account of the price earnings ratios of similar companies and market conditions at the time. Underwriters may be approached to take up any unwanted shares for a small commission and this ensures the success of the venture whatever the market conditions on the day. There are a variety of ways in which a new issue can take place.

Very large companies that are already household names may succeed in going public by issuing a prospectus and inviting investors to subscribe. These cases are very rare. More usually a larger company sells the shares to a merchant bank which in turn offers them to the investing public at a slightly higher price. This *offer for sale* may be composed partly of new shares to raise capital for the company, and partly of existing shares where the original shareholders wish to realize some of their capital. Privatization issues normally take this form. An *offer for subscription* sounds very similar, but here the shares are offered to the general investing public by the company. Another difference is that if sufficient shares are not applied for, the offer may be withdrawn.

Small companies can avoid some of the advertising and other expenses by obtaining stock exchange permission for a *placing*. Instead of offering shares to the general public by an offer for sale, shares are placed initially with large institutional investors. Somewhat similar is an *intermediaries offer* when shares are allocated to stockbrokers and other intermediaries for onward sale to the general public.

An *open offer* is where an existing listed company keeps some or all of the new shares being offered for its existing shareholders. Occasionally one hears of an *introduction* when a company with a large number of existing shareholders, or with a listing abroad, wants a quotation on the London Stock Exchange. No new shares are involved necessarily, but sufficient shares must be made available to allow the market to function.

Offer by tender

When fixing the price of shares for an offer for sale or placing, account will be taken of the standing of similar companies with regard to financial yardsticks such as p/e ratio, dividend yield, and dividend cover. Occasionally a company comes to the market which is rather unique in the sense that no other companies in the same field already have a quotation. Such a company is a suitable candidate for the sale by *tender* approach.

When the government privatized Amersham in 1981, it offered the shares at a fixed price, but considerably underestimated the substantial premium that investors were willing to pay for such a high-technology company. Attempts were made to persuade the government that any future issues would use the tender method, but this was not implemented until 1987 with the partial tender offer for British Airports.

When an offer for sale is by tender, applications are invited from investors at or above a stated minimum price. All shares are eventually issued at the same striking price which represents the lowest price at which the last shares on offer are taken up. Those investors who are very keen to buy will offer a very high price hoping this will secure an allocation of shares at a lower striking price.

Example

Let us assume that company X offers 500,000 shares for sale at a minimum price of £2 each and gets the following tender bids:

Number of shares	Tender price
7,500,000	£2.00
1,350,000	£2.10
625,000	£2.20
300,000	£2.30
125,000	£2.40
50,000	£2.50
25,000	£2.80

Ignoring the possibility of large applicants being scaled down, the striking price would be fixed at £2.30, being the highest price at which all 500,000 shares can be sold. Applicants who tendered less than £2.30 would receive no shares.

RIGHTS ISSUES

Companies with an existing stock market quotation can also issue new shares. When they issue them for cash and offer them first to existing shareholders, it is known as a *rights issue*, whereas when they are given free it is called a *scrip issue*. It is important to understand the reasons for these issues and the effect on the share price of the company concerned.

The simplest to understand is a rights issue, when a company raises more capital either to finance more assets or to repay borrowed capital and so reduce its gearing. Existing shareholders are first given the right to buy the new shares *pro rata* to the number of shares they already own.

Example

A company offers its shareholders one new share at £1.50 for every five they already hold. This is known as a 1 for 5 rights issue.

The year 1991 was a bumper one for rights issues, well exceeding the £7 billion raised in 1987 at the height of the 1980s boom. The mid-1990s was also a busy time for rights issues as companies replaced debt with equity as the economy started another growth phase. This lowering of gearing, temporarily, made future borrowing possible to finance their own expansion.

When a rights issue is first announced it may have a depressing effect on the existing share price. This is partly because of the threat of a larger than normal number of shares coming on to the market, due to some existing shareholders being unwilling or unable to put up more money. It is also a response to the size of the discount offered by the company, as the new shares will usually be offered at a price at least 10 per cent lower than the market price to ensure the success of the issue.

After a rights issue has been effected, the market price can be estimated from the following formula:

$$\text{Ex-rights price} = \text{Subscription price} + \left\{ \text{£ discount} \times \frac{\text{Number of shares pre issue}}{\text{Number of shares post issue}} \right\}$$

Example
In the case of the 1 for 5 issue at £1.50 previously mentioned, let us assume the market price stood at £1.74 before the issue was announced. After the issue the share price of both old and new shares should be:

$$\text{£1.50} + \left\{ 24\text{p} \times \frac{5}{6} \right\} = \text{£1.70}$$

Very often share prices may not conform with the above pattern. This is possibly because at the time of the issue the company makes an updated forecast of future profits and dividends. If this is better, or worse, than market expectations before the rights issue, then the share price will move accordingly. Shareholders who do not wish to exercize their rights can sell them in the market, provided the subscription price is less than the current market price. To reduce expenses for small investors, the company sometimes does this on their behalf after the expiry date.

SCRIP ISSUES

A scrip issue is a very different animal to a rights issue. Here the company issues new shares to existing shareholders on a *pro-rata* basis, but receives no cash for them. The mechanism of a scrip issue is to capitalize reserves, meaning that the issued share capital is increased while the reserves are depleted by the same amount. This is merely a book entry in the balance sheet and may be thought of little purpose.

There are a number of reasons why scrip issues occur. Creditors or bankers may insist on it as a safeguard to their interests. Certain reserves can be used for dividend payments if cash is available and this could be at the expense of creditors who are owed money. Once reserves are made up into permanent share capital, dividends can no longer be paid from this source.

Companies usually express dividends as x pence per share, as opposed to the previous practice of declaring them as a percentage of the par value of a share. This latter practice can be misleading for employees in particular, who may not see that the dividend is a return on all shareholders' funds and not just on the original issued capital. After a scrip issue the amount of dividend per share will be less than before as it is now paid on a greater number of shares.

Very often scrip issues are a public-relations exercise with employees and shareholders, based on their inadequate knowledge of company finance. Small investors prefer low-priced shares to high-priced ones for psychological reasons. A £10 share is really just as valuable as 10 £1 shares. Scrip issues have the effect of lowering the market price of a share *pro rata* to the size of the issue.

Example
If a company makes a 1 for 2 scrip issue then the price should fall by one-third, leaving the investor no better and no worse off. Take two shares which stand at £3 each before a 1 for 2 scrip issue. After the issue a shareholder will still hold £6 (3 x £2) value as before.

As with rights issues, the share price may not respond as described if a dividend forecast accompanying the scrip issue does not equate with market expectations beforehand.

Dividend cover

We saw with preference shares that the market price was based on the size of the dividend payment. This is not the case with ordinary shares because very few companies pay out all their profit as dividends. A combination of inflation and growth means that firms need extra capital each year to finance the increased value of fixed assets and working capital. The prime source of this extra capital is retained profit.

The proportion of profit paid out as dividend is ascertained from the *dividend cover* expressed as:

$$\text{Dividend cover} \quad = \quad \frac{\text{Earnings per share}}{\text{Dividend per share}}$$

Example
Where earnings per share is 24p and the dividend is 8p net, the dividend cover is three times, meaning that one-third of the profit is paid out as dividends.

This financial ratio is used as a measure of risk to the dividend should profits decline in future years. It is also used to express the proportion of earnings retained, in this case two-thirds.

Dividend yield

The dividend yield is the gross dividend expressed as a percentage of the current market price. Dividend yields are usually measured gross because any individual's tax liability is unknown, and also because the return offered on most other alternative investments is also expressed in gross terms.

Example

Using the same example of an 8p net dividend, this is equivalent to a 10p gross dividend with the rate of tax on investment income set at 20 per cent (8p x 100/80 = 10p). If the market price of the share is £1.60 then:

$$\text{Gross dividend yield} \quad = \quad \frac{10p}{160p} \quad \times \quad \frac{100}{1} \; \% \quad = \quad 6.25\%$$

This can now be compared with returns on other investments or other shares. It must be remembered that dividends are only part of the return received by investors. This is because retained profits are also expected to increase the market price of the shares over time. For this reason ordinary shares cannot be valued just by reference to their dividend yield. All earnings should be taken into account irrespective of whether they are retained or distributed as dividends. A more valid approach is to use the comparative p/e ratio mentioned earlier to value ordinary shares.

Dividend policy

In the case of small private companies, the shareholders are usually either directors or members of their families. The dividend policy of these companies takes into account the need to retain profits as additional capital, as well as considering the needs and tax status of the shareholders regarding dividend income.

Public companies with a stock market quotation must consider their shareholders when framing their dividend policy. We have seen that the dividend yield at any moment in time is not a means to valuing shares. Shareholders do expect their company to pursue a consistent dividend policy and not use retained profits as the sole source of new finance. Should a company have pursued a policy, say, of distributing one half of its profit over a number of years, then this policy will be expected to continue. Any reduction of dividends to fund high capital expenditure will be greeted by a sharp fall in the market value of the shares. Although this does not immediately have any effect on the company, it makes future rights issues more difficult, and could lead to an opportunistic takeover bid.

An exception to this rule appeared in the severe recession of the early 1990s. In some instances, companies that still paid dividends, but were perceived to be imprudent, found that their share price fell as a result. In other cases, companies that cut their dividends to affordable levels were rewarded by a rise in their share price.

Further reading

Rappaport, A (1996) *Creating Shareholder Value: The new standard for business performance,* The Free Press, San Francisco.

Samuels, JM, Wilkes, FM and Brayshaw, RE (1995) *Management of Company Finance,* ITP, London.

Walsh, C (1995) *Key Management Ratios,* FT/Pitman, London.

Self-check questions

1. What is the market value of a non-redeemable 11 per cent preference share of £1 if the current rate of dividend on new shares is 9 per cent?
2. What are the advantages and disadvantages to an investor of holding preference shares?
3. What are the three main ways of valuing ordinary shares?
4. What is goodwill?
5. Takeover activity often increases at times when share prices are high. Why is this so?
6. Differentiate between market-makers and brokers.
7. Name the different ways a new issue can come to the market.
8. Why do shares often fall in value when a rights issue is announced?
9. Why do companies make scrip issues?
10. Define dividend cover.
11. What is the gross dividend yield on a share with a market value of £1.60 when the net dividend is 9p and the notional rate of tax on investment income is 20 per cent?

20

Mergers, takeovers and buy-outs

INTRODUCTION

The terminology used in this connection is not as precise as first appearances might suggest. A *merger* is when two or more companies join together voluntarily under the umbrella of a newly formed holding company. The parties concerned have equal status in the discussions leading up to the merger even when the companies involved are unequal in size.

A *takeover* is when one company buys out the shareholders in another company. It implies the unwillingness of one party and the use of force by the other. Very often this is not the case, as with an agreed takeover. This represents a merger in many ways, except that no new holding company is formed and the larger company usually buys the issued shares of the smaller company. Should the smaller company take over the larger company, this is known as a *reverse takeover*.

In recent years *management buy-outs* have become more frequent. When a particular activity no longer fits into the corporate plan of a holding company, it may decide to divest itself of that subsidiary. Sometimes group overheads charged to the subsidiary result in an inadequate return on capital. Occasionally companies go into receivership with potentially profitable activities submerged by other loss-making subsidiaries. All of these situations yield potential candidates for a buy-out by their management and other employees.

More recently still, *management buy-ins* have occurred where a management team is brought together with the purpose of identifying a suitable company for acquisition, usually in conjunction with venture capitalists and other financiers.

REASONS FOR MERGERS AND TAKEOVERS

The reasons for mergers and takeovers are somewhat different from those of management buy-outs. Any amalgamation should fit in with the corporate strategy of the principal company involved. The purpose is to make the combined companies more profitable, and stronger, than was the sum of their separate parts. Very often economies of scale are cited as the justification for mergers and takeovers. These are described as technical, financial, marketing, managerial and risk-bearing economies resulting from the integration of activities.

Integration can take one or more of three forms:

- vertical;
- horizontal;
- lateral.

1. *Vertical integration* occurs when two companies at different stages join together under common ownership. A company can integrate forward to the market outlets or backward to the raw material and component supplies.

Example
An example of forward vertical integration is a shoe manufacturer taking over a chain of shoe shops, while a manufacturer taking over a leather tannery represents backward vertical integration. The main economies will be financial, resulting from the co-ordination of production and marketing functions and the elimination of middlemen profits.

2. *Horizontal integration* occurs when two companies at the same stage combine together. The purpose may be to eliminate competition or to broaden the product range and geographical coverage. Many economies are possible in this situation including technical, marketing, managerial and financial benefits.

Example
A chain of retail stores operating in the north takes over another chain of stores operating mainly in the south and west of the country.

3. *Lateral integration* is the third possibility, being a diversification from existing activities into a totally different industry. An attraction here could be that the particular industrial cycles do not coincide, so that risks are spread.

Example
A construction company buys a shipping company or an engineering company buys a chain of recruitment agencies

Occasionally a financial economy occurs through the workings of the tax system. If one company has accumulated tax losses, or unclaimed capital allowances, it may be possible for them to be offset against profits of another company if both are part of the same group. Although chancellors have tightened up the rules over the years, losses can be worth taking over and may be the main attraction to a predator.

Asset-stripping days seem to be behind us, but there will always be opportunist bids where a company appears to be lowly valued in the market. This may follow a particularly bad set of annual results or may be the result of years of poor management. New owners may be willing to take a long hard look at the component parts, weeding out unprofitable or misplaced activities. Money raised from such divestments, or from the sale and leaseback of properties, may go some way to funding the original purchase price.

Another reason for amalgamations of companies may be the need for management succession. Where the founder owners of a private company have no suitable successors within the family, they may seek a merger or takeover with a larger public company to safeguard their investment.

VALUATION OF A BUSINESS

Control of a business rests with shareholders who own the voting shares. Where voting powers are vested in the ordinary shares, the value of a business is the total value of these shares. Occasionally, voting rights are vested in preference or other special categories of ordinary shares, but these are rare occurrences.

In the previous chapter we saw that there are the following different approaches to valuing ordinary shares:

- asset value;
- earnings value;
- stock market value.

1. *Asset value.* Each share is represented by a proportionate part of the assets owned by the company after allowing for the payment of all debts. If we revalue these net assets and divide by the number of issued ordinary shares, we arrive at an asset value per share. An additional amount may be added for goodwill as discussed previously.
2. *Earnings value.* The earnings per share is the amount of profit earned for each ordinary share after tax, interest and preference dividends have been allowed. A search is made to find quoted comparable companies and their average price/earnings ratio is used as a basis for valuing the shares of the company in question.
3. *Stock market value.* This value is relevant in mergers and takeovers involving public limited companies quoted on the stock exchange. Very few bids succeed at the existing stock market price unless it has been pushed too high on takeover rumours, or major shareholders agree to sell at a lower price. A higher price than the prebid stock market value is needed because market prices are based on willing buyers and sellers at the margin. To tempt all existing shareholders to sell their shares may require substantially higher prices and 20–50 per cent premiums are not uncommon, especially in boom times.

TACTICS

The price a bidder is prepared to pay for another company depends on a number of factors. Obviously an assessment of the asset value and earnings value can be made, bearing in mind the broad changes that the new management propose. As previously mentioned, no bid is likely to succeed at a price below stock market value, where this exists. Any additional payment for goodwill over and above tangible asset value depends on the reason for the bid and the strengths of the two parties.

Tactics are not very relevant in a merger where the good faith of both companies' management is paramount. In a takeover, particularly if it is opposed, battle lines are drawn very much as in chess. Each side proceeds with caution, one move at a time, anticipating and countering the other side's move.

The bidder usually tries to gain a foothold by acquiring itself, or through associates, a stake in the other company. If this is done through normal market purchases, the effect on the other company's share price may lead to speculation of an impending bid. This can be avoided by spreading such purchases over a long period of time, but it is not possible to build up a large stake secretly due to preventive measures in the City Takeover Code.

Defending an unwanted bid depends on that management's record and the proportion of total shares under their control. If the company has just announced poor results and the directors own only a tiny proportion of the total issued shares, then any price significantly above the present market price will be hard to resist. On the other hand a company with a good track record of profit and dividend growth, together with a substantial director interest in the shares, may be able to fight off an unwelcome bid or demand such a high price that the bidder withdraws.

Very few bids are either successful at the first attempt or withdrawn on first refusal. Sometimes three or four increased bids are made in response to the defending management's arguments, all of which are given space in the national financial press as well as being mailed personally to each shareholder. Once 90 per cent acceptance of a bid has been achieved, the remaining 10 per cent can be compulsorily acquired at the same price. Even when 90 per cent acceptance is not achieved, but voting control passes to the predator, the remaining minority shareholders should think their position over carefully. There is no guarantee that the new parent will follow dividend policies to their liking and it may be wiser to accept the bid rather than be 'locked in' without an effective voice.

MONOPOLIES AND MERGERS COMMISSION

Mergers and takeovers are not allowed to take place without due regard to the public interest, particularly where a reduction in competition would result from the proposed amalgamation of companies. The Office of Fair Trading can request an investigation by the Monopolies and Mergers Commission, who report back to the Department of Industry, whose Minister can accept or reject the findings. Such a reference can effectively kill off a proposal as the necessary investigations may take up to six months and the resulting uncertainty causes difficulty in share dealings of the companies involved.

CONSIDERATION

This refers to the form in which the purchase price is paid. Possible types of consideration are ordinary or preference shares, loan stock, convertible securities, or cash itself. Only cash counts as an actual disposal for capital gains tax of individual investors. This may prove unpopular with large shareholders to whom it would apply, and who would prefer to receive payment in securities which do not count as a disposal. Gains of several thousand pounds are exempt in any tax year, so small shareholders are not influenced in the same way.

Payment can be effected in preference shares or loan stock, both of which have a fixed rate of return. These will not be so popular with the ordinary shareholders being bought out, as their investment requirements are usually growth of dividend income and an increasing value of their capital. Neither preference shares nor loan stock participate in the changing prosperity of the parent company, but they do enhance the gearing benefits for the latter company's ordinary shareholders.

A compromise often reached is to offer a mixture of securities and cash in exchange for the shares in the recipient company. Another alternative is to offer to pay in convertible loan stock. This starts its life as a conventional loan with a fixed rate of interest, but carries the right to be converted into a predetermined number of ordinary shares in the parent company at a future date. From the bidders' point of view no dilution of equity is involved immediately, and a lower rate of interest can be offered than that acceptable on a pure loan stock. When conversion takes place at a future date, it is anticipated that earnings from the company taken over will have grown sufficiently to offset any dilution of equity earnings in the parent company.

Sometimes the management of the two companies cannot agree on the value of the one to be taken over because of uncertainty as to the level of its future profits. This situation can be resolved by the offer of a performance-related purchase price when the initial down-payment is supplemented by later additional payments on achievement of agreed profit targets.

Case study

The following short case study illustrates the valuation of a company's shares in an agreed takeover context. A large public company has just been approached by the directors of EZ Engineering Ltd (a smaller private company) with a view to merging the two companies. The latest balance sheet of EZ Engineering Ltd showed:

Balance sheet as at 31 December 1999

	£000	£000
Fixed assets:		
Freehold land and buildings (at cost)		350
Plant and machinery (net)		600
Vehicles, etc (net)		100
		1,050
Current assets:		
Stocks and work-in-progress	400	
Debtors	250	
	650	
Creditors due within a year:		
Trade creditors	150	
Bank overdraft	175	
Tax payable	125	
	450	
Net current assets		200
Total assets less current liabilities:		1,250
Creditors due after a year:		
6% debenture (repayable in January 2001)		
		400
Net assets		850
Capital and reserves:		
Called-up £1 share capital		500
Profit and loss account		350
		850

The directors of EZ Engineering Ltd have also disclosed the following information:

1. On a going-concern basis the values of assets and current liabilities are all reasonable except that a recent professional valuation puts the freehold land and buildings at £550,000.
2. In a liquidation, stock and work-in-progress would fetch only about £250,000, and redundancies would cost another £250,000.
3. After-tax profits have been static in real terms in recent years at £150,000, and this level is expected to be maintained in the current year. The pre-tax figure was £275,000 and a normal return would be 20 per cent on total assets.
4. Public companies of a similar size to EZ Engineering Ltd have been averaging price/earnings ratios of 5 recently on the stock market.

Calculate and discuss the various methods of valuing the ordinary shares of EZ Engineering Ltd on the basis that its directors are willing sellers, and state reasons for the valuation you think most reasonable to both parties.

Calculation of value of ordinary shares

	Book value	Break-up value	Going concern value
(a) Asset basis	£	£	£
Fixed assets	1,050,000	1,250,000	1,250,000
Current assets	650,000	500,000	650,000
	1,700,000	1,750,000	1,900,000
Current liabilities	450,000	450,000	450,000
	1,250,000	1,300,000	1,450,000
Debentures	400,000	400,000	400,000
	850,000	900,000	1,050,000
Redundancy costs	nil	250,000	nil
Value of assets owned by shareholders	£850,000	£650,000	£1,050,000
Number of ordinary shares	500,000	500,000	500,000
Value per share	£1.70	£1.30	£2.10

(b) Earnings basis	
Maintainable annual profit after tax	£150,000
Number of ordinary shares	500,000
Earnings per share	30p
Comparative price/earnings ratio	5
Value per share	£1.50

Conclusions:

1. Four different valuations have emerged ranging from £1.30 asset value on a liquidation to a £2.10 value of the assets as a going concern. Although the directors of EZ are willing sellers, they cannot be expected to accept themselves, nor recommend to other shareholders, a price below liquidation value. This, therefore, sets a minimum value of £1.30 per share as this can be achieved should the company stop trading and sell its assets on a piecemeal basis.

2. Book value of assets is not very meaningful, as it does not represent the value obtainable for the assets whether it keeps going or is wound up. The going-concern value of assets would be more appropriate if the company was using these assets to full effect. A 20 per cent pre-tax return on total assets of £1.9 million suggests EZ should be earning £380,000, which is well in excess of the £275,000 actually achieved. For this reason EZ directors cannot expect to receive £2.10 per share nor would any extra payment for goodwill be justified.

3. Shares in similar public quoted companies can be bought on a price/earnings ratio which value EZ at £1.50 per share. Stock market prices always relate to marginal purchases and a buyer of a controlling interest would expect to pay substantially more. However, EZ directors wish to sell out and

with the 6 per cent debentures repayable in a year's time, they are not in a strong bargaining position.

4. All things considered, it might seem appropriate to value the shares in EZ at around £1.50, being more than break-up value but valuing the assets on the basis of the earnings they produce. The eventual agreement will depend on the willingness of the public company directors to buy, and the EZ directors to sell out.

Further reading

Samuels, JM, Wilkes, FM and Brayshaw, RE (1995) *Management of Company Finance*, ITP, London.
Watson, D and Head, T (1998) *Corporate Finance*, FT/Pitman, London.

Self-check questions

1. What are the reasons for mergers and takeovers?
2. Whose clearance is required before large takeovers and mergers are allowed to proceed?
3. What are the three bases on which the value of ordinary shares can be calculated?
4. What is the difference between a management buy-out (MBO) and a buy-in (MBI)?

21
Company taxation

INTRODUCTION

The existence of a central government with the power to levy taxes means that it can influence a business's investment decisions through the tax system. There are two aspects to taxation, one being negative and the other positive. The negative side is the payment of tax on profits, while the positive side is the receipt of tax allowances on specified capital expenditure which reduces taxable profits and hence the tax payments.

Corporation tax is the system of taxation which applies to profits of all limited companies, as opposed to income tax, which applies to profits of the self-employed and partnerships. Differences between the two systems are confined mainly to the tax rates and the timings of the tax payments. If we examine the principles of corporation tax first then the differences of the income tax system can be contrasted later.

RATES OF CORPORATION TAX

There are two rates of corporation tax, either of which can apply, depending on the size of the taxable profit for the year. As from April 1999, the normal rate is 30 per cent, with a small companies rate of 20 per cent for those businesses whose profits are relatively small. There is effectively a gradual increase in the rate of tax for companies whose profits fall within the band where the 20 per cent rate ceases to apply, but the full 30 per cent rate is not yet applicable.

The accounting year for many companies will not cover the same 12 months as the tax year which runs from 1 April one year to the following 31 March. If the rate of tax did alter from one tax year to the next and the company accounting year straddled both tax years, then the year's profit is apportioned *pro rata* for the number of months which fall into each tax year. The two rates of tax can then be levied on the respective part of the profit which falls into each tax year.

Example
A company made a taxable profit of £4m in its accounting year ended 31 December. This year straddles two tax years when the rate of tax was 35 per cent and 30 per cent respectively. One-quarter of the profit will be taxed at 35 per cent for the period 1 January to 31 March, and the remaining three-quarters of the profit will be taxed at 30 per cent for the period 1 April to 31 December.

CORPORATION TAX ASSESSMENT

The profit on which corporation tax is assessed (£4 million in the above example) is not identical with the profit as disclosed in the firm's profit and loss account, but is an adjusted profit figure after some costs have been disallowed and some other allowances received. The statement in Figure 21.1 shows the main adjustments that take place, assuming now that the company's accounting year coincided with the tax year so that corporation tax is all at the 30 per cent rate.

		£
Profit as per profit and loss account		4,040,000
Add back disallowed expenses:		
Depreciation	200,000	
Entertainment	10,000	
Political contributions	5,000	
Provision for possible bad debts	1,000	216,000
		4,256,000
Deduct:		
Capital allowances		256,000
Taxable profit		£4,000,000
Corporation tax payable is £4.0m × 30% = £1.2m.		

Figure 21.1 *Corporation tax assessment*

It can be seen from this statement that there are significant adjustments which affect the taxable profit, of which the most important is depreciation. The amount charged for this by a company in its profit and loss account is added back to profit as though it had never been deducted, for the sole purpose of calculating the taxable profit. It is never possible, therefore, for a company to reduce the size of the tax bill by charging extra depreciation in any one year that large profits happen to be made. Whatever figure a company charges for depreciation, the Inland Revenue will add back. The taxable profit each year comprises sales less all allowable operating costs (excluding depreciation) less specified tax allowances as discussed next.

CAPITAL ALLOWANCES

It would be unfair if companies were disallowed depreciation and given nothing in its place. This is because depreciation is the yearly charge for buildings, plant and machinery, vehicles and office equipment. The only difference between the cost of these fixed assets, as opposed to the costs of wages, materials and overheads, is the time they last. Firms could not provide goods and services to customers without investing in these physical assets, unless they chose to lease or rent them. In this case the lease or rent payments are included as expenses in the profit and loss account and tax relief is automatically obtained.

The Inland Revenue have their own system of depreciation allowances which are called *capital allowances* or writing-down allowances. These are available to firms which buy new physical assets of the specified categories, although some allowances are restricted to specific industries. Figure 21.2 is a list of the main rates of capital allowances as at July 1998.

Industrial buildings	4% per annum allowance on a straight-line basis for 25 years.
Plant and machinery	25% per annum allowance on a reducing balance basis except for long-life plant and machinery (25 years plus) when it is reduced to 6% pa For one year only from 2 July 1998, small and medium-sized enterprises can claim a first year allowance of 40%, reverting to 25% on the reducing balance in subsequent years.

Figure 21.2 *Rates of capital allowances as at July 1998*

The capital allowances on industrial buildings are restricted to firms operating in specified industrial classifications. The other allowances apply to all industries. From this it can be deduced that no allowance is normally given for buildings used by service industries, although the equipment, furniture, and vehicles they use are eligible. Exceptions to this rule apply to hotels that possibly may receive the industrial buildings allowance. Another exception may be commercial buildings, including integral plant and machinery, when these are located in an enterprise zone and special allowances apply.

It may have struck you that some of these tax allowances, on say plant and machinery, may be significantly higher than the equivalent depreciation rate used in a firm's profit and loss account computations. This is because the Chancellor uses the size of tax allowances as an economic regulator and does not attempt to relate allowances to individual company needs.

Tax allowances on motor cars are most likely to coincide with the firm's practice on depreciation. Most firms use the 25 per cent writing-down allowance on reducing capital balance when calculating their car depreciation charge to include in the profit and loss account. Managers are no longer able to run a Rolls-Royce at the expense of other taxpayers because tax allowances are restricted to a maximum figure which effectively excludes all luxury vehicles. In the case of a car costing £12,000, the allowances shown in Figure 21.3 apply.

	£	
Purchase cost of car	12,000	
Year 1 – capital allowance	3,000	(25% of £12,000)
Written-down value – year 1	9,000	
Year 2 – capital allowance	2,250	(25% of £9,000)
Written-down value – year 2	6,750	
Year 3 – capital allowance	1,687	(25% of £6,750)
Written-down value – year 3	5,063	

Figure 21.3 *Capital allowances of 25 per cent on reducing value of a £12,000 car*

The capital allowance is seen to fall substantially each year, but the written-down value never actually reaches zero on this basis of calculation. This is not a problem in practice as assets are generally grouped into pools of like assets.

Balancing charges and allowances

Whenever an asset is sold, a balancing up with the Inland Revenue takes place. This is to ensure that the correct amount of capital allowances has been received over the asset's life with the company. If the sale price does not equate with the written-down value for tax purposes then either a *balancing charge* or *balancing allowance* is appropriate. The former applies when the sale price exceeds the written-down value on the grounds that too many allowances have been given. Conversely, when the sale price of the asset is less than the written-down value, an additional allowance, called a balancing allowance, is required.

Example
Assume the car illustrated in Figure 21.3 was sold for £3,000 after three years' use. This is less than its book value of £5,063, so a balancing allowance of the £2,063 difference is required. On the other hand, if the car realized £6,000, the tax collector would claim back excess allowances of £937 previously granted in a balancing charge. This would result in the firm paying back £937 x 30 per cent = £281 tax when it settled the tax bill for the year in which the sale took place.

When appraising new investment projects, the availability of these tax allowances should be incorporated into the cash flows, as must the tax payments on profits earned by the project. Tax saved by claiming these allowances will occur in the year the tax payment would otherwise have taken place. We must now look to see when tax is due for payment.

CORPORATION TAX PAYMENTS

Until 5 April 1999, when a limited company made a dividend payment, it paid a *net* dividend to shareholders and a tax payment to the Inland Revenue.

Example
On a net dividend of £800 the tax payment is £200, being equivalent to income tax at the 20 per cent rate on the gross dividend of £1,000. Such tax was deemed to be an advance payment towards the company's total corporation tax liability and was called *advance corporation tax (ACT)*. The shareholder received the net dividend of £800 together with a tax credit of £200, so his or her gross dividend was £1,000. If the shareholder was not liable for tax, the £200 *tax credit* could be reclaimed from the Inland Revenue. Conversely, if the shareholder was liable for the 40 per cent higher rate of tax, the Inland Revenue sent a tax bill in due course for the remaining 20 per cent tax.

Most companies made two dividend payments within any 12 months, namely, the interim and final dividend relating to their accounting year. This resulted in two payments of advance corporation tax being made which were offset from the company's total corporation tax liability for the year. The balance or *mainstream* tax payable became due nine months after the company accounting year end. There was therefore some delay from the making of profits to the payment of corporation tax on them. This is the reason for the assumed one-year time lag on tax payments in the cash flow models used in investment appraisal, as mentioned in Chapter 17.

As from 6 April 1999 all the above changed. Advance corporation tax is now abolished and companies no longer have to account for it at the time dividend payments are made. This will help the cash flow for the vast majority of companies (over 650,000) which are classified as medium- or small-sized. They will now pay corporation tax as one total sum nine months after their accounting year end and thereby benefit from the abolition of advance corporation tax. The largest companies (about 20,000 in total), however, are going on to a system of quarterly tax payments based on estimated current year profits, which is being phased in over four years starting 1999.

The nature of the above tax payments relating to the profits of any one year makes it very difficult to generalize about exactly when tax is paid. As explained above, it all depends on the size of the company concerned and, in the case of large companies, the stage reached with the new payment system.

When appraising investments, we need to incorporate tax payments and tax savings into the yearly cash flows. A good rule of thumb is to assume an average delay of one year in the payment of all tax on profits for small- and medium-sized companies. In the case of tax saved via capital allowances for these companies, the delay depends on precisely when in the accounting year the capital expenditure took place. Either a one-year or two-year lag should be assumed as appropriate.

In the case of large companies, no time delay in tax transactions should be assumed when quarterly payments of corporation tax are fully implemented.

INCOME TAX

Previous discussion has centred on limited companies which come under the auspices of the corporation tax system. Some business people trade in their own name, or as a partnership, without ever forming a limited company. Profits of these self-employed persons come under the income tax system which also applies to employees.

Unlike limited companies, the self-employed do not pay dividends and any drawings or salary they pay themselves are not allowed when computing the taxable profit. Profits from running a business are deemed to be the income of the individual or partner. Like limited companies, the various capital allowances on new investment all apply. The remaining profits are taxed in bands at rates presently varying from 20 per cent to 40 per cent after the personal allowances for the particular individual have been deducted.

Collection of income tax from employees takes place weekly or monthly under the PAYE system. The Inland Revenue cannot operate the same system with the self-employed because the income or profits are not known until the accounting year ends. In practice it takes a few months to prepare and audit accounts, so the delay is even longer. To overcome this problem the Inland Revenue initially charges income tax in the current year based on the level of tax paid in the previous tax year. Equal payments on account are made on 31 January in the current tax year and on 31 July in the next tax year. Any adjustment necessary is made when the current year's profits are determined.

Example
A self-employed person's accounting year ends 31 August. The profit for the accounting year ended 31 August 1998 falls in the tax year 1998/99. This profit will be used as the basis for assessing income tax for the tax year 1998/99, but advance payments on 31 January 1999 and 31 July 1999 will be initially assessed by reference to the amount of tax paid in the preceding year.

When incorporating tax payments and tax savings into investment appraisals, the timing must be taken into account. In the case of self-employed persons it is advisable to assume no time lag in tax payments. It may be appropriate, however, to assume a time lag of one year when incorporating the benefit of capital allowances into the net cash flows, particularly when the capital expenditure occurs early in the accounting year.

A practical difficulty occurs here when the size of the profits is such that higher rates of tax are payable. The benefit of capital allowances shows up in reduced taxable profits, starting at the highest rate of tax which would have been payable if the investment had not taken place. If the size of the capital allowance is such that a number of bands of taxable income are eliminated, then the tax saved should be calculated at the different marginal rates of tax applicable in that case.

CAPITAL GAINS TAX

A capital gain takes place when a possession such as a building or asset is sold for more than was paid for it. There are various exemptions and reliefs available to individuals which reduce the amount of the gain and the tax payable on it.

Individuals and self-employed persons are taxed on any chargeable gains as if it were taxable income. They, therefore, pay capital gains tax at the relevant rate depending on the size of their other taxable income. A limited company includes any capital gains with its profits from trading activities each financial year. All the company's profit is then assessed for corporation tax.

In practice, both companies and unincorporated businesses may not pay tax on certain gains. This is because *roll-over relief* allows them to reinvest the proceeds from the sale of fixed assets in new qualifying assets. This defers the payment of capital gains tax until the disposal of the new assets. As this process can be repeated *ad infinitum*, capital gains tax may not be a problem for businesses able to take advantage of this relief.

VALUE ADDED TAX (VAT)

The standard rate of VAT is 17.5 per cent at the time of writing and has been since April 1991. This tax has little influence on business decisions, although it may have an affect on a company's cash flow. VAT is collected by the Customs and Excise in multi-stages and not just at the time of sale to the final consumer. When a firm buys goods and services, it pays input tax to the suppliers as part of the invoice settlement. When the buying firm in turn sells goods or services, it charges output tax to its customers, but pays only the difference between output VAT and input VAT to the tax collector.

Some materials may go through a number of processing stages in different firms before eventually being bought by a final consumer, so some VAT is collected at each stage. The tax point occurs at the invoice date rather than the date cash is paid in settlement of credit transactions. However, small businesses have the option of accounting for VAT on a cash basis, ie when invoices are actually settled.

It is possible for the cash flow of a firm to be adversely affected by having to pay input tax to suppliers before tax has been received from customers. This will partly depend on the credit periods for purchases and sales. Where a much longer credit period is granted to customers than is received from suppliers, the balance of tax due to the tax collector may have to be paid before it is actually received.

Sales of some goods and services are zero-rated, which means no VAT is levied on the final consumer. New house buildings are a case in point. Building firms will pay input tax on all building materials and services they buy in from other firms, which they then claim back from the tax collector. If they pay suppliers' invoices which include VAT before they get the refund from the tax collector, then their cash flow is adversely affected. It may be possible to arrange a monthly settlement in these cases in place of the more normal quarterly one.

The greatest criticism of VAT by business people is probably on the grounds of the extra administration required, particularly in very small businesses where office staff are minimal.

Further reading

Melville, A (1998) *Taxation*, FT/Pitman, London.
Rowes, P (1998) *Taxation and Self-assessment*, Letts, London.

Self-check questions

1. Do all companies pay the same rate of corporation tax irrespective of the size of profit made?
2. Does the capital allowance on an asset in any one year always have the same value as the company's own depreciation charge?
3. If a company pays corporation tax at 30 per cent, will the tax charge for the year exactly equal 30 per cent of the net profit?
4. In the case of a medium-sized company, when is corporation tax paid to the Inland Revenue?
5. What is the written-down value of an asset costing £25,000 that has been depreciated at 20 per cent pa for three years on the reducing balance method?
6. How does the Inland Revenue collect income tax from self-employed persons when it does not know how much profit they made in the current tax year?
7. Do firms actually bear the cost of the VAT they have to pay on the goods and services they buy in from other firms?

22
Overseas transactions

INTRODUCTION

The UK is a prominent country in international trade, exporting approximately one-fifth of its total output of goods and services and importing roughly the same amount in exchange. This means that many firms are directly involved with imports and exports or own subsidiary companies which operate in foreign countries. A knowledge of exchange rates, the financing of foreign trade, the minimizing of risk and the accounting treatment of profits arising abroad is, therefore, very important.

EXCHANGE RATES

When a UK exporter quotes a price to a foreign customer, it has to decide whether to quote in pounds sterling, in the importer's currency, or in some other recognized currency such as the dollar or euro. When quoting in sterling the exporter will know with certainty the value receivable and be able to estimate the profit on the deal. However, if the exporter quotes a price in a foreign currency then the profit is subject to the uncertainty of fluctuations in the rate of exchange between sterling and that currency, up until the time payment is made.

Example
A UK shoe manufacturer agrees to sell a consignment of shoes to a French importer for 100,000 francs. At the time the contract was signed, the rate of exchange between the two currencies was £1 = 8 francs. The importer suffers no exchange rate risk as it is paying in its own currency of francs. The exporter, however, could make a larger or smaller profit on the contract depending on what happens to the exchange rate up to the time payment takes place. Initially it expects to be able to convert the 100,000 francs into £12,500 at the rate of

£1 = 8 francs. If the rate of exchange for the £ went up to £1 = 9 francs, the exporter would receive £11,111 on conversion of the francs. Conversely, if the £ had gone down to £1 = 7 francs it would receive £14,285.

The UK abandoned the system of fixed exchange rates in favour of a floating rate in the early 1970s. Then in October 1990, we joined the Exchange Rate Mechanism (ERM) at a quasi-fixed rate of £1 = 2.95DM, but allowed to move 5 per cent either side of that rate. In September 1992, the UK was forced to leave the ERM after an unprecedented attack by currency speculators anticipating a devaluation, or realignment, of the pound against other hard European currencies, such as the mark. The pound is still freely floating and in mid-1998 was about £1 = DM 3.10, but three months later had' fallen over 10 per cent to DM 2.76.

Protection for importers and exporters is now more important than ever when exchange rates can fluctuate without end-stops. In the last year or two, the pound has gone up some 20 per cent against the main European currencies. This rise has not necessarily been uniform, but composed of a series of sharp movements in small periods of time. Any contract that was settled during one of these periods of violent change could have resulted in a substantially altered profit to that originally envisaged.

Economic and monetary union (EMU) is progressing in Europe, although the UK has not yet (September 1998) agreed to join the single currency (euro) which is intended to replace completely national currencies in 2002. The advantages claimed for a single European currency are:

- a market in which companies can trade without exchange-rate risk threatening their profitability;
- elimination of transaction costs caused by currency conversion;
- establishment of an international currency for European trade similar to the dollar and yen in their own continents.

Until such time as the UK joins the single currency after it is implemented, UK companies will not share these benefits to the extent that other EC members will.

MINIMIZING EXCHANGE RATE RISK

It would seem therefore that in foreign trade either the importer or the exporter is exposed to the risk of an adverse movement in the exchange rate. Which party it is depends on which currency is used to fix the contract price. Whether a UK firm is exporting or importing, it will bear no exchange risk if the contract price is expressed in pounds sterling. However, the firm is exposed to exchange risk if the contract is priced in any other currency.

Pricing in a foreign currency makes the deal more attractive to the foreign importer who knows its commitment exactly because it is expressed in its own currency. This does not necessarily mean the UK firm has to bear the risk of an adverse movement in the exchange rate until payment is received. There are a number of methods by which this risk of pricing in a foreign currency can be minimized or eliminated. These include:

- use of the same currency;
- money market hedging;
- forward contract;
- option contract;
- futures contract;
- covering.

Use of the same currency

If an importer (or an exporter) makes both purchases and sales abroad in the normal course of their business, then equal values of transactions in the same foreign currency will cancel out any exchange risk.

Money market hedging

Waiting until the date of a foreign currency transaction exposes the UK exporter or importer to exchange-rate risk. An importer, say, paying for goods receivable in six months' time in a foreign currency, can eliminate exchange risk by buying the foreign currency now. In fact, the importer needs to buy slightly less than the whole amount of foreign currency needed if it can be invested to earn interest for the six-month interval.

Forward contract

One of the simplest and most effective ways of eliminating exchange risk is to deal forward. A forward contract fixes the rate of exchange now between sterling and a foreign currency, for conversion of that currency into pounds at a later date, say three months or even a year hence. Depending on the time interval and which way the currencies involved are expected to move, the forward rate can be either at a discount or a premium to the *spot rate* of exchange obtainable now.

Example
Suppose an exporter of goods priced in dollars can obtain a spot rate of £1 = $1.600 with the three-month forward rate quoted at 0.40 cents discount. By entering into a forward contract with a bank, it is guaranteed to be able to exchange the dollars it receives in three months' time into sterling at a rate of £1 = $1.6040. Should the pound fall in value to only $1.50 during this time, it would have been better off taking the risk itself as it would have received more pounds for the dollars it received. On the other hand if the pound rose to £1 = $1.70, it would have received less pounds for the dollars so the forward contract would have been worthwhile.

The forward contract guarantees receipt of a fixed value in pounds at very little extra cost. Such a contract cannot guarantee that the exporter would not have been better off taking the risk itself, but few would want to expose themselves to such risks in an increasingly volatile market quite outside their normal trading experience.

A variation on forward contracts is possible where importers or exporters do not know the precise date of payment with certainty. They can enter into a forward contract with an option to convert during part of this period. For example, a *three months forward option over third month contract* means that the trader can convert the foreign currency into pounds at the agreed rate at any time during the third month.

Option contract

With a forward contract the conversion of foreign currency must take place at the specified future point in time. However, if a UK exporter or importer is fairly sure that the exchange rate will move in its favour before payment is made, it can take out an *option contract*. By paying an initial premium, it is allowed to exchange the future foreign currency at the present exchange rate so covering itself should its judgement prove to be wrong. The crucial difference is that it does not have to take up the option and if its judgement proves to be correct, and the exchange rate does move in its favour, it simply lets the option lapse.

Futures contract

Nowadays, it is possible to deal in all sorts of items for future delivery. Futures markets exist internationally for financial securities, raw materials, other commodities and foreign currencies for delivery at intervals up to a year hence. The UK has such a futures market called The London International Financial Futures Exchange (LIFFE), but it discontinued its futures currency market through lack of sufficient business.

Futures contracts are for a fixed value so a number of contracts may be needed to make up the required amount of foreign currency. This may be one of the reasons for its unpopularity in the UK.

Covering

Another way to allow for exchange risk applies when an exporter expects to be paid in a foreign currency at a future date. If it borrows the same amount of foreign currency *now* and converts it into sterling at today's spot rate, it can repay the foreign debt it incurred by the proceeds of the export contract. Provided it reinvests the loan, any loss is limited to the difference between the rate of interest paid on the loan and that earned on the short-term deposit in this country. This method of exchange risk avoidance may be more appropriate to large contracts of lengthy duration.

OTHER RISKS

Apart from the above risk associated with exchange-rate movements, there is also the risk of non-payment for goods by a foreign buyer. This risk can be avoided by taking out insurance, a role once the province of the Export Credit Guarantee Department, but which has now passed into the private sector for short-term cover.

Risk of non-payment may also be avoided if an exporter receives orders through a *confirming house* which acts as an agent for overseas buyers. Such institutions may arrange for the shipment of goods to their foreign importer as well as guarantee payment to the exporter so that it is little different from a sale on the home market.

METHODS OF PAYMENT

For internal trade in the UK it is quite usual for credit to be granted for a period of some weeks or even a few months. Normal terms in many industries are for payment to be made by the end of the month following the month of delivery, which in effect means between four to eight weeks' credit.

An increasing amount of export trade is being conducted on this same basis being known as an *open account*. Payment never results in the physical movement of currency, but by the adjustment of bank balances in the two countries concerned. This can be effected by telegraphic transfer or a banker's draft.

A *confirmed and irrevocable letter of credit* is frequently used to settle payments in international trade. Such a document is a letter from the importer's bank to a UK bank guaranteeing payment to the exporter for goods on production of certain documents, for example, a bill of lading, invoice and insurance certificate.

An exporter can draw up a *bill of exchange* on the importer who accepts it by signing it, thereby agreeing to pay a sum of money at a specified time to the bearer or a named party. If the specified time is some months away, the exporter can sell it to a bank or discount house at a discount that reflects the interest cost involved. If a bank puts its name to a bill, it *accepts* it, so guaranteeing payment and making it easy for the exporter to discount it for ready cash.

Another way of satisfying payment for exports is by *countertrade*. One method requires the exporter to buy goods or services of equal value from the importer's country. Payments for exports and imports would still be made in cash or on credit terms. A simpler type of countertrade is *barter* where goods are swapped for goods and no money changes hands.

FINANCING FOREIGN TRADE

In many cases exporters will view the financing of foreign trade in the same light as financing domestic trade. A mix of owners' capital and borrowed capital will provide the working capital required for both exports and domestic sales. A documentary credit or discounted bill of exchange may actually result in cash being received earlier on export trade than from sales at home.

Should further finance be required in the form of a bank loan or overdraft, the existence of ECGD guarantee will greatly facilitate proceedings and possibly reduce the rate of interest. A variation on this theme occurs with *buyer credit financing* where the buyer pays the exporter on delivery from a bank loan guaranteed by the ECGD or other insurer. From time to time government tries to stimulate exports via special bank lending arrangements so investigation of this source is always worth while.

Invoice factoring is another way of financing export trade and is somewhat similar to the factoring system used in the home market. Money is not advanced until the sale takes place when the factor buys the sales invoice and collects the debt from the foreign importer without recourse to the exporter. In this way working capital requirements are reduced, although not necessarily eliminated.

A similar new source of finance for exporters is now provided by *forfaiting*. When an export sale takes place, the forfaiter buys the sales invoice, or promissory note, at a discount. This is less risky when the importer's bank has guaranteed payment at the due date. For large projects in developing countries, the World Bank or UK Government aid may be a source of finance for the scheme, thereby providing an export market for UK construction and engineering companies that would not otherwise be possible.

EXCHANGE CONTROL

At the time of writing, exchange control no longer exists in the UK. This means that firms and individuals are free to invest abroad and firms can import goods without regard to foreign exchange availability or otherwise. This is not the case with many other countries whose balance of payments position demands that they ration out their scarce holdings of foreign currency by imposing exchange control. Such control specifies the amounts and purposes for which foreign exchange will be made available. A country may, for example, prohibit or impose limits on the amount of profits remittable as dividends by foreign subsidiaries to their parent company in the UK.

Separate from exchange control there may also exist a system of tariffs or quotas which prohibit or limit the importing and exporting of specified goods and services. There are international agreements specifying when, and how, such restrictions are to be used. These restrictions may be intended to prevent unfair competition, to protect developing industries, or to restrict trade for political and security reasons.

FOREIGN SUBSIDIARIES ACCOUNTS

Subsidiary companies operating abroad will keep their accounting records in the currency of that country. From such records the trial balance and hence the profit and loss account and balance sheet will be produced. If a foreign subsidiary's accounts are consolidated with the parent and other subsidiaries into group accounts, then they must be converted from the local currency to pounds sterling.

The balance sheet of a foreign enterprise is translated into sterling at the closing rate of exchange at the group year-end. Owing to a movement in exchange rates between the two currencies, any exchange difference between yearly balance sheets is dealt with in reserves. The profit and loss account is translated at either the year-end or the average exchange rate.

The consolidation of foreign subsidiaries is something of a grey area in accounting where alternative treatments of specific items may be found, for example, when the year-end of the foreign subsidiary and the UK parent are non-coterminous. The precise policy adopted by a company should be spelt out in the statement of accounting policies contained in its annual report.

TRANSFER PRICING

The term *transfer pricing* refers to the price at which goods and services are sold or transferred from one unit to another, when both are parts of a more global undertaking. Take, for example, a holding company which owns two subsidiaries, one of which manufactures ventilation equipment while the other installs the same, in addition to other makers' equipment. The performance of each subsidiary, if measured in terms of return on capital, will have to take account of the transfer price of the equipment between the two units. Too low a price will result in a low return for the manufacturer and a high return for the installer, and vice versa for a price set too high. Prices should be set at normal commercial rates, that is at arm's length, but agreement on this could be a contentious point for the managers of the two units concerned.

Transfer pricing is also relevant when holding companies trade with their foreign subsidiaries. In this case two further points will have to be considered. One relates to the level of taxation on company profits in the different countries and the tax treatment of distributed profits. It may seem advisable to let the bulk of the profit arise in the country where tax rates are low by transferring out at a high price or transferring in at a low price. But tax authorities around the world are aware of these practices and give them close attention. Some major trade countries, such as the USA, Germany, Japan and the UK, issue detailed regulations on the criteria used to fix arm's length transfer prices.

Prior to the UK government enacting new legislation, the Inland Revenue issued a consultative document in October 1997 containing the following proposals to coincide with the inception of self-assessment by companies for year endings 1 July 1999 onwards:

1. A company's taxable profit must reflect all related party dealings at arm's length prices. It was previous practice for the Inland Revenue itself to make adjustments to a company's declared taxable profit for any non-arm's length pricing.
2. Certain joint ventures are now included.
3. Companies are required to create and retain documentation to justify their transfer prices.

4. Penalties are to be introduced for fraudulent or negligent tax returns regarding the adjustment of taxable profit for arm's length pricing.

Another point about transfer pricing relates to exchange control regulations. If a UK company desires overseas subsidiaries to remit dividends, but these are blocked or restricted by foreign governments' exchange control regulations, then a solution might be to transfer out at a high price. This has the effect of artificially inflating the UK parent's profits and deflating the profit of the foreign subsidiary which would not have been allowed to remit the same funds as dividends.

Obviously both UK and foreign governments are aware of these possibilities and may try to regulate such practices. Trade unions too have been known to question transfer prices from the point of view that profits are a relevant factor in pay negotiations.

Further reading

Brealey, RA and Myers, SC (1996) *Principles of Corporate Finance,* McGraw Hill, New York.
Elliott, J (1998) International transfer pricing, *Management Accounting*, March.
Samuels, JM, Wilkes, FM and Brayshaw, RE (1995) *Management of Company Finance*, ITP, London.

Self-check questions

1. What risk does a UK exporter take when it prices in pounds sterling?
2. What risk does the foreign importer take on the same deal?
3. How can an exporter eliminate some of the risks involved in such trade?
4. What special sources of finance are available to exporters?
5. Why are foreign subsidiaries not always able to remit dividends back to their UK parent?
6. What does the term transfer pricing mean?
7. Why are national governments interested in transactions between arms of the same multinational company?

Appendix 1

Financial Reporting Standards (FRS) as at September 1998

Issued

Cash Flow Statements (FRS 1) – requires companies to provide a primary financial statement analysing cash flows under specified headings. — 1996 (rev)

Accounting for Subsidiary Undertakings (FRS 2) – aims to present financial information relating to a parent company and its subsidiary undertakings as a single entity, ie group accounts. — 1992

Reporting Financial Performance (FRS 3) – requires the analysis of turnover and profit, separating continuing activities from discontinued activities. Also requires earnings per share (EPS) to include all profits and losses disclosed in the profit and loss account. — 1992

Capital Instruments (FRS 4) – cracks down on financial engineering and requires debt and equity to be defined not by their legal form, but the underlying commercial reality. Finance costs of non-equity or debt should be a constant charge on the carrying amount of the liability which may differ from the actual interest payments made. — 1993

Reporting the Substance of Transactions (FRS 5) – tackles the thorny issue of off-balance sheet finance regarding the ownership and control of an asset. Specifically it refers to loan transfers, sale and repurchase agreements, consignment stocks, securitized mortgages and factoring of debts. — 1994

Acquisitions and Mergers (FRS 6) – defines 'acquisition accounting' and 'merger accounting' for use when accounting for business combinations. Criteria are laid down before any combination can be treated as a true merger. — 1994

Fair Values in Acquisition Accounting (FRS 7) – sets out the principles to identify the fair values of assets and liabilities and associated goodwill on acquisition. Cracks down on creative accounting via the manipulation of goodwill by the creation of reorganization/future loss provisions which are now excluded.   1994

Related Party Transactions (FRS 8) – this standard was inevitable following a number of high profile corporate collapses. It requires a company to disclose significant transactions with other companies it controls or can influence, and transactions with directors or members of their household.   1995

Associates and Joint Ventures (FRS 9) – defines how to include their results in the consolidated financial statements of the investing party.   1997

Goodwill and Intangible Assets (FRS 10) – stipulates that purchased goodwill and other intangibles should be capitalized as assets and depreciated over their useful economic lives, presumed not to exceed 20 years.   1997

Impairment of Fixed Assets and Goodwill (FRS 11) – sets out the method for measuring the extent of any impairment.   1998

Provisions, Contingent Liabilities and Contingent Assets (FRS 12) – sets out the principles for recognizing and measuring these items and any accompanying notes in financial statements   1998

Derivatives and Other Financial Instruments: Disclosures (FRS 13) – the disclosure of information relating to financial instruments in financial statements, with the object of facilitating risk assessment.   1998

Earnings Per Share (FRS 14) – sets out the basis for calculating and presenting earnings per share figures in the financial statements.   1998

Notes: In addition to the above FRSs, there are a number of older Statements of Standard Accounting Practice (SSAPs) still wholly or partly applicable.

Small companies, and other entities that would qualify if they had been incorporated, are exempt from the above standards if the following standard is applied:

Financial Reporting Standard for Smaller Entities (FRSSE) a composite accounting standard applicable to smaller entities as defined by companies legislation.   1997

Appendix 2

List of acronyms

ABB	activity-based budgeting
ABC	activity-based costing
ABM	activity-based management
ACCA	The Association of Chartered Certified Accountants
APB	Auditing Practices Board
ARR	accounting rate of return
ASB	Accounting Standards Board
CAPEX	capital expenditure
CAPM	capital asset pricing model
CCA	current cost accounting
CFROI	cash flow return on investment
CGT	capital gains tax
CIMA	The Chartered Institute of Management Accountants
CIPFA	The Chartered Institute of Public Finance and Accountancy
CPP	current purchasing power
DCF	discounted cash flow
ECGD	Export Credit Guarantee Department
EOQ	economic order quantity
EPS	earnings per share
EVA	economic value added
FIFO	first-in-first-out
FRS	financial reporting standard
FRSSE	financial reporting standard for smaller entities
GAAP	generally accepted accounting practice
GDP	gross domestic product
HCA	historic cost accounting
IASC	International Accounting Standards Committee
ICAEW	The Institute of Chartered Accountants in England and Wales

ICAS	The Institute of Chartered Accountants in Scotland
IRR	internal rate of return
JIT	just-in-time
LIFO	last-in-first-out
MBI	management buy-in
MBO	management buy-out
MRP	material requirements purchasing
MRP II	manufacturing resource planning
NPV	net present value
OPT	optimized production technology
P/E (R)	price/earnings (ratio)
PLC	public limited company
PPBS	planning, programming and budgeting system
PV	present value
ROCE	return on capital employed
ROE	return on equity
SORP	statement of recommended practice
SSAP	statement of standard accounting practice
SVA	shareholder value analysis
TQM	total quality management
VAT	value added tax
WACC	weighted average cost of capital

Appendix 3
Glossary of terms

accrual – outstanding expense for an accounting period which has not yet been paid or invoiced.

acid test ratio – also known as the quick or liquidity ratio. A measure of liquidity obtained by dividing debtors, cash and short-term investments by creditors due within 12 months.

asset – any possession or claim on others which is of value to a firm. See also *fixed assets* and *current assets*.

associated company – a company in which another company owns a substantial shareholding exceeding 20 per cent, but not more than 50 per cent of the total.

balanced scorecard – a performance measurement system that combines financial, operational, innovative and customer service measures.

balance sheet – a statement of the financial position of a firm at a point in time showing the assets owned and the sources of finance.

beta – a measure of risk used in assessing the volatility of a share price and the cost of equity capital.

book value – the original or historic cost of an asset less depreciation.

break-even point – the level of output or sales value at which total costs equal total revenue.

budgetary control – financial plans to meet objectives in accounting periods, against which actual results are compared.

capital allowance – the Inland Revenue's equivalent of a company's depreciation charge. Allowances are granted on purchases of certain new assets and reduce taxable profits.

capital employed – the permanent and longer-term capital used by a company comprising share capital, reserves and borrowings.

capital gains tax – the tax payable by individuals or companies on the profit made from the sale of certain assets.

cash flow – the definition depends on the context in which the term is used, but it is generally regarded as the profit after adding back the depreciation charge for the period.

cash flow statement – a financial statement showing the internal and external sources and uses of cash during a period of time.

consolidated accounts – a combined profit and loss account and a combined balance sheet for a holding company and its subsidiaries.

contribution – the difference between sales and the variable cost of goods sold, before charging fixed costs.

convertible loan – this starts life as a conventional loan, but gives the holder the right to transfer into a specified number of ordinary shares at a later date.

corporation tax – the tax levied on a limited company's profit. There is one standard rate (30 per cent from April 1999), but a small companies rate applies to those companies with insufficient profit to be taxed at the higher level.

cost code – a numbering system used to describe every cost, income, asset and liability.

cost: direct or indirect – a direct cost is one which can be specifically allocated to a product, as in the case of materials used and labour expended. An indirect cost cannot be directly related to any particular product, but is more general in nature. Indirect costs are alternatively called overheads and direct costs are sometimes referred to as prime costs.

cost reduction – the reduction in the unit cost of a product or service without impairment of quality.

cost: variable or fixed – a variable cost varies in total pro rata to the volume of production. A fixed cost stays the same total sum over a range of output levels.

creditor – any party to whom the business owes money, usually divided into two time categories.

current assets – cash and other short-term assets in the process of being turned back into cash. For example, stocks and debtors.

current cost accounting – a procedure for adjusting items in a company profit and loss account and balance sheet for the effects of inflation.

current liabilities – short-term sources of finance from trade creditors, bank overdraft, dividend and tax provisions awaiting payment.

current ratio – a measure of liquidity obtained by dividing current assets by current liabilities.

debenture – a legal document acknowledging a debt by a company. It sets out details of the interest payment on the loan and the repayment of the capital. Also, it will contain details of any company assets pledged as security in a fixed or floating charge.

debtor – a credit customer or other party who owes money to the firm.

debt ratio – the relationship of total debts to total assets.

deferred tax – corporation tax which is not payable at one specific time, but which may become payable at a future date.

depreciation – a proportion of the original or current cost of a fixed asset which is charged as an expense in a company profit and loss account.

dividend – a periodic profit distribution to shareholders in proportion to the amount of shares held.

dividend cover – a measure of the security of the dividend payment obtained by dividing the profit after tax by the total dividend.

dividend yield – the income obtained from the dividend as a percentage of the current market price of a share.

double entry bookkeeping – the method of recording financial transactions whereby every item is entered as a debit in one account and a corresponding credit in another account.

earnings yield – the earnings per share expressed as a percentage of the current market price of an ordinary share.

equity – the total amount of shareholders' investment in a company comprising both issued share capital, retained profits, and all other reserves. It equals the value of all the company's assets after deducting all debts owing to outside parties and is sometimes called 'net worth'.

factoring – the acquisition of finance from a specialist company against the security of sales invoices which that company collects.

fixed assets – assets kept by the firm for the provision of goods or services to customers. They are not sold in the normal course of business and include buildings, plant and machinery, vehicles, furniture and office equipment.

fixed budget – a budget left unchanged irrespective of actual activity levels achieved.

flexible budget – a budget which is constructed to change in accordance with the actual level of activity achieved.

forfaiting – a specialist form of finance for exporters.

gearing – the relationship of prior charge capital to owners' capital.

goodwill – the benefit accruing to a business due to its name and reputation. It is valued as the difference between the purchase price of a business and the value of the net assets acquired.

gross profit – the difference between sales and the cost of goods sold before charging general overhead expenses.

gross profit margin – gross profit expressed as a percentage of sales.

group accounts – see consolidated accounts.

historic cost accounting – the recording of transactions at the actual cost incurred at the time of purchase irrespective of the item's current value.

holding company – the parent company which owns a controlling interest in one or more subsidiaries.

income tax – the tax levied on the income of employees and on the profits of self-employed persons.

invoice discounting – the acquisition of finance from a specialist company against the security of sales invoices without the administrative services provided by full factoring.

inflation accounting – see current cost accounting.

intangible assets – assets of a non-physical nature including goodwill, patents, trade marks and royalty agreements.

internal rate of return (IRR) – a measure of the true rate of profitability expected on a project. It represents the maximum rate of interest earned on the diminishing capital balance of an investment year by year.

invoice discounting – a form of factoring where a specialist finance company advances money against the security of customer invoices.

liquidity ratio – a measure of liquidity obtained by dividing debtors, cash, and short-term investments by current liabilities.

marginal costing – a system of costing used for decision-making which is based on the analysis of costs into fixed and variable categories.

minority interests – the proportion of a subsidiary company which is owned by outside shareholders as opposed to the parent or holding company. Cannot apply to wholly owned subsidiaries.

net present value – the net present value is the sum of all negative and positive present values of a project's yearly cash flows, indicating that project's viability when positive.

net profit – the profit after all deductions except tax and dividends.

net profit margin – net profit expressed as a percentage of sales.

ordinary shares – the class of capital entitling the holders to all remaining profits after interest and preference dividends have been paid. They are also entitled to all residual assets once other claimants have been repaid on liquidation.

overtrading – a liquidity problem caused by insufficient working capital to support the level of sales.

payback period – the number of years taken to recover the original sum invested.

preference shares – a class of capital entitling the holders to a fixed rate of dividend prior to any ordinary share dividend. On liquidation they are also entitled to the repayment of their capital before ordinary shareholders are repaid.

present value – the equivalent value now of a sum of money receivable in a later year.

price/earnings ratio – a ratio used for comparing market prices of different companies' ordinary shares. It is calculated by dividing the market price of the share by the earnings per share.

profit and loss account – sometimes called the income statement. It summarizes the income and expenditure of a company to arrive at the net profit or loss for the period.

ratio – two figures usually extracted from the profit and loss account and/or balance sheet expressed as a percentage, a true ratio, or a function.

realization – an accounting concept which states that profit is earned when a sale takes place and not when cash from that sale is received.

related company – a modern version of an associated company introduced by the Companies Act 1981. It refers to a non-group company in which voting shares are held long term with a view to exerting influence for the holding company's benefit. The holding can be any size up to 50 per cent when it would assume subsidiary status.

reserves – 'revenue reserves' are retained profits which can be distributed as dividends. 'Capital reserves' are not available for distribution as they have not arisen from normal trading activities. They occur when fixed assets are revalued or sold at a profit and when a company sells new shares at a premium.

return on capital employed (ROCE) – profit before tax and interest charges expressed as a percentage of capital employed.

rights issue – an invitation to existing shareholders to subscribe for new shares when a company requires further capital.

scrip issue – a free or bonus issue of new shares to existing shareholders in proportion to their existing holding. No new capital is received by the company which translates existing reserves into share capital.

share capital – money subscribed by shareholders in a limited company for ordinary or preference shares. Issued share capital is the amount of money actually received while authorized capital is the total amount the directors are empowered to issue at that time.

share premium account – the excess money received by a company when it sells shares for more than their par value. It is a capital reserve and must be distinguished from the issued share capital in the balance sheet.

standard costing – a system of costing whereby predetermined product costs are compared with actual costs to highlight significant variances which are then investigated.

standard hour – a measure of the volume of work achievable in one hour.

subsidiary – a company which is controlled by another company which owns more than 50 per cent of the voting shares.

sunk cost – a cost already incurred as a result of a previous decision and which cannot be changed by a subsequent decision.

target cost – a market-driven cost target used in product development.

throughput – sales revenue earned minus direct material costs.

transfer price – the price at which one company sells to another in the same group.

trial balance – the list of debit and credit balances on individual accounts from which a profit and loss account is prepared.

turnover – an alternative word for sales.

turnover of capital – the relationship of sales to capital employed, stating the number of times each £1 of capital has generated £1 of sales in a year.

value added statement – a financial statement showing the wealth created by a company in a period of time and how it was distributed to the interested parties.

variance – the difference between a budget or standard and the actual amount.

virement – the ability to transfer expenses from one budget head to another.

working capital – that part of a firm's total capital which is tied up in stocks, work-in-progress and granting credit to customers. It is equal to current assets less current liabilities.

Z score – a combination of certain accounting ratios used to predict business failure.

Appendix 4
Compound interest factors of £1

Purpose: The table opposite shows the *future value of £1* at any rate of interest between 1 per cent and 20 per cent for any number of years up to 20. Compound interest adds interest on to the running total of the original capital plus accumulated interest to date.

The main use of the table in an investment appraisal context is to inflate current value cash flows to their future money or nominal value. The table can be applied to any sum of money by multiplying that sum by the relevant factor read off the table.

Example: Find the value of £4,600 in three years' time with inflation at a constant 4 per cent per annum.

Answer: £4,600 x 1.125 = £5,175

Formula: The table is constructed from the following formula when interest is calculated once yearly at the year-end.

$(1+i)^n$ where i = the rate of interest as a decimal (ie 4% = .04)
n = the number of years.

Year	1%	2%	3%	4%	5%	6%	7%	8%	9%	10%	11%	12%	13%	14%	15%	16%	17%	18%	19%	20%
0	1.000	1.000	1.000	1.000	1.000	1.000	1.000	1.000	1.000	1.000	1.000	1.000	1.000	1.000	1.000	1.000	1.000	1.000	1.000	1.000
1	1.010	1.020	1.030	1.040	1.050	1.060	1.070	1.080	1.090	1.100	1.110	1.120	1.130	1.140	1.150	1.160	1.170	1.180	1.190	1.200
2	1.020	1.040	1.061	1.082	1.103	1.124	1.145	1.166	1.188	1.210	1.232	1.254	1.277	1.300	1.323	1.346	1.369	1.392	1.416	1.440
3	1.030	1.061	1.093	1.125	1.158	1.191	1.225	1.260	1.295	1.331	1.368	1.405	1.443	1.482	1.521	1.561	1.602	1.643	1.685	1.728
4	1.041	1.082	1.126	1.170	1.216	1.262	1.311	1.360	1.412	1.464	1.518	1.574	1.630	1.689	1.749	1.811	1.874	1.939	2.005	2.074
5	1.051	1.104	1.159	1.217	1.276	1.338	1.403	1.469	1.539	1.611	1.685	1.762	1.842	1.925	2.011	2.100	2.192	2.288	2.386	2.488
6	1.062	1.126	1.194	1.265	1.340	1.419	1.501	1.587	1.677	1.772	1.870	1.974	2.082	2.195	2.313	2.436	2.565	2.700	2.840	2.986
7	1.072	1.149	1.230	1.316	1.407	1.504	1.606	1.714	1.828	1.949	2.076	2.211	2.353	2.502	2.660	2.826	3.001	3.185	3.379	3.583
8	1.083	1.172	1.267	1.369	1.477	1.594	1.718	1.851	1.993	2.144	2.305	2.476	2.658	2.853	3.059	3.278	3.511	3.759	4.021	4.300
9	1.094	1.195	1.305	1.423	1.551	1.689	1.838	1.999	2.172	2.358	2.558	2.773	3.004	3.252	3.518	3.803	4.108	4.435	4.785	5.160
10	1.105	1.219	1.344	1.480	1.629	1.791	1.967	2.159	2.367	2.594	2.839	3.106	3.395	3.707	4.046	4.411	4.807	5.234	5.695	6.192
11	1.116	1.243	1.384	1.539	1.710	1.898	2.105	2.332	2.580	2.853	3.152	3.479	3.836	4.226	4.652	5.117	5.624	6.176	6.777	7.430
12	1.127	1.268	1.426	1.601	1.796	2.012	2.252	2.518	2.813	3.138	3.498	3.896	4.335	4.818	5.350	5.936	6.580	7.288	8.064	8.916
13	1.138	1.294	1.469	1.665	1.886	2.133	2.410	2.720	3.066	3.452	3.883	4.363	4.898	5.492	6.153	6.886	7.699	8.599	9.596	10.699
14	1.149	1.319	1.513	1.732	1.980	2.261	2.579	2.937	3.342	3.797	4.310	4.887	5.535	6.261	7.076	7.988	9.007	10.147	11.420	12.839
15	1.161	1.346	1.558	1.801	2.079	2.397	2.759	3.172	3.642	4.177	4.785	5.474	6.254	7.138	8.137	9.266	10.539	11.974	13.590	15.407
16	1.173	1.373	1.605	1.873	2.183	2.540	2.952	3.426	3.970	4.595	5.311	6.130	7.067	8.137	9.358	10.748	12.330	14.129	16.172	18.488
17	1.184	1.400	1.653	1.948	2.292	2.693	3.159	3.700	4.328	5.054	5.895	6.866	7.986	9.276	10.761	12.468	14.426	16.672	19.244	22.186
18	1.196	1.428	1.702	2.026	2.407	2.854	3.380	3.996	4.717	5.560	6.544	7.690	9.024	10.575	12.375	14.463	16.879	19.673	22.901	26.623
19	1.208	1.457	1.754	2.107	2.527	3.026	3.617	4.316	5.142	6.116	7.263	8.613	10.197	12.056	14.232	16.777	19.748	23.214	27.252	31.948
20	1.220	1.486	1.806	2.191	2.653	3.207	3.870	4.661	5.604	6.727	8.062	9.646	11.523	13.743	16.367	19.461	23.106	27.393	32.429	38.338

Note: The above compound interest factors are based on year-end interest calculations.

251

Appendix 5
Present value factors of £1

Purpose: The table opposite shows the *present value of £1* at any rate of interest between 5 per cent and 40 per cent for up to 50 years. Compound interest is deducted from future money to find its equivalent value now, ie as at Year 0.

The main use of the table in an investment appraisal context is to reduce future cash flows to their present value as at Year 0. This process is known as discounting. The table can be applied to any sum of money by multiplying that sum by the relevant factor read off the table.

Example: Find the present value of £57,900 receivable in five years' time using a 14 per cent rate of interest.

Answer: £57,900 x 0.519 = £30,050

Formula: The table is constructed from the following formula when interest is calculated once yearly at the year-end.

$(1+i)^{-n}$ where i = the rate of interest as a decimal (ie 14% = .14)
n = the number of years.

Year	5%	6%	7%	8%	9%	10%	11%	12%	13%	14%	15%	16%	17%	18%	19%	20%	21%	22%	23%	24%	25%	26%	27%	28%	29%	30%	35%	40%
0	1.000	1.000	1.000	1.000	1.000	1.000	1.000	1.000	1.000	1.000	1.000	1.000	1.000	1.000	1.000	1.000	1.000	1.000	1.000	1.000	1.000	1.000	1.000	1.000	1.000	1.000	1.000	1.000
1	.952	.943	.935	.926	.917	.909	.901	.893	.885	.877	.870	.862	.855	.846	.840	.833	.826	.820	.813	.807	.800	.794	.787	.781	.775	.769	.741	.714
2	.907	.890	.873	.857	.842	.826	.812	.797	.783	.769	.756	.743	.731	.718	.706	.694	.683	.672	.661	.650	.640	.630	.620	.610	.601	.592	.549	.510
3	.864	.840	.816	.794	.772	.751	.731	.712	.693	.675	.658	.641	.624	.609	.593	.579	.564	.551	.537	.524	.512	.500	.488	.477	.466	.455	.406	.364
4	.823	.792	.763	.735	.708	.683	.659	.636	.613	.592	.572	.552	.534	.516	.499	.482	.467	.451	.437	.423	.410	.397	.384	.373	.361	.350	.301	.260
5	.784	.747	.713	.681	.650	.621	.593	.567	.543	.519	.497	.476	.456	.437	.419	.402	.386	.370	.355	.341	.328	.315	.303	.291	.280	.269	.223	.186
6	.746	.705	.666	.630	.596	.564	.535	.507	.480	.456	.432	.410	.390	.370	.352	.335	.319	.303	.289	.275	.262	.250	.238	.227	.217	.207	.165	.133
7	.711	.665	.623	.583	.547	.513	.482	.452	.425	.400	.376	.354	.333	.314	.296	.279	.263	.249	.235	.222	.210	.198	.188	.178	.168	.159	.122	.095
8	.677	.627	.582	.540	.502	.467	.434	.404	.376	.351	.327	.305	.285	.266	.249	.233	.218	.204	.191	.179	.168	.157	.148	.139	.130	.123	.091	.068
9	.645	.592	.544	.500	.460	.424	.391	.361	.333	.308	.284	.263	.243	.225	.209	.194	.180	.167	.155	.144	.134	.125	.116	.108	.101	.094	.067	.048
10	.614	.558	.508	.463	.422	.386	.352	.322	.295	.270	.247	.227	.208	.191	.176	.162	.149	.137	.126	.116	.107	.099	.092	.085	.078	.073	.050	.035
11	.585	.527	.475	.429	.388	.350	.317	.287	.261	.237	.215	.195	.178	.162	.148	.135	.123	.112	.103	.094	.086	.079	.072	.066	.061	.056	.037	.025
12	.557	.497	.444	.397	.356	.319	.286	.257	.231	.208	.187	.168	.152	.137	.124	.112	.102	.092	.083	.076	.069	.062	.057	.052	.047	.043	.027	.018
13	.530	.469	.415	.368	.326	.290	.258	.229	.204	.182	.163	.145	.130	.116	.104	.093	.084	.075	.068	.061	.055	.050	.045	.040	.037	.033	.020	.013
14	.505	.442	.388	.340	.299	.263	.232	.205	.181	.160	.141	.125	.111	.099	.088	.078	.069	.062	.055	.049	.044	.039	.035	.032	.028	.025	.015	.009
15	.481	.417	.362	.315	.275	.239	.209	.183	.160	.140	.123	.108	.095	.084	.074	.065	.057	.051	.045	.040	.035	.031	.028	.025	.022	.020	.011	.006
16	.458	.394	.339	.292	.252	.218	.188	.163	.141	.123	.107	.093	.081	.071	.062	.054	.047	.042	.036	.032	.028	.025	.022	.019	.017	.015	.008	.005
17	.436	.371	.317	.270	.231	.198	.170	.146	.125	.108	.093	.080	.069	.060	.052	.045	.039	.034	.030	.026	.023	.020	.017	.015	.013	.012	.006	.003
18	.416	.350	.296	.250	.212	.180	.153	.130	.111	.095	.081	.069	.059	.051	.044	.038	.032	.028	.024	.021	.018	.016	.014	.012	.010	.009	.005	.002
19	.396	.331	.277	.232	.194	.164	.138	.116	.098	.083	.070	.060	.051	.043	.037	.031	.027	.023	.020	.017	.014	.012	.011	.009	.008	.007	.003	.002
20	.377	.312	.258	.215	.178	.149	.124	.104	.087	.073	.061	.051	.043	.037	.031	.026	.022	.019	.016	.014	.012	.010	.008	.007	.006	.005	.002	.001
25	.295	.233	.184	.146	.116	.092	.074	.059	.047	.038	.030	.025	.020	.016	.013	.011	.009	.007	.006	.005	.004	.003	.003	.002	.002	.001	.001	.000
30	.231	.174	.131	.099	.075	.057	.044	.033	.026	.020	.015	.012	.009	.007	.005	.004	.003	.003	.002	.002	.001	.001	.001	.001	.000	.000	.000	.000
35	.181	.130	.094	.068	.049	.036	.026	.019	.014	.010	.008	.006	.004	.003	.002	.002	.001	.001	.001	.001	.000	.000	.000	.000	.000	.000	.000	.000
40	.142	.097	.067	.046	.032	.022	.015	.011	.008	.005	.004	.003	.002	.001	.001	.001	.001	.000	.000	.000	.000	.000	.000	.000	.000	.000	.000	.000
45	.111	.073	.048	.031	.021	.014	.009	.006	.004	.003	.002	.001	.001	.001	.000	.001	.000	.000	.000	.000	.000	.000	.000	.000	.000	.000	.000	.000
50	.087	.054	.034	.021	.013	.009	.005	.003	.002	.001	.001	.001	.001	.000	.000	.000	.000	.000	.000	.000	.000	.000	.000	.000	.000	.000	.000	.000

Note: The above present value factors are based on year-end interest calculations.

Appendix 6
Cumulative present value factors of £1 per annum

Purpose: The table opposite shows the *cumulative present value of £1* receivable each year at any rate of interest between 5 per cent and 40 per cent for up to 50 years. Compound interest is deducted from these future yearly sums to find its equivalent value now (Year 0).

The main use of the table in an investment appraisal context is to reduce future cash flows to their present value as at Year 0. This process is known as discounting. The table can be applied to any *constant* sum of money by multiplying that sum by the relevant factor read off the table. Where the yearly cash flows vary from year to year, this table cannot be used.

Example: Find the present value of £13,700 receivable at the end of each of the next five years using a 14 per cent rate of interest.

Answer: £13,700 x 3.433 = £47,032

Formula: The table is constructed from the following formula when interest is calculated once yearly at the year-end.

$$\frac{1-(1+i)^{-n}}{i} \quad \text{where } i = \text{ the rate of interest as a decimal (ie 14\% = .14)}$$
$$n = \text{ the number of years.}$$

n Year	5%	6%	7%	8%	9%	10%	11%	12%	13%	14%	15%	16%	17%	18%	19%	20%	21%	22%	23%	24%	25%	26%	27%	28%	29%	30%	35%	40%
1	.952	.943	.935	.926	.917	.909	.901	.893	.885	.877	.870	.862	.855	.847	.840	.833	.826	.820	.813	.807	.800	.794	.787	.781	.775	.769	.741	.714
2	1.859	1.833	1.808	1.783	1.759	1.736	1.713	1.690	1.668	1.647	1.626	1.605	1.585	1.566	1.546	1.528	1.510	1.492	1.474	1.457	1.440	1.424	1.407	1.392	1.376	1.361	1.289	1.224
3	2.723	2.673	2.624	2.577	2.531	2.487	2.444	2.402	2.361	2.322	2.283	2.246	2.210	2.174	2.140	2.106	2.074	2.042	2.011	1.981	1.952	1.923	1.896	1.868	1.842	1.816	1.696	1.589
4	3.546	3.465	3.387	3.312	3.240	3.170	3.102	3.037	2.974	2.914	2.855	2.798	2.743	2.690	2.639	2.589	2.540	2.494	2.448	2.404	2.362	2.320	2.280	2.241	2.203	2.166	1.997	1.849
5	4.329	4.212	4.100	3.993	3.890	3.791	3.696	3.605	3.517	3.433	3.352	3.274	3.199	3.127	3.058	2.991	2.926	2.864	2.804	2.745	2.689	2.635	2.583	2.532	2.483	2.436	2.220	2.035
6	5.076	4.917	4.767	4.623	4.486	4.355	4.231	4.111	3.998	3.889	3.784	3.685	3.589	3.498	3.410	3.326	3.245	3.167	3.092	3.021	2.951	2.885	2.821	2.759	2.700	2.643	2.385	2.168
7	5.786	5.582	5.389	5.206	5.033	4.868	4.712	4.564	4.423	4.288	4.160	4.039	3.922	3.812	3.706	3.605	3.508	3.416	3.327	3.242	3.161	3.083	3.009	2.937	2.868	2.802	2.508	2.263
8	6.463	6.210	5.971	5.747	5.535	5.335	5.146	4.968	4.799	4.639	4.487	4.344	4.207	4.078	3.954	3.837	3.726	3.619	3.518	3.421	3.329	3.241	3.156	3.076	2.999	2.925	2.598	2.331
9	7.108	6.802	6.515	6.247	5.995	5.759	5.537	5.328	5.132	4.946	4.772	4.607	4.451	4.303	4.163	4.031	3.905	3.786	3.673	3.566	3.463	3.366	3.273	3.184	3.100	3.019	2.665	2.379
10	7.722	7.360	7.024	6.710	6.418	6.145	5.889	5.650	5.426	5.216	5.019	4.833	4.659	4.494	4.339	4.192	4.054	3.923	3.799	3.682	3.571	3.465	3.366	3.269	3.178	3.092	2.715	2.414
11	8.306	7.887	7.499	7.139	6.805	6.495	6.207	5.938	5.687	5.453	5.234	5.029	4.836	4.656	4.486	4.327	4.177	4.035	3.902	3.776	3.656	3.544	3.437	3.335	3.239	3.147	2.752	2.438
12	8.863	8.384	7.943	7.536	7.161	6.814	6.492	6.194	5.918	5.660	5.421	5.197	4.988	4.793	4.610	4.439	4.278	4.127	3.985	3.851	3.725	3.606	3.493	3.387	3.286	3.190	2.779	2.456
13	9.394	8.853	8.358	7.904	7.487	7.103	6.750	6.424	6.122	5.842	5.583	5.342	5.118	4.910	4.715	4.533	4.362	4.203	4.053	3.912	3.780	3.656	3.538	3.427	3.322	3.223	2.799	2.469
14	9.899	9.295	8.745	8.244	7.786	7.367	6.982	6.628	6.302	6.002	5.724	5.468	5.229	5.008	4.802	4.611	4.432	4.265	4.108	3.962	3.824	3.695	3.573	3.459	3.351	3.249	2.814	2.478
15	10.380	9.712	9.108	8.559	8.061	7.606	7.191	6.811	6.462	6.142	5.847	5.575	5.324	5.092	4.876	4.675	4.490	4.315	4.153	4.001	3.859	3.726	3.601	3.483	3.373	3.268	2.825	2.484
16	10.838	10.106	9.447	8.851	8.313	7.824	7.379	6.974	6.604	6.265	5.954	5.669	5.405	5.162	4.938	4.730	4.536	4.357	4.190	4.033	3.887	3.751	3.623	3.503	3.390	3.283	2.834	2.489
17	11.274	10.477	9.763	9.122	8.544	8.022	7.549	7.120	6.729	6.373	6.047	5.749	5.475	5.222	4.990	4.775	4.576	4.391	4.219	4.059	3.910	3.771	3.640	3.518	3.403	3.295	2.840	2.492
18	11.690	10.828	10.059	9.372	8.756	8.201	7.702	7.250	6.840	6.467	6.128	5.818	5.534	5.273	5.033	4.812	4.608	4.419	4.243	4.080	3.928	3.786	3.654	3.529	3.413	3.304	2.844	2.494
19	12.085	11.158	10.366	9.604	8.950	8.365	7.839	7.366	6.938	6.550	6.198	5.877	5.584	5.316	5.070	4.844	4.635	4.442	4.263	4.097	3.942	3.799	3.666	3.539	3.421	3.311	2.848	2.496
20	12.462	11.470	10.594	9.818	9.129	8.514	7.963	7.469	7.025	6.623	6.259	5.929	5.628	5.353	5.101	4.870	4.657	4.460	4.279	4.110	3.954	3.808	3.673	3.546	3.427	3.316	2.850	2.497
25	14.094	12.783	11.654	10.675	9.823	9.077	8.422	7.843	7.330	6.873	6.464	6.097	5.766	5.467	5.195	4.948	4.721	4.514	4.323	4.147	3.985	3.834	3.694	3.564	3.442	3.329	2.856	2.499
30	15.372	13.765	12.409	11.258	10.274	9.427	8.694	8.055	7.496	7.003	6.566	6.177	5.829	5.517	5.235	4.979	4.746	4.534	4.339	4.160	3.995	3.842	3.701	3.569	3.447	3.332	2.857	2.500
35	16.374	14.498	12.948	11.655	10.567	9.644	8.855	8.176	7.586	7.070	6.617	6.215	5.858	5.539	5.251	4.992	4.756	4.541	4.345	4.164	3.998	3.845	3.703	3.571	3.448	3.333	2.857	2.500
40	17.159	15.046	13.332	11.925	10.757	9.779	8.951	8.244	7.634	7.105	6.642	6.234	5.871	5.548	5.258	4.997	4.760	4.544	4.347	4.166	3.999	3.846	3.703	3.571	3.448	3.333	2.857	2.500
45	17.774	15.456	13.606	12.108	10.881	9.863	9.008	8.283	7.661	7.123	6.654	6.242	5.877	5.552	5.261	4.999	4.761	4.545	4.347	4.166	4.000	3.846	3.704	3.571	3.448	3.333	2.857	2.500
50	18.256	15.762	13.801	12.234	10.962	9.915	9.042	8.305	7.675	7.133	6.661	6.246	5.880	5.554	5.262	5.000	4.762	4.545	4.348	4.167	4.000	3.846	3.704	3.571	3.448	3.333	2.857	2.500

Note: The above present value factors are based on year-end interest calculations.

Appendix 7
Answers to self-check questions

Chapter 1

1. Profit and loss account and balance sheet.
2. See text.
3. Financial accounting; management accounting; and possibly financial management.
4. Generally accepted accounting practice.
5. *Financial Reporting Standard for Smaller Entities (FRSSE).*
6. No – not yet.
7. See text.
8. See text.

Chapter 2

1. A single entry bookkeeping system is the simplest for a self-employed person to use, but a basic computerized double entry system might be suitable for some people, given a little training.
2. A receipts and payments account is a summary of all cash received and paid out during a period of time. The opening cash balance starts off the receipts side whilst the closing cash amount balances off the payments side.

3.
Gosforth Gardeners Association
receipts and payments account

Receipts:		Payments:	
Cash at start of year	1,270	Bulk purchase of seeds, etc	2,510
Members' annual subscriptions	560	Purchase of equipment	1,500
Sale of seeds, etc	2,250	Cash at end of year	520
Hire fees received	450		
	£4,530		£4,530

4. Expenses – debit
Liabilities – credit
Assets – debit

5. Debit entry in the named Suppliers Account.
Credit entry in Bank Account.

6.

Bank a/c

Capital a/c	1,500	Equipment a/c	1,200
Sales a/c	28,000	A. Wholesaler a/c	16,000
Balance	2,700	Van hire a/c	3,600
		Drawings a/c	6,000

Capital a/c

		Bank a/c	1,500

Equipment a/c

		Bank a/c	1,200

Purchases a/c

A. Wholesaler a/c	17,000		

A. Wholesaler a/c

Bank a/c	16,000	Purchases a/c	17,000
Balance	1,000		

Sales a/c

		Bank a/c	28,000

Van hire a/c

Bank a/c	3,600		

Drawings a/c

Bank a/c	6,000		

John Deel trial balance at year end

Bank a/c	2,700	A. Wholesaler a/c	1,000
Equipment a/c	1,200	Capital a/c	1,500
Van hire a/c	3,600	Sales a/c	28,000
Purchases a/c	17,000		
Drawings a/c	6,000		
	£30,500		£30,500

7.

Baker's profit and loss account

Purchases	47,200	Sales	86,500
Wages	22,700		
Rent, etc	7,300		
Sundry expenses	2,700		
Profit	6,600		
	£86,500		£86,500

Baker's balance sheet

Fixtures, etc	6,300	Capital	6,000
Bank balance	9,800	+ Profit	6,600
			12,600
		Creditors	3,500
	£16,100		£16,100

8. A chart of accounts is the numbering system used by any organization to identify each ledger account in its bookkeeping system.

9. A journal is a book of prime entry where financial transactions of a similar type are entered in chronological order. For example, all sales are entered in a sales day book. Transactions are posted from a journal to the two relevant ledger accounts which are an integral part of the double entry system.

Chapter 3

1. Revenue account; income and expenditure account; profit and loss account.

2. False. Some monies received or paid out may relate to the previous year or the following year. Monies received during the year may be new loans while money paid out may be for additional assets, both of which go in the balance sheet and not the profit and loss account.

3. Depreciation has two aspects. First is the diminution in value of an asset through use and consequent wear and tear. Second is the charge of depreciation as an expense against income in a profit and loss account, reflecting the amount of asset value consumed in that period of time.

4. £8,192.

5.

Profit and loss account for month

Rent	500	Sales	3,600
Depreciation	100		
Cost of sales (3,000–1,500)	1,500		
Wages	600		
Sundry expenses	200		
Electricity	150		
	3,050		
Profit	550		
	£3,600		£3,600

Balance sheet

Shop fittings (4,800–100 depn)	4,700	Capital at start	9,000
Stock	1,500	+ Retained profit	550
Prepayment of rent	1,000		9,550
Bank balance	3,500	Creditors	1,000
		Accrued expense (electricity)	150
	£10,700		£10,700

Chapter 4

1. A balance sheet is like a coin – it has two faces but only one value, reflecting the dual aspects of double entry bookkeeping. The assets owned by a company must be financed with capital provided by somebody; both have the same total value. Modern balance sheets no longer show this equality of assets with liabilities in the way they used to with a side-by-side presentation.
2. Fixed assets and current assets.
3. Shareholders' funds (ie share capital plus retained profits) and borrowings.
4. Goodwill built up over the years is difficult to value because such value does not represent money spent on it in any identifiable way, nor may its value stay constant over time if things go wrong. For these reasons, it is not placed in the balance sheet as an asset although it may well have substantial value in a takeover situation.
5. Operating leases relate to short-term hire where ownership of the hired asset remains with the lessor. Finance leases on the other hand are more long-term and confer on the hirer most of the benefits of ownership except the legal title. Finance leases are very similar to hire purchase.
6. Raw materials, work-in-progress and finished goods.
7. Some outstanding customer invoices will never be paid in full due to dispute or business failure. For this reason, companies provide for an amount of bad debts, based on past experience. The balance sheet value of debtors, reduced by this bad debt provision, will always be less than the total value of all customer invoices outstanding at the balance sheet date.
8. Preference shares are paid a fixed rate of dividend before ordinary shares and receive their capital back in full on a liquidation (funds allowing!) before ordinary shareholders are paid the balance of funds remaining. Dividends on ordinary shares can vary from year to year.

Chapter 5

1. Only a trained analyst or accountant could identify the cash movements from a profit and loss account and balance sheet.
2. See Figure 5.2 in text.
3. Compare the depreciation charge with payments to acquire tangible fixed assets. This approach has the weakness that it makes no allowance for inflation.
4. Not necessarily. It may have drawn on past liquid resources (eg sold financial investments) or raised new finance. It could also have run down stocks or cut capital expenditure.

Chapter 6

1. Because the Inland Revenue tax the whole profit (before any drawings are deducted) as income.
2. They may allow interest on capital and/or pay partners' salaries before dividing the residual profit in the agreed proportions.
3. Retained profit is the profit *after* the tax and dividend provisions have been deducted.
4. Consolidated accounts are prepared for a parent company and its subsidiaries to give a view of the group's profit or loss, assets and liabilities, as if it was one single entity.
5. Minority interests are the value of shareholders' funds in subsidiary companies owned by outside shareholders as opposed to the parent company.

Chapter 7

1. A historic cost profit is calculated by deducting from income the original cost of expenses consumed in a period. A current cost profit is calculated by deducting from income the current cost of expenses (cost of sales, depreciation etc) consumed at the time of sale. This is usually achieved by recording all transactions at their historic cost and adjusting the historic cost profit at a later stage.
2. The firm will retain insufficient cash to replenish the stocks and replace fixed assets at their inflated cost.
3. Cost of sales adjustment, depreciation adjustment, monetary working capital adjustment and the gearing adjustment.
4. Any increase or decrease in the value of an asset is matched by a corresponding change in the reserves.

Chapter 8

1. Value added is the wealth created by a company in a period of time. It is measured by deducting from sales the cost of all bought-in goods and services consumed.
2. A profit and loss account.
3. It could calculate ratios and compare them with previous periods, for example, added value per employee or added value/sales per cent.
4. The four parties to whom the value added is distributed are employees, government, providers of capital and the company itself.
5. Employees.

Chapter 9

1. A ratio is a pair of figures extracted from the annual accounts and expressed as a true ratio, or as a percentage, or as a multiple. Ratios are used to measure the profitability, performance, and liquidity of a company.
2. Return on capital = Profit margin × Rate of turnover of capital.

3. Very few ratios have an ideal value with the possible exception of the 1:1 quick ratio. Their use lies in comparison with previous years' ratios, with target ratios, or with competitors' ratios.
4. The quick ratio of liquid assets/current liabilities.
5. Interest cover for company A is 2 times and for company B over 3 times. Company A is therefore more vulnerable should profits fall.
6. Ratios that measure economy, efficiency and effectiveness are more relevant in the public sector than the profit-related ratios used in the private sector. However, some public services are finding ratios like return on capital employed have some application.
7. A Z-score is a combination of ratios used to help predict corporate failure.

Chapter 10

1. Number of warranty claims; time spent on rework; per cent defect rates on own products.
2. A balanced scorecard is a framework from which a set of performance measures can be developed, looking at more than just financial measures.
3. Benchmarking is concerned with seeking out best practices and implementing them to enhance performance.
4. Internal benchmarking; external benchmarking (competitive and noncompetitive); best practice benchmarking.

Chapter 11

1. Costing is concerned with the detailed breakdown of revenue expenditure.
2. Invoices, timesheets and stores issue notes.
3. A cost unit is a product or service provided to either internal or external customers. A cost centre is a location within an organization, typically a department or section of a department, or an activity.
4. Indirect costs have no specific link to the product or service being provided to customers. They include support services and general administrative functions.
5. (a) Lighting of courts will vary with amount of usage.
   (b) Raw materials going into the final products.
   (c) Coal, oil, gas, etc, from which the electricity is generated is a variable cost to the generating company. The energy supplied to regional distribution companies is a variable cost to them.
6. On the basis of time or output or some combination of both. Typical payment systems are hourly rates, measured day work, incentive schemes, or premium bonus systems.
7. FIFO, LIFO, standard price, or weighted average price.
8. ABC crosses departmental boundaries to identify the activities incurring overhead costs and subsequently charging products for the activities they have consumed. A departmental overhead recovery system charges overheads to products benefiting from each department's services, using time or cost as its basis.

Chapter 12

1.   £

	£
Direct materials	180.00
Machine time – 3 × £50	150.00
Selling, dist., etc – 3 × £40	120.00
	450.00
Profit on cost	50.00
Selling price to quote	£500.00

2. A profit margin of 15 per cent is needed to give a 30 per cent return on capital when the turnover of capital rate is two times.
3. Process costing.
4. By comparison with published data from other authorities or with its own past/target unit costs.
5. Either *volume* or *market value* are used to separate joint product costs at separation point.
6. Target costing is concerned with setting a realistic selling price and driving down costs to a level that leaves the required profit margin.

Chapter 13

1. Firm B is cheaper for mileage under 117 per day while firm A is cheaper for mileage in excess of that figure.
2. £15,000 profit.
3. Yes – the contribution of £15,000 on product C would be more than offset by the additional contribution of £24,000 on product A.
4. Yes – it is still worth tendering an even lower price which covers the direct materials cost and makes some contribution to the wages which have to be paid anyway. (Obviously firms cannot continue making such losses for long periods of time).
5. Contribution per unit of product = £25 – £14 = £11.
Total contribution required = (20% × £1.5m) + £0.8m = £1.1m.
Number of sales required = £1.1m/£11 = 100,000.
6. Ranking order is ZYX on a contribution per hour basis. Only products Z and Y should be produced, using up all available labour.
7. When it is cheaper to buy-in than the marginal cost of internal provision.
8. Throughput is the rate at which money is generated through sales. It is defined as total sales minus direct materials costs only.
9. The difference between throughput and contribution relates to the treatment of variable costs other than direct materials, eg direct labour and variable overheads. They are deducted from sales when calculating contribution, but are not deducted from sales when calculating throughput.
10. The primary ratio of throughput as a percentage of total factory cost (excluding material costs).

Chapter 14

1. A standard hour is a measure of the amount of work which can be done in one hour under standard conditions.
2. The activity ratio relates the actual work produced to the budgeted work for that period calculated by:

$$\text{Activity ratio} = \frac{\text{Actual standard hours}}{\text{Budgeted standard hours}} \%$$

3. Plant layout, method study, work measurement, value engineering, value analysis, etc.
4. Adverse.
5. The labour efficiency variance compares the standard hours allowed with the actual hours taken for the work done evaluated at the standard rate per hour.

Formula: (Actual hours – Standard hours) Standard rate.

Note: The expression within the bracket is to arrive at the difference which is then interpreted as favourable or adverse. It does not matter, therefore, whether standard or actual hours is placed first.

6. Budgeted profit for the week 1,100 × £6			£6,600
Variances:	(F)	(A)	
Sales price (£32-£31) 900	900		
Sales volume (1,100–900) £6		1,200	
Material price (50p-55p) 12,600		630	
Material usage (12,600–10,800) 50p		. 900	
Labour rate (£6-£6) 1,800	-	-	
Labour efficiency (1,600–1,800) £6	1,200		
Variable O/H expenditure £2,100-£1,800		300	
Fixed O/H expenditure £5,700-£5,500		200	
Fixed O/H volume (1,100–900) £5		1,000	
	2,100	4,230	£2,130(A)
Actual profit for the week			£4,470

7. Material cost variance = £20 (F)
   (SC £4,500 – AC £4,480)
   Material price variance = £320 (F)
   3,200 × (£1.50 – £1.40)
   Material usage variance = £300 (A)
   (3,300m – 3,200m) £1.50

Chapter 15

1. The factor which limits or sets the level of activity for the budget period around which all budgets must be based.
2. Current level of sales; market research; sales representatives' reports; order book; seasonal trends; economic outlook.

3. A cash budget literally budgets the cash flowing into and out of a company on a monthly basis for the budget period.
4. A flexible budget calculates the costs that should have been incurred for the level of activity actually achieved and compares these costs with the actual costs to calculate variances. It, therefore, excludes the variances caused when actual costs are compared with fixed budgeted costs for a dissimilar level of activity.
5. Budgetary control and standard costing are both planning and control techniques setting standards of performance against which actual results are compared. This throws out variances for investigation where significant, and allows top management to practise management by exception. Their difference lies in the unit of comparison. Standard costs transcend departments and are product-based. Budgets are department-based and more global.
6. Closing stock 750

Production requirements	10,000
	10,750
Opening stock	350
Purchases required	10,400 kg

7. PPBS is applied in local authorities and other large public bodies. It transcends department boundaries and plans for programmes that last a number of years. Budgets, however, focus on functional departmental expenditure for one year only.
8. Traditional methods of budgeting focus on departments as the unit for planning and control. ABC focuses on activities as the planning unit, which transcends all departmental boundaries.

Chapter 16

1. High gearing is a large proportion of fixed return capital (primarily borrowings) to total capital employed or to shareholders' funds.
2. 17.7 per cent.
3. 20 per cent approx. (solved by calculating the IRR as in Figure 13.3).
4. 7.8 per cent.
5. Cost of equity capital $= \dfrac{10p}{£1.50} \% + 10\% = 16.7\%$

6. 14.6%.

Chapter 17

1. Expansion, new product, diversification, replacement, cost saving, alternative choice and alternative financing of investments.
2. 5.6 years.
3. £2,848.
4. NPV $= + £5,095.$
5. 21 per cent approx.

6. 18.2 per cent.
7. Conclusion: The investment is worthwhile as there is a surplus NPV of £299 using a cumulative PV table at 14 per cent.
8. When an investor receives annual interest of £100 on a £1,000 investment, his or her nominal return is 10 per cent. If inflation exists, the real return will be less as some of the interest is needed to maintain the purchasing power of the £1,000 investment. The real return is the nominal return less the rate of inflation.
9. The real IRR is 15 per cent.

Chapter 18

1. Working capital is the amount of capital employed in the current assets after deducting the short-term sources of finance, ie the current liabilities. Therefore working capital is defined as current assets less current liabilities.
2. By calculating the current relationship of working capital to sales and applying that ratio to the increased sales expected.
3. N/A.
4. Bank and trade references; credit agency reports; analysis of latest annual accounts; informal grapevine through own sales representatives.
5. 21 per cent approx.
6. 83 days.
7. Raw materials, work-in-progress and finished goods.
8. Size of buffer stock; re-order level; reorder quantity.
9. Benefits from JIT include lower stock-holding costs and reduced interest charges on capital employed.

Chapter 19

1. £1.22.
2. The advantages are that a preference dividend must be paid before any dividend is paid to other types of shareholder and in a liquidation preference shares are repaid before other shareholders. The disadvantages are that the rate of dividend does not increase if profits increase and any surplus capital remaining on a liquidation goes to the ordinary shareholders.
3. Stock market value; asset value; comparative earnings value (via p/e ratio).
4. Goodwill is the name, reputation, and know-how of a firm which brings customers back and allows a firm to earn more profit than a new entrant to the industry. If one firm buys out another firm and pays more for the tangible assets than they are worth, the extra payment is for goodwill.
5. When share prices are high, price/earnings ratios will also be high. Takeovers can be financed by the issue of fewer new shares at high prices than is the case when share prices are low.
6. Market makers fix the prices at which they will buy and sell shares in a selected number of companies. Brokers act as intermediaries, or agents, between clients and the market-makers, carrying out buying or selling instructions. Both market-makers and brokers are members of the stock exchange.

7. Issue by prospectus; offer for sale at fixed price; offer by tender; offer for subscription; placing; introduction; intermediaries offer; open offer.
8. Because the new shares are offered at a discount to the previous market price and this discount is now spread over all the old and new shares. Also because of the threat of new shares not being taken up by existing holders which will cause a temporary excess supply.
9. A scrip issue makes permanent the use of retained profits as extra share capital. It is sometimes required as a condition of a loan to safeguard the lender. Otherwise it is largely cosmetic, bringing down the market value of the shares *pro rata* to the size of the issue. Shareholders like more shares even though they are of the same total value. The dividend will now appear to be less per share after the issue which may help to prevent employee misunderstandings.
10. Dividend cover is the number of times the profit after tax covers the net dividend payment. The greater this figure then the more secure the dividend payment.
11. Gross dividend yield $= \dfrac{9p \times 100}{\pounds1.60 \times 80}$ % $= 7\%$

Chapter 20

1. Economies of scale through integration of the activities of the combined firms. These may be technical, marketing, managerial, financial, or risk spreading.
2. Office of Fair Trading; Monopolies and Mergers Commission and Department of Trade and Industry.
3. Assets basis, earnings basis and stock market price.
4. An MBO is where existing managers take over their company while an MBI is where outside managers take over a company. In both cases the management team will put up some of the capital, the remainder being provided by banks and venture capitalists.

Chapter 21

1. No – there is a small companies rate of corporation tax in addition to the standard rate.
2. No – in the case of, say, plant and machinery, the capital allowance is 25 per cent pa but no company will depreciate such items at that rate if they are expected to last, for example, ten years.
3. No – mainly because of the answer in question 2, the taxable profit will only equal the company's net profit by coincidence.
4. Nine months after the accounting year-end.
5. £12,800.
6. By initially basing the tax payment for the current tax year on the level of tax paid in the previous tax year, with a final adjustment later when actual profits are known.

7. No – firms are only collectors of VAT which is borne by the final consumer of the goods and services. Any VAT which one firm pays on its supplies is deducted from the VAT collected from its customers and only the balance forwarded to the Customs and Excise.

Chapter 22

1. No exchange risk is involved when exporters price in their own currency.
2. The importer faces the risk that its own currency will fall in value against the pound and it will have to pay more when settlement is made.
3. If the exporter prices in a foreign currency, it will be exposed to exchange risk which can be covered in the forward exchange market. The risk of non-payment can also be insured against.
4. Bills of exchange can be discounted immediately. Bank loans or overdrafts can be more easily obtained with insurance cover. Buyer credit financing enables an importer to pay the exporter immediately from a loan guaranteed by the ECGD or another party. Invoice factoring results in immediate payment.
5. Because of exchange control regulations in the foreign country or tax penalties on dividend remissions.
6. Transfer pricing means the price at which one company sells to another company within the same group.
7. Transfer pricing between different arms of a multinational company could be used to take profit in low-tax paying countries, at the expense of higher tax-rate countries. It can also be used as a means of avoiding dividend restrictions which are designed to conserve scarce foreign currency.

Appendix 8
Further questions

Part 1 The annual accounts

1. Claire Smith started her own business by renting a shop to hire out videos. Prepare T accounts, a trial balance, a profit and loss account and a balance sheet from the following list of her first month's transactions:

	£
Opened business bank account with	4,000
Bought shop fittings for displaying video tapes	1,000
Paid first month's rent	300
Bought stock of video tapes to hire out	2,500
Paid first week's wages	200
Banked first week's sales	300
Paid second week's wages	250
Banked second week's sales	500
Paid third week's wages	250
Bought more video tapes to hire out	600
Banked third week's sales	800
Paid fourth week's wages	250
Banked fourth week's sales	1,100
Paid electricity bill for the month	100
Paid first month's rates to local authority	150

2. Explain the precise meaning of 'profit' by reference to any relevant accounting conventions (*essay question*).

3. The following balance sheet items are in mixed-up order. Put them in groups under correct headings, using the layout currently recommended.

	£
Stocks	92,825
Tangible fixed assets	116,612
Called-up share capital	44,985
Cash at bank and in hand	8,632
Finance debt (due within year)	7,543
Finance debt (due after a year)	28,303
Investments (in related company)	717
Share premium account	33,891
Other creditors (due within year)	73,617
Profit and loss account	88,279
Debtors	74,402
Other creditors (due after a year)	3,525
Provisions for liabilities and charges	13,045

4. A firm buys a piece of equipment for £40,000 and expects it to last for six years after which it will be worth about £2,000. (a) Use the *reducing balance method* to calculate what the balance sheet value of the equipment will be in four years' time;(b) Explain how this method varies from the *straight-line method* and what factors determine the use of each one.

5. The following annual accounts relate to an advertising agency:

Balance sheet as at 30 April

	£000	£000	£000
Fixed assets (net of depreciation)			875
Current assets:			
Stocks and work-in-progress	310		
Debtors	770		
Bank balance	100	1,180	
Less Creditors due within year:			
Trade creditors	620		
Proposed dividend	45	665	
Net current assets			515
Total assets less current liabilities			1,390
Creditors due after one year:			
12% Debentures			700
Total net assets			690
Share capital and reserves:			
Issued share capital			450
Profit and loss account			240
			690

Profit and loss account for year ended 30 April

	£000
Sales	3,100
Cost of work done	1,375
Gross profit	1,725
Overhead expenses	1,055
Debenture interest	84
Net profit	£586

(a) Calculate the following ratios and compare them with the trade average shown in brackets:

(i)   Gross profit margin (50 per cent).
(ii) Net profit margin before interest (25 per cent).
(iii) Return on capital employed (35 per cent).
(iv) Turnover of capital (1.4 times).
(v)   Current ratio (2.2:1).
(vi) Debtors' collection period (75 days).

(b) State whether the performance of this agency is better or worse than the trade average for each ratio and give one suggestion for improvement for each adverse ratio you find.

6. A colleague cannot understand why the firm you both work for needed to increase its bank overdraft at the end of the year in which the firm made a record profit. Give possible reasons why this may be so. You have at your disposal the following balance sheets for this Year 2 and the previous Year 1:

	Year 1	Year 2
Tangible fixed assets at cost	700	868
Less depreciation	120	148
	580	720
Investments in new subsidiary co.	—	120
Current assets:		
Stock	160	240
Debtors	100	120
Cash	4	—
	264	360
Creditors due within a year:		
Taxation	60	40
Other creditors	120	140
Proposed dividend	40	20
Bank overdraft	—	106
	220	306
Net current assets	44	54
Total assets less current liabilities	624	894
Capital and reserves:		
Called-up share capital	264	434
Share premium account	—	40
Profit and loss account	360	420
	624	894

Part 2 Management accounting

7. A firm plans to sell 3,000 units of its industrial suction cleaner in the coming year. Fixed overhead costs attributed to this product are budgeted to be £39,000 pa.

   Direct costs per unit of product are:

   - Direct labour 3 hours at £5.20 per hour
   - Direct materials and components £16.26
   - Direct expenses £3.19
     The capital employed on this production is £240,000 and the firm aims to make a 20 per cent return on capital.
     Calculate the selling price needed to achieve this objective.

8. Precision Ltd manufacture a metal fastener for the motor trade and its management want your advice. The following information is available:

   (a) The product takes 12 minutes labour time to make, at £6 per hour.
   (b) Raw materials cost 25p per unit.
   (c) Variable overheads amount to £4 per hour.
   (d) Fixed overheads amount to £90,000 pa.
   (e) The proposed selling price is £3.10.

   Management require you to produce the following information:

   (i) A calculation of the break-even point.
   (ii) A chart to illustrate the break-even point.
   (iii) A calculation of the number of units needed to be sold to earn a 20 per cent return on the £0.2 million capital employed in this area.

9. Explain why absorption costing is a dangerous tool to use when examining the effects of a change in the level of activity (*essay question*).

10. JHL Ltd has budgeted the following figures for its three product lines for next year:

	A	B	C	Total
	£000	£000	£000	£000
Sales value	960	960	320	2,240
Variable costs	864	768	240	1,872
Fixed costs (allocated and apportioned)	48	72	100	220
Profit (loss)	48	120	(20)	148

The management of JHL Ltd are particularly concerned about product C and are considering various alternatives:

Alternative 1 – to cut product C's selling price by 10 per cent which is expected to increase demand for product C by about 40 per cent.

Alternative 2 – to substitute a new product D for product C. Estimated sales for product D are £280,000 in the first year and variable costs are estimated at 55 per cent of sales value. In this case some £32,000 additional fixed costs directly attributable to D will be incurred but £18,000 of fixed costs directly attributable to C will be saved.

Alternative 3 – to drop product C completely, but not introduce any new product, nor increase sales of product A or B. In this case, the £18,000 of fixed costs directly attributable to product C will be saved.

Calculate the effect on the total profit of the firm of each alternative course of action and state your preferred choice.

11. Your firm makes one-off equipment to customers' own specifications. You have just received an order which has been costed out at £20,000 on an absorption (total) costing basis and with a 20 per cent mark-up gives a selling price of £24,000. The customer declines to place the order at this price and offers to pay £19,000. Explain the circumstances that might persuade you to accept this order at the customer's price (*essay question*).

12. The standard material cost of fabric specified for a particular garment is £10.50 comprising 3 metres at £3.50 per metre. The standard time allowed for making up the garment is 15 minutes paid at the rate of £5 per hour.

Last week 1,000 garments were made using 3,200 metres of fabric which was purchased at £3.30 per metre. The total time taken to make up these garments was 230 hours which were paid at the standard rate.

(a) Calculate the material cost variance and the material price and usage variances.

(b) Calculate the labour cost variance and the labour rate and efficiency variances.

(c) Suggest any possible reasons why these variances may have occurred.

13. The following statement shows the actual profit for one month to be less than that originally budgeted. The firm in question makes a small standardized product in large volume for use in the engineering industry.

Standard costing profit and loss account for the month

	(F)	(A)	£
Budgeted profit			10,000
Variances:	(F)	(A)	
Sales price variance	1,900		
Sales quantity variance		4,000	
Material price variance		2,000	
Material usage variance	1,500		
Labour rate variance	—	—	
Labour efficiency variance		1,600	
Variable o/h expenditure variance	200		
Fixed o/h expenditure variance	500		
Fixed o/h volume variance		2,000	
	4,100	9,600	5,500
Actual profit for the month			£4,500

You are required to give possible reasons for each of the variances disclosed in the statement and to say how they resulted in a worse profit than expected.

Part 3 Financial management

14. (a) Explain the term *capital gearing*.

   (b) Discuss the advantages and disadvantages of a company increasing its level of capital gearing (*essay question*).

15. (a) What is the cost of equity capital that is implied in the following information?

   Market price per ordinary share £3.00

   Forecast net dividend per share for current year £0.12

   Notional rate of income tax on dividends 20 per cent

   Recent annual growth rate of profits 15 per cent pa

   (b) Calculate the weighted average cost of capital using the cost of equity above and assumea debt/equity ratio of 25:75. All the debt has a fixed rate of interest of 9 per cent. Assume corporation tax is 30 per cent.

   (c) Explain why the weighted average cost of capital is less than the cost of equity alone.

16. A firm is considering buying a machine which costs £80,000 and is expected to last five years, when its scrap value will be about £2,000 only. Taxable savings are estimated to be £40,000 each year and the rate of corporation tax is 30 per cent. Capital allowances of 25 per cent on the reducing balance can be claimed, but no allowances are available on the £30,000 working capital required for the duration of the project. The real cost of capital is 10 per cent and this is regarded as the minimum requirement.

   (a) Set out the yearly cash flows and find their net present value using the table at Appendix 5.

   (b) Find the IRR by interpolation and state your conclusions as to the worthwhile nature of this project.

17. A firm is considering whether or not to replace a machine which makes metal frames for umbrellas. The remaining life of the machine is put at four years. The product sells for £2 each at a volume of about 60,000 pa.

   Three alternative courses of action have been suggested by the production engineer as follows:

   (a) Keep the existing machine which originally cost £40,000 four years ago and is being depreciated at 12.5 per cent pa on a straight-line basis. The total annual cost of this method (including depreciation) amounts to £85,000 and requires all the existing working capital of £25,000.

   (b) Buy a new machine costing £250,000 less a trade-in allowance of £10,000 on the old machine. The total annual running costs would amount to £95,000 including £60,000 depreciation. Further working capital of £5,000 would be required, making £30,000 working capital in total.

   (c) Cease the manufacture of frames and sell the existing machine to another firm for £20,000 plus a royalty of 20p per unit they sell. Sales volume would be as that expected from own manufacture. The existing working capital would be recovered in full immediately.

Calculate which is the most attractive alternative on a net present value basis if the cost of capital is 16 per cent and state your recommended course of action bearing risk in mind.

18. New Enterprise Ltd set up in business on 1 January as a supplier of specialized chemicals to a small number of other firms. Its management have made the following plans and estimates for the year:

   (a) On 1 January the company will purchase premises for £60,000 and furniture, fittings and office equipment for £16,000. The latter will be depreciated over 10 years on a straight-line basis, but the premises will not be subject to depreciation.
   (b) Sales will be only £5,000 in January, but will hold steady at £20,000 every month thereafter except in July and August when they will reach £50,000 per month.
   (c) The gross profit margin (ie sales less cost of sales), will be held at 40 per cent of the selling price.
   (d) On 1 January the company will purchase £8,000 of stock and maintain this level throughout the year.
   (e) Trade creditors demand payment on the last day of the month in which the purchase was made.All sales are on credit and it is expected that 80 per cent will be received by the end of the month following the month of sale, and the remaining 20 per cent received a month later again.
   (g) Overheads, wages and salaries will amount to £6,000 each month, except in July when it will be double that figure. Payment of these expenses will be at the end of the same month as incurred.
   (h) There will be no tax or dividend payments during the year.

You are required to:

   (i) Prepare a monthly cash budget for the year and use it to state the amount of share capital needed to be issued on 1 January if the company is never to borrow money during the year.
   (ii) Prepare a forecast profit and loss account for the year and a projected balance sheet as at 31 December based on the above assumptions
   (iii) Suggest a scheme of financing (other than all equity) that may be more suitable, given the seasonal nature of the business.

19. Mr Smith is the Managing Director of Smiths Ltd, a medium-sized private company, all of whose shares are owned by himself and his wife. As he is nearing retirement age and as he has no family, he has decided to sell out to a larger public company, but is unsure of the value of his shares. The following information is available for Smiths Ltd:

Balance sheet

	£000		£000
Issued £1 ordinary shares	800	Land and buildings	2,000
Profit and loss account	2,452	Plant and equipment	1,100
	3,252	Motor vehicles	220
10% loan	600		3,320
Other creditors	720	Stocks	582
		Debtors	590
		Cash	80
	£4,572		£4,572

The following values have been assessed by an independent valuer on a going-concern basis:

	£000
Land and buildings	2,440
Plant and equipment	1,152
Motor vehicles	208
Stocks	400
Debtors	480

The profit after tax and interest was £340,000 in the previous year and is expected to be about £360,000 in the current year, a rise of over 5 per cent pa. The annual dividend last year was £160,000.

The dividend yields and price/earnings ratios of three companies in the same field as Smiths Ltd are as follows:

	Divd yield %	P/E ratio
Company A	6.0%	8.0
B	4.8%	10.8
C	5.3%	9.7

Advise Mr Smith.

20. Explain the procedures you would adopt for credit sales in order to limit the amount of working capital tied up in debtors and to minimize bad debts (*essay question*).

21. Explain why the tax charge for the year, shown in the profit and loss account, is not identical to the profit before tax charged at the current rate of corporation tax (*essay question*).

21. What steps can an exporter take to limit exposure to exchange rate risk? (*essay question*).

Index

Index